# DOUBLE
# ACE

## ALSO BY ROBERT CORAM

*Boyd: The Fighter Pilot Who Changed the Art of War*
*American Patriot: The Life and Wars of Colonel Bud Day*
*Brute: The Life of Victor Krulak, U.S. Marine*

# DOUBLE ACE

## THE LIFE OF ROBERT LEE SCOTT JR., PILOT, HERO, AND TELLER OF TALL TALES

# ROBERT CORAM

Thomas Dunne Books ⚑ St. Martin's Press   New York

THOMAS DUNNE BOOKS.
An imprint of St. Martin's Press.

DOUBLE ACE. Copyright © 2016 by Robert Coram. All rights reserved. Printed in the United States of America. For information, address St. Martin's Press, 175 Fifth Avenue, New York, N.Y. 10010.

www.thomasdunnebooks.com
www.stmartins.com

Designed by Steven Seighman

The Library of Congress Cataloging-in-Publication Data is available upon request.

ISBN 978-1-250-04018-3 (hardcover)
ISBN 978-1-4668-3542-9 (e-book)

Our books may be purchased in bulk for promotional, educational, or business use. Please contact your local bookseller or the Macmillan Corporate and Premium Sales Department at 1-800-221-7945, extension 5442, or by e-mail at MacmillanSpecialMarkets@macmillan .com.

First Edition: August 2016

10  9  8  7  6  5  4  3  2  1

For JFA

*That is what we are supposed to do when we are at our best—make it all up—but make it up so truly that later it will happen that way.*
—ERNEST HEMINGWAY

# CONTENTS

| | | |
|---|---|---|
| OVERTURE | | 1 |
| 1. | GEORGIA BOY | 7 |
| 2. | FAILURE | 17 |
| 3. | WEST POINT | 25 |
| 4. | BUGLING | 33 |
| 5. | FLYING AND DRIVING | 39 |
| 6. | LEARNING THE TRADE | 49 |
| 7. | DARK NIGHTS OF THE SOUL | 57 |
| 8. | THE FORTRESS FALLS | 61 |
| 9. | WEDDING BELLS AND DISTANT TRUMPETS | 67 |
| 10. | EXTRA DUTY | 73 |
| 11. | ORCHIDS AND PIGS AND, OH MY, THE TRAINING COMMAND | 79 |
| 12. | CALIFORNIA DREAMING | 87 |
| 13. | WAR TOCSINS | 93 |
| 14. | "YOU ARE NOT BLOODED" | 103 |
| 15. | HOLD MY BEER . . . | 109 |
| 16. | THE FLIGHT TO DESTINY | 119 |
| 17. | AT THE END OF THE WORLD | 129 |
| 18. | THE HUMP | 145 |
| 19. | FLYING TIGER | 151 |
| 20. | GLORY | 155 |
| 21. | LEAVING CHINA | 167 |
| 22. | HOME IS THE HERO | 179 |
| 23. | ON THE ROAD AGAIN | 185 |
| 24. | THE BOOK . . . AND THE MOVIE | 193 |

25. Good Reviews . . . and Bad                    203
26. Movie Star                                    209
27. Chiaroscuro                                   217
28. Twilight                                      225
29. The More Things Change . . .                  235
30. Still in the Race                             243
31. Resurrection                                  253
32. At Last                                       261
33. One More Mission                              277
34. Mission Accomplished                          287

Acknowledgments                                   303
Bibliography                                      305
Index                                             311

# DOUBLE
# ACE

# OVERTURE

ROBERT LEE SCOTT JR. WAS A HERO.

He flew into battle alone against the enemies of his country, and he emerged victorious. He also wrote one of the most important books of his time, a book that influenced the lives of thousands. For a time in the mid-1940s, Robert Scott was one of the most famous people in America.

Fighter pilot. Hero. Famous author. Scott was these and many other things.

He was a man who talked too much and with too little regard for the truth. He was an inveterate and dazzling storyteller, a devilish charmer, and a roguish fellow who had more than a little of the carnival barker in his makeup.

He was a professional Southerner, a lifetime performance artist who, in telling stories of his adventure-jammed life, often left facts behind and cavorted through vales of hyperbole, believing, as do many Southerners, that the story would become true in the telling.

Mothers influence their sons in ways both beneficial and burdensome. Scott's mother wanted her firstborn son to be famous, and with words like velvet-sheathed blades, she poked and prodded him until he achieved her great desire.

Nothing could be commonplace for Scott; events had to be dramatic, obstacles had to be mountainous, and enemies had to be so powerful that when he triumphed—as was his destiny—Scott's mother would nod in approval.

Scott had two younger siblings—a sister and a brother—and they would say that Rob (the family called him Rob) was an only child; that from the time he was born, he was his mother's life, and that they grew up almost as outsiders in their family.

Scott's mother—he called her "Mama"—was a teacher forced by marriage into the role of housewife, and what energy she had left after cleaning and dusting and cooking and scrubbing, she used to drive Rob toward greatness.

Scott responded well to his mama's admonitions. All his life he would add extra effort to whatever chore was set before him. Doing a job well was not enough; every job had to be perfect, because his mama expected perfection. Of course, perfection is impossible and thus Scott, from an early age, was afflicted with an itch that could not be scratched, an ambition that could not be satisfied, and a hope that could not be fulfilled. For Rob, the inevitable failures of childhood became lifelong scars.

Robert Scott and his oversized personality came out of an undersized town: Macon, Georgia, a piddling and nondescript town in the middle of the state where wind sighs in the tall pines, the heat of the sun is fierce, and people see visions in cloud formations.

In Macon, the favorite pastime was replaying battles from what the locals called the War of Northern Aggression; that, and worshipping ancestors who had served the Glorious Cause. The town was barely touched by the Civil War—Sherman had fired a few shots in that direction to keep Macon's militia in place as he raced past en route to Savannah—but the town's inhabitants preferred to believe that they had been invaded and ravished; that because of Sherman's assault, the chickens stopped laying eggs and the cows stopped giving milk. Generations of Macon's children grew up obsessed by the Civil War and roiling with ever-fresh anger at "the Damnyankees"—a phrase expressed by Southerners as a single word to show their everlasting contempt.

Given that Scott's first and middle names came from Robert E. Lee, one of the most venerated men in Southern history, he would have been horrified at being compared to a Yankee general, especially a man as vilified in Georgia as William Tecumseh Sherman. But the comparisons are many and cannot be denied.

- Both men spewed so much verbiage that their words distort their historical image.
- Both men were dramatic and theatrical.

- Both men were inveterate womanizers who felt considerable remorse late in life for their weakness.
- Both men were prone to lengthy and debilitating bouts of depression.
- Both men loved geography and had a genius for knowing and remembering terrain, an invaluable gift in war.
- Both men can be considered gifted to the point of genius in their individual fields of warfare: Sherman laid waste to a large part of southeastern America. Scott laid waste to enemy forces in the air and on the ground in southeastern China.
- Finally, both men were warriors, and warriors must be judged by their deeds in war, not by their human frailties. Sherman and Scott were among the most brilliant soldiers of their times in their separate wars.

Like it or not, Sherman and Scott were two peas in the same pod.

An invisible wall built with bricks of prejudice and sealed with the mortar of inferiority surrounded Macon, and about the best a Macon boy could hope from life was mediocrity. But you would never know this by the attitude of local boys. They rolled their shoulders, hustled their testicles, and looked around with angry and defiant eyes, ready to take on all comers. They would tell you in a heartbeat that they were as good as any sumbitch from New York City and that they could do anything in life that they wanted to do. But deep inside, in words that were never spoken, they believed that only the wealthy and privileged ever climbed the invisible wall.

Scott, pushed by his mother, resolved early in life that not only would he climb the wall, he would travel farther, fly higher, and do greater things than anyone from Macon had ever done; he would do all this and more, by God.

And he did.

In World War II, he was an Army ace, a bona fide national hero at a time when America so desperately needed heroes. He came home in early 1943 as Americans waited for their country to invade Europe. Scott traveled America making speeches to galvanize defense workers, to support the war effort, and to encourage people to buy war bonds to finance the war. His speeches were war stories from far-off China, and pictures of the time show hundreds of people staring at him with enthralled looks on their faces. During his speech-making tour a host suggested he write a book about his combat experiences. He was too busy to write, but he was a talker, so he took off three days to *dictate* a book. *God Is My Co-Pilot* sold hundreds of thousands of copies and influenced several generations of boys to become pilots. It was one of the most famous books of the time, and it was made into an iconic movie that is still aired on late-night television.

For decades Scott was trailed by big-name journalists who wanted to write down every word he spoke, by adulatory young people who wanted to gaze upon this mythic man, and by Hollywood movie stars who wanted to borrow the luster that his company would bring to their careers; that and more these movie stars wanted.

The wonder of all this, to paraphrase Dr. Samuel Johnson, was not so much that Scott did these things well, but that he could do them at all. Scott was the most unlikely of men to achieve such success. His intellect was as average as his ability. He was a small-town Southerner who had the values and the insecurities of a small-town Southerner. In addition, Scott spent much of his life running from and covering up the shame of flunking out of high school. His failure to meet even this minimum level of achievement was a lifelong embarrassment. Even when he was an old man and famous, he did not care to speak of that crippling experience.

Scott compensated for all of this by maintaining an unshakable belief in his own destiny. His mama had told him time and time again that he would grow up to be a great and famous man. How could she be wrong?

Scott and his family attended the Tattnall Square Baptist Church every Sunday morning and Wednesday night along with the weeklong revival every summer. There they worshipped the hard and unbending God of the Old Testament. Scott grew up having an easy relationship with the Almighty, whom he referred to as "the Big Sky Boss." Scott viewed the Deity's main job as protecting him from the many Philistines seeking to block his destiny. There were many times when Scott's dreams were thwarted, many times when his career was threatened, many times when superiors did not recognize his destiny. But in each instance, events that can only be described as providential opened the way. Scott led a life illuminated by moonbeams and covered with pixie dust. He was fortune's child.

Scott had a wide streak of what he called "cussedness"—a defiance of authority and a compulsion to swim against the tide. When he saw something that had never been done before, something that was often dangerous, sometimes illegal, and usually forbidden, he frequently took daring action that, had it failed, would have made him a candidate for a Darwin Award. But most of the time his audacity and boldness carried the day.

In the South, there is an expression that covers this sort of behavior: "Hey, y'all. Hold my beer and watch this."

Scott first gained fame as a military man in a time of war. He exploded out of nowhere in an obscure place and—for his profession—as a relatively old man. To go to war and to stay there, he fought the very system he had sworn to defend. He disdained military regulations, ignored military policy, and defied his superiors. At the end of his military career, Scott wore the star of a brigadier general on his shoulders, but his actions continued to be those of a second lieutenant. Throughout his life, Scott did just what he wanted to do; he never grew up. Some would say that Scott was an impulsive and selfish man.

Scott's story is an American story. It is the story of a boy from the outback of his country, a mama's boy who dreamed impossible dreams and who saw his dreams come true. Everything in life he ever wanted, he got—a claim few men can make.

Often, and publicly, he attributed his success to "Mama." He sent her letters from around the world, and the letters were longer and more frequent than those he sent his wife. Scott once wrote that his mama "inspired me to seek an eternal goal and never to be satisfied with where I was but to keep pressing on to the next horizon."

After Scott became a retired general—that is, after his accomplishments had guaranteed him a place in military and literary history, and when he could be expected to coast through his final years—he embarked upon one of the great solo expeditions of modern times, walking a significant part of the Great Wall of China. The bureaucratic obstacles, the physical challenges, and the remote territory he traversed made this an expedition in the old sense of the word. He was seventy-two years old when he did it.

And then a few years later he found the strength, drive, and desire to build one of the largest aviation museums in America. It would benefit his home state for generations to come.

After the 1950s, Scott's military legacy suffered. But by the 1980s a new generation of officers discovered Scott and resurrected his reputation. As an old man, he again knew the fame that had been his as a young man.

By then Scott knew that flunking out of high school did not really matter. But he also knew the South, and he knew there were those who would never forget. They would only die. Maybe this one last job, this one last campaign, this great gift to his part of Georgia, would be what he would be remembered for. Maybe this would be the final brushstroke in painting over his great failure. Maybe this was an accomplishment that would stretch beyond the grave and make his mama proud.

Maybe.

# 1

## GEORGIA BOY

FEW MEN HAVE EVER KNOWN THEIR LIFE'S WORK AT SUCH AN EARLY AGE or with such unwavering certitude as did Robert Lee Scott Jr. He was not quite four years old that warm morning of October 19, 1911, when he stood on the ground of Central City Park in Macon, squeezed his mother's hand, and stared with unblinking eyes at the jumbled wreckage of a small fabric-covered airplane and the broken body of its pilot.

The dead pilot was twenty-six-year-old Eugene Ely, the first man to fly an airplane off a U.S. Navy ship and the first to land on one, now a barnstormer and one of the most famous aviators in America. A few days earlier, to draw crowds for his performance at the state fair, he flew his Curtiss biplane low over Macon, the first man ever to fly over the city, according to the *Macon Telegraph*. After Ely's first performance on Saturday, the *Telegraph* wrote that the "Aviator Catapulted his Cloud-Cleaver into Convolutions" above the crowd with "apparently a most reckless disregard of safety."

The newspaper story, and the fact that Monday was Farmer's Day at the fair—a day that drew a larger than usual crowd for the livestock sales—pulled in several thousand spectators. Ely was scheduled to make three flights that day, and he had promised an even more exciting exhibition than he had flown on Saturday.

The sky was clean and clear and perfect for flying. The park was filled with women in white dresses and men in suits and lots of neatly dressed young people all waiting to see Ely perform his famous "ocean wave" maneuver. When Ely had flown off of the USS *Birmingham* he had dipped so close to the surface of the water that his propeller blew up a big cloud of spray into which his aircraft almost disappeared. The finale of Ely's barn-storming act sought to replicate that maneuver. He would dive his aircraft toward a declivity or behind a mound of dirt and seemingly disappear only to emerge triumphantly, engine roaring, as he clawed for the sky.

But on this day Ely misjudged time and distance and botched the delicate equation of when he should pull out of his dive. He stalled, crashed, and broke his neck. His death would be a national story.

Scott's mother, Ola Burckhalter Scott, did not believe in shielding her son from the tragedies of life. Other than Sherman's visit, this was the biggest thing ever to happen in Macon, and if Rob wanted to look at Ely's body, if he wanted to watch his neighbors take Ely's gloves and tie and belt and shoes and even pieces of his airplane as souvenirs, then let him watch. In years to come, when the people of Macon talked of the crash and showed the souvenirs they had taken from Ely's corpse, her son, her Rob, could nod and say, "I was there."

Ola looked around at the crowd that had come to see Ely's performance. She looked down at Rob, and in that moment she wanted him to know the fame that Ely had known. She wanted her son to know the adoration of the crowd. She leaned down and whispered in his ear, "You are going to grow up and be an aviator and you will be as famous as he is." She told Rob that he would fly the same sort of airplane that Ely had flown. In coming years she would tell him countless times, "From the moment you saw that crash, I knew you would be a flyer."

Thus, Rob never had a moment of indecision about his life's work, never went through the false starts of many boys regarding their careers. His earliest memory was of wanting to be a fighter pilot. To find glory in the skies was his destiny. His mama had told him so.

Robert Lee Scott Jr. was born on April 12, 1908, in Waynesboro, Georgia, a small town near the South Carolina border. His sister, Elizabeth, was born in Americus, Georgia, in 1911, and his brother, Roland, in Macon in 1915.

The births were scattered about because Rob's father, Robert Lee Scott, had trouble finding his niche in life. He was from Aiken, South Carolina, and he attended Clemson Agricultural College but dropped out and became a railroad conductor and a supervisor at a peach orchard, and when the family moved to Macon not long after Rob was born, he operated the S&S Grocery on Poplar Street. The store went bankrupt, something the family rarely talked about. The elder Scott finally found his calling as a traveling salesman for high-end men's clothing. Photographs show him as a big, raw-boned, and unsmiling man in a three-piece suit and bow tie. Because he traveled around three states and was away so much, it fell to his wife to take care of their three children and the house he bought at 511 East Napier Avenue.

Ola Burckhalter, like her husband, came out of Aiken, South Carolina, where her family had a farm on the Whiskey Road. Few Southern women of her time attended college, but Ola graduated from the South Carolina Coeducational Institute, a school that described itself in a newspaper ad as a "Christian Military Institute" where "teachers take the place of parents" and where, as did most female students, Ola took a course of study that trained her to be a teacher. After graduation she taught school for several years in Aiken. For a woman of her time, Ola was relatively well-educated, enough so that when she settled in Macon she thought that she was a bit better than her neighbors, and that Rob was better than his little Macon friends.

It was in the Burckhalter home near Aiken that Ola and Robert were married, on June 26, 1907, and it was on the Burckhalter farm that Rob spent his summers while growing up. He spent little time with the Scott family, and in later years he would dismiss them as "dirt farmers."

All parents say they love their children equally and that they play no favorites. But this is a lie. The parents know it and the children know it. If a parent has a favorite child, that parent usually tries to hide it. But sometimes not. Ola did not.

From the time Rob was born it was as if Ola believed in primogeniture. Elizabeth's and Roland's earliest memories were of how Rob was the bright shining star at the center of his mother's world, and that they were only small planets on the far and dark edges of the universe.

As did many Southern boys, Scott grew up with two overlapping influences: the Civil War and ancestor worship. He talked of the Civil War as if he were in a lull between battles, and he boasted that one of his great-grandfathers had died at Bull Run. He did have a great-grandfather on the paternal side, William Thomas Scott, who was wounded at Gettysburg, which is about as good as it gets when it comes to bragging rights, but why Rob traded an ancestor wounded at Gettysburg for a fictional ancestor who died at Bull Run is unknown.

Rob's maternal great-grandfather Jarrett D. Burckhalter enlisted in a South Carolina unit in 1863, but according to his service record he was "never paid" and "never reported" for duty.

One of Scott's memories of the summers in South Carolina was how his grandfather always wore a Confederate hat that he said had belonged to his father. Scott grew up thinking that his great-grandfather Burckhalter was a hero, when in fact he was a deserter.

For Scott, the "home place," that mythical taproot into the past so treasured by Southerners, was not Macon, but was instead the Burckhalter farm on the Whiskey Road in the rural countryside south of Aiken.

Perhaps it was the rural origin, the closeness with the outdoors, and the independence that is part of a rural heritage that caused Ola to give Rob a long leash at an early age. For a mother who was so possessive, so ambitious for her son, she gave him extraordinary freedom. He was a city boy with the freedom and independence of a country boy.

The first of many such examples was in 1919, when Rob was an eleven-year-old paperboy delivering the *Macon Telegraph*. One morning he read on the front page that famed Army aviator Billy Mitchell would be leading a flight of nine fighter planes from Canada to Miami and that the pilots would stop in Macon to refuel their aircraft and have lunch with the mayor at the Dempsey Hotel. Rob's heroes were Billy Bishop and Eddie Rickenbacker, Allied fighter aces of World War I; Manfred von Richthofen, Germany's famous "Red Baron"; and Billy Mitchell, the flamboyant commander of American air forces in Europe during World War I. Now one of those heroes was coming to Macon.

Rob rode his bicycle across town to the airport to see the sleek little fighter planes land and to look upon the goggled faces of Mitchell and his pilots. Rob's desire to be a flyer seemed more than he could contain. After the pilots drove away to lunch, Scott considered stowing away in the baggage compartment of one of the aircraft. But the compartment was too small, and instead he waited until Mitchell and the pilots returned, and when they fired up their engines and taxied for takeoff, he ignored the shouted warnings from city fathers and ran along behind the aircraft, oblivious to the dust and dirt being thrown into his face by the prop blast, and as the aircraft took off down the grass strip he ran behind them, arms outstretched, chasing the airplanes that he knew would one day take him away from Macon. Rob watched the aircraft form up and he kept his eyes upon them until they were tiny specks far to the south and he could no longer hear the deep rumble of their engines. They would be in Miami before sundown. Canada to Miami in a single day. If airplanes could do that, Rob thought, they could take him around the world.

The next year Rob joined Boy Scout Troop 23 and, pushed by his mama, he set about to earn twenty-one merit badges and become an Eagle Scout. One of the first badges he sought was in aviation, which called for him to build a model airplane and fly it. But a model was not ambitious enough for Rob, and so he built a glider, almost full-sized, and covered it with canvas cut from the tent of a traveling evangelist preacher. With the help of several friends Rob hoisted the glider to the roof of the tallest house in the neighborhood. There he strapped himself in, had his friends release a restraining rope, and plummeted down the steep roof. As the glider cleared the roof, the main spar broke and Rob plummeted into the top of a rosebush, uninjured and unabashed. That was his first, albeit brief, flight. Later he would say it was the only time he ever crashed an airplane.

In practicing for a merit badge in archery, Rob found he was a natural at leading a moving target, that is, shooting not where the target was, but where it would be when the arrow reached it. He became a master of the snap shot, the quick reflex shot, and the intuitive shot taken without apparent aim. When his mother complained that feral cats were getting inside the chicken coop and eating her baby chicks, Rob switched to steel-tipped hunting arrows, sat on the back steps, and began shooting cats. He timed his shots to pin the running cat to a wooden fence post. That soon eliminated the feline threat.

The Ocmulgee River flowed along the eastern edge of town, and most Macon mothers forbade their children to go anywhere near its swirling brown waters. But in warm weather, which was most of the year, Rob would go alone to the river's edge, disrobe, hold his clothes above his head, and back-stroke his way out to a small island. There he darkened his face with the juice of berries and adopted his self-bestowed Indian name, "Eagleheart." Rob built a lean-to and hunted on the island. He caught fish, cooked hush puppies over a small fire, and slept on a sandbar.

When Scott was fourteen he took all the money he had saved from being a paperboy and from cutting lawns—the grand total of seventy-five dollars, which in 1922 was a small fortune for a boy his age—and attended an auction where disassembled and boxed surplus Army aircraft—the Curtiss JN-4, the famous "Jenny" of early aviation—were being sold. As the auctioneer moved to each box, Scott shouted, "Seventy-five dollars." But each aircraft was bought by a man who was acquiring them as training planes for an airline. The buyer grew weary of Scott's importunate shouts, and told him he could buy the next aircraft and then to get out.

It was okay with his mama that Rob had bought an airplane and stored it in the garage. It seemed half of Macon knew of the boxed aircraft and talked of it. But Ola ignored the talk. The box stayed in the garage for months, and then a streetcar driver came to the door and identified himself as a former World War I pilot. He offered to help Rob assemble the aircraft and then teach him how to fly if, in turn, Rob would let him use the aircraft on weekends to perform at air shows around the state. And that was how Rob learned to fly. His lessons took place at Central City Park, the same place where Ely had crashed and died.

The lessons did not last long, because the World War I pilot crashed the Jenny. He was uninjured, but the fragile little aircraft was destroyed.

Rob entered Lanier High School, one of the most prestigious public schools in Georgia. It was named for the poet Sidney Lanier, and its athletic teams were called "the Poets"; they were feared by their opponents as a mighty force. The school motto was "We Lead," and Lanier's Junior Reserve Officers Training Course would be consistently ranked among the best in America. Around Macon, Lanier students were recognized by their short hair, no-nonsense demeanor, and courtesy toward their elders. "Lanier Men" were ambitious and motivated, and it was a given that they would serve with distinction in the military and in business. They were afforded a respect and deference rarely granted to high school students.

Lanier was sited atop the crest of a long slope that dipped down toward Macon and the river. Wednesday was parade day at Lanier, and around midmorning people in Macon would begin looking at their watches, staring up the hill, and waiting. At precisely 11:30 there would be a thunderous clash of drums followed by the martial thrust of horns, and the Poets would begin marching, all keeping the Army standard pace of 105 steps to the minute, feet hitting the ground with every boom of the drum. And as the parade began, many people in Macon did an unconscious shuffle to get in step with the drum, in step with the Lanier Men, until the city was marching with the Poets, and school and city were one.

Hard-bitten career Army sergeants served as ROTC instructors at Lanier and taught cadets how officers should conduct themselves, including the finer points of etiquette upon visiting brothels: "Determine the price, conduct your business, pay for services rendered, and depart as gentlemen," the sergeants taught. "This is a business transaction. Do not fall in love."

Rob never had the self-discipline and sense of mission to fit in at Lanier. He played only intramural sports and never distinguished himself academically.

In the spring of 1923 came an event that awakened Rob's curiosity about the outside world, stirred his nascent passion for life, and released the obsessive streak that would characterize his personality. He was fifteen, and boys of that age rarely have a blinding moment of realization about the outside world, a heart-stopping instant of awareness about a distant culture, a breathtaking appreciation of the accomplishments of others. But that is what happened to Rob, and afterward his life was never the same.

Pursuing a merit badge in first aid, Rob visited a local doctor who had agreed to instruct him in basic emergency medical procedures. In the waiting room, Rob looked at the magazines piled on a table and plucked out the March 1923 issue of *National Geographic*. The magazine fell open to a story by Adam Warwick about the Great Wall of China. Out of the magazine fell a bulky and folded white thickness that, when opened, proved to be a 45½ × 9½–inch black-and-white panorama of a section of the Great Wall. The bold headline read, "THE GREAT WALL OF CHINA NEAR NANKOW PASS," and underneath was a boiling caption: "For more than two thousand miles this Long Rampart, the most stupendous structure ever raised by the hand of man, writhes along the mountain peaks, dips deep into valley and canyon, and pursues its desolate way across windswept plateau and desert sands. Its myriad cloud-capped towers stand in solemn stillness, where they were stationed twenty centuries ago, as though condemned to wait the march of Time until their builders return."

The photograph and the overwrought writing transfixed Rob. He stared, eyes wide and heart pounding. In the foreground was a man wearing sandals and blousy pants and a long tunic-like shirt secured around his waist by a cord. Atop his head was a close-fitting cap. The man's hands were behind him, pulling a rope attached to three heavily laden camels. In the background behind the camels the Great Wall, marked by frequent towers, stretched up and across barren hills until it disappeared over a distant mountain peak. In front of the man the wall stretched across a rise, then to a tower atop a far peak, and then it disappeared on the back side of the mountain.

The opening sentence of Warwick's story said that the only work of man's hands that would be visible to the human eye from the moon was the Great Wall of China. The photograph gave the boy from Macon, Georgia, his first real sense of an outside world; an awareness that there were places beyond the city-limit sign that he had never heard of.

Rob had been an avid reader as far back as he could remember. He had read Edgar Rice Burroughs's novels of Tarzan, and he was fascinated by Africa. But there were no pictures in the novels, and it was an Africa that had to be imagined. Now he had this grand picture of the Great Wall of China, along with a description of the geography traversed by the wall.

As Rob read of the Long Rampart, his eyes widened and his heart pounded. He had never, in his wildest dreams, imagined a wall that could traverse some two thousand miles. He read the story and feelings washed over him that he had never known before. There in the doctor's waiting room the fifteen-year-old boy nodded to himself as he made a solemn resolution: One day he would walk the length of the Great Wall of China. He would see both ends of the ancient man-made wonder and all that lay between.

It is not uncommon for young boys to dream big dreams. But often those dreams are transitory and replaced by other dreams. For Rob, walking the Great Wall would become a lifelong obsession. Perhaps it was because of his determination to leave Macon, and nothing more exemplified that desire than a place on the other side of the world. When he unfolded the panorama he was overcome by a vision and a determination that would never leave him.

When Rob came out of the doctor's inner office and passed the waiting-room table stacked with magazines, he reached down, plucked out the panorama, and kept walking.

Some may consider it a trivial thing to take something from a magazine in a doctor's waiting room, but for the rest of his life, when Scott told this story he would hang his head and say, "I stole that photograph. I was a Boy Scout in there working on a merit badge, and I stole something."

But Rob's guilt was not as great as his obsession. He took the monochromatic photograph home, unfolded it and tacked it on the wall of his room, and studied it for hours, often finding something new: a small group of people in front of the camel driver, almost hidden because their clothes were the color of the earth; a few people clambering over the heavy stones where the wall had been breached; what appeared to be a shadowy gully behind the camel driver; and always the dark foreboding landscape over which crawled the wall.

Rob carried the photograph with him for most of the rest of his life. Long after it had become tattered, long after the creases split and had to be taped, long after the paper crumbled, Scott still carried it.

Not long after seeing the photograph, Rob became a weekend hobo. He began hopping freight trains in Macon, dodging railroad detectives who were even rougher than the hoboes who rode their rails. As a result, he spent some nights in various Georgia jails. And the next morning, when the police called his mother, more often than not Robert Senior was traveling and could not be reached to pick up Rob. The police would release him with admonitions either to become a paying customer, or to stay off the trains. Covered with contrition, Rob nodded, said, "Yes, sir," and immediately went to the edge of town, where he hopped aboard the next train bound for Macon.

Some skepticism is called for about this hobo business. But proof is found in the *Lanerian*, Rob's high school yearbook, where his nickname was "Jail-bird," and the class prophecy predicted that he would become the chief of police in Griffin, a town between Macon and Atlanta where Rob spent a night in jail. The yearbook also described him as the "wittiest" of his class-mates. (Years later Scott's work would require a security clearance. The FBI conducted a background check and the investigators were curious about why he was known as "Jailbird.")

When Rob had earned twenty-one merit badges and became an Eagle Scout, he put his merit badge sash over his shoulder and the badges covered the front of the sash. His mama glanced at the sash and said, "How many do the Scouts have?"

"Seventy-five." (Actually, the number was more than 130.)

"Why don't you earn all seventy-five?" She turned and walked away.

Rob eventually earned seventy-two merit badges, which he said was more than any other Boy Scout in the Southeast. But his mama never praised him. Instead she always reminded him of the three badges he never earned.

After Scott became a national figure, he was often asked to speak to Boy Scouts and he rarely turned down an invitation. And in every speech he said he was a failure because he had never earned those last three merit badges.

As a Scout, Rob became a skilled amateur ham-radio operator. Because the Macon detachment of the Georgia National Guard needed a radio op-erator, on November 10, 1924—when Rob was sixteen—he joined the Guard. Rob was underage, but that was a trivial matter to Guard officers in the South, many of whom grew up hearing of underage relatives who had served in the Civil War. Besides, Rob was six feet tall, looked older than his age, and was a Lanier Man.

Rob continued to spend afternoons and occasional weekends in the woods along the river, and he became an accomplished fisherman and bird hunter, adept at wing shooting. He learned when shooting into a covey of quail or a flock of doves to pick out a single target, lead it, then shoot, and mentally to compute the speed of the bird, the vector of the shotgun pellets, and that invisible spot in the air where the bird would be when the pellets got there, and to do all this instinctively and in an instant. He learned well, and many times Rob brought home quail, doves, and ducks for the family table.

Rob was comfortable being alone in the woods and along the riverbanks, at home in the outdoors.

# 2

## FAILURE

THE SS *INNOKO* OF THE BLACK DIAMOND LINE, A 411-FOOT CARGO VESsel, departed Philadelphia in early June, 1924, bound for Rotterdam and Madrid, scheduled to return to Philadelphia in mid-August. But tramp steamers go where they must go, and in Madrid the captain of the *Innoko* received orders for Bordeaux and then via the Mediterranean Sea, the Suez Canal, and the Red Sea to Aden and on to Bombay, Calcutta, Singapore, and Shanghai before returning to the U.S. in February. Because the vessel was five months behind schedule, an able-bodied seaman (he had graduated from deck boy at the end of his first cruise the year before) named Robert Lee Scott Jr. was hopelessly behind when he returned to Lanier. To graduate with his classmates in June 1925 was impossible.

When Scott walked back into his classroom at Lanier, he was so tired from his trip that he fell asleep at his desk. A few minutes later he was nudged by his teacher, who said, "We've missed you, Robert. Where on earth have you been?"

Scott stood up, threw his arms wide, and said, "Why, sir, I've been around the world."

The teacher paused, turned to the blackboard, and pulled down a map of the world, mumbling, "All the way around the world?" He looked up and said, "Well, we thought you were never coming back. Why don't you come up here, take this pointer, and show us the route you took? And while you are at it, tell us the most interesting memories you have."

Rob seized the pointer, stabbed at the map, and was off and running, talking of his voyage. He talked for much of the rest of the day.

Rob spent the remainder of the school year telling endless and fanciful stories about his boat trip, as if stories of far and fabled lands would compensate for his lack of academic progress.

Scott flunked his senior year of high school.

In middle Georgia in 1925, only poor white trash, boys who would never go to college, and boys who would never amount to anything flunked out of high school. In retrospect, and given Scott's later accomplishments, flunking out may seem a trivial thing. But not at that place, and not at that time. Those who flunked out of high school were *sorry*—perhaps the most laminated criticism that could be leveled against a Southern boy. Now Scott was no longer a promising Lanier Man, and the stigma was great. This business of gallivanting around the world on a boat was unthinkable for a goal-oriented Poet. And now, at seventeen, Robert Scott found that not only was his intellectual ability in question, his *character* was in question. He knew that no matter how long he lived and no matter how great his accomplishments, to the people of Macon he would always be the boy who flunked his senior year.

Southerners spread misery and pain on their neighbors the way they spread butter and syrup on their biscuits, and there is no statute of limitations, no time in the future when the mention of a person's name will not automatically elicit the missteps of that person's life. It is all very low-key and in the light of "Did you know that . . . ?" or "Do you remember he was the one that . . . ?"

And that's just the way things were for Scott.

Scott's mother had always sung softly as she worked around the house, usually hymns from the previous Sunday's church service, but now she stopped singing. She was silent with the shame of her favored son having disgraced his family.

Rob's father became even more taciturn and found ways to avoid his friends. For the first time in his life, Rob saw tears in his father's eyes and he knew, although his father never said so, that his father had given up on him.

On Sundays when the Scott family attended church, their faces were stern, even for Baptists, and after the service they did not linger.

For the remainder of his long life, Scott never admitted to anyone that he had flunked his senior year at Lanier.

It was perhaps out of despair that he turned on his younger brother, Roland, now ten years old, and convinced Roland that he had flat feet and should wear arch supports. Roland did not have flat feet, and the supports caused him considerable discomfort. But his big brother Rob had convinced his parents that Roland had flat feet and should wear arch supports all day every day. And Roland did just that for several years, until a doctor delivered the obvious news that his feet were fine. Roland never decided if Rob had perpetuated this hoax out of mischief or out of a mean streak.

After Rob flunked out of Lanier, he reacted in over-the-top defiance. The Philistines were upon him, and he had to maneuver sharply and boldly if he was to achieve his destiny as a fighter pilot.

The only way to be sure of flying fighters was to become a commissioned officer in the Army Air Service. And the best way to be guaranteed a career as a regular officer was to go to the United States Military Academy at West Point. Rob, who had just flunked out of high school, began telling people around Macon that he planned to attend West Point and become a fighter pilot, or, as they were called at the time, "a pursuit pilot."

Scott does not talk of the reaction, but it is likely the people of Macon thought Rob was delusional.

That summer Scott visited his grandfather Burckhalter, who, as is the way of grandfathers, put his arm around his grandson, consoled him, and said he knew Rob would see his dreams come true. "You just keep your heart in the heavens, son," his grandfather said. He took off his Confederate hat, waved it in the air, pointed to an adjacent field, and said, "One day you'll fly back here in your own airship, and you'll light right in that field. And I'll be waiting for you."

Rob's father went to the local congressman seeking an appointment to West Point for his son, but he was told that both primary and alternate appointments were filled for the next several years. That avenue was closed.

Then Rob tried for an appointment through the Army National Guard, but he flunked the math section of the test. Another avenue closed and more disappointment for Rob's parents.

Later Rob would say that in 1926 he attended both Mercer University, in Macon, and the Military College of the South (better known as the Citadel), in Charleston, South Carolina, and that he flunked out of both. Records show that he did apply to those schools—probably during his senior year at Lanier—and was accepted. But the acceptance was based on graduation from high school, and those institutions would not have allowed him to enroll, which is why records do not show that he ever attended either. Rob, like his great-grandfather Burckhalter, signed up but never showed up.

Rob told the story of flunking out of two colleges to disguise the embarrassing truth: He was back at Lanier taking remedial courses. And even more embarrassing, he needed the help of a tutor. Most embarrassing of all, the tutor was his younger sister.

Rob even registered under the name "R. Scott," rather than his usual "Robert Lee Scott, Jr." To complete his humiliation, Rob's teachers at Lanier laughed when he insisted he was going to West Point. "You are having trouble graduating from high school," he remembers one teacher saying. "And West Point is one of the most rigorous and demanding colleges in the country."

The patronizing attitude of his teachers may have been informed in part by Rob's continued preoccupation with Scouting.

Rob was an archery instructor with the Scouts. But to his teachers, he was eighteen years old and still playing with bows and arrows. Most unbecoming for a Lanier Man.

County school records show that "R. Scott" graduated in June 1926, a year behind his class. Rob did not play intramural sports during his last year at Lanier, and he took no part in extracurricular school activities. Rob appears in no pictures in the *Lanerian* that year. He was the invisible senior.

His mother's singing voice remained stilled, and she shuffled around the house, mute and bent.

"That just killed me," Rob said.

His mama was his "character barometer," and when he prayed, he never asked God to make him rich or powerful, but a thousand times he turned his face skyward and prayed to please his mama: to win merit badges, to pass the West Point exam, and, oh, yes, please God let me be a fighter pilot.

Praying to be a fighter pilot was a logical prayer, he said. After all, didn't everyone in heaven have wings?


When Rob was nineteen, his then-twelve-year-old brother, Roland, joined Troop 23 of the Boy Scouts. Rob went to his mama and said, "I don't want Roland trading on my reputation," and convinced his mother to pull Roland from the larger and prestigious Troop 23 and transfer him into the smaller and more obscure Troop 13.

For years afterward, Roland wondered why his older brother would do such a thing.

Only one avenue remained for Scott to reach West Point, and that avenue was not unlike walking a high wire over a yawning abyss. Because if Scott failed, not only would his dream end, but he would be embarked on a course that, while honorable, was often only for those who can't go to college or who don't want to spend their lives working at a menial job in Macon. It was something of a tradition for many Southern boys, but it was not a path to aviation and there was little chance for glory.

Rob joined the regular Army as an enlisted man.

His mother was quiet as he left home on the morning of June 29, 1927. She smiled, kissed his cheek, and hugged him. She stared in disappointment as he folded himself into the passenger seat of the family car next to his father. He turned and waved. She nodded tightly. His father said little on the drive to Fort McPherson, an Army post on the south side of Atlanta.

Scott went to Fort McPherson because it was there that enlisted men seeking an appointment to West Point could attend a special preparatory school. But before he could take a test to enter the preparatory school, he had to learn how to be a soldier and how to perform the duties expected of a newly enlisted private in Company F of the Twenty-second Infantry Regiment. He washed dishes in the mess hall. He stood sentry duty. He marched.

Anyone who has ever served as an enlisted man knows the mindless nature of being a private. But in the evenings, Rob took out the photograph of the Great Wall, gently unfolded it, and dreamed of the day when he would walk the very place where that picture was taken. And as he folded it he promised himself that he would make his mama proud.

He studied. At night after lights out, he read under the covers with a flashlight. He read in the latrine. He studied as he had never studied in his life. Because Scott was not a gifted student, he relied on the power of his memory. He drilled the math and history and English into his brain, and when he took the test he passed and was put into the special group of young enlisted men—they came from throughout the Army—who would take the entrance exam for admission to West Point. The instructors were young lieutenants who had recently graduated from West Point. They knew full well what the entrance exam required and what the first year at the academy demanded.

Now Rob learned the real meaning of study. Fewer than a dozen of some eight hundred applicants would receive an academy appointment. Scott had to be one of those few, or he would revert to being a private in the regular Army.

Rob listened in class and he asked questions. The instructors thought that teaching enlisted men was good duty, and they were helpful to the privates. They knew that the looming test would weed out those applicants not qualified to be cadets and, by extension, officers in the United States Army. Rob took copious lecture notes and studied until the early hours of the morning. Applicants flunked out daily and as the size of the class diminished, Rob's life was classwork, bookwork, and homework.

In the spring of 1928, Rob took the entrance exam for West Point and returned to the quotidian duties of a private. Test results would not be announced for several months.

Rob was twenty years old. If he failed the test, he would be too old for a second attempt.

Rob was pulling guard duty one day in early June when he was ordered to report to his superior officer. In the office, Rob stood at attention. He was six feet tall and a skinny 150 pounds. He looked good in a uniform. He had a large and slightly lopsided hound-dog mouth that seemed always on the edge of a smile, dancing and devilish blue eyes, and more than his share of self-confidence. But he was sober and unsmiling as he stared at a spot on the wall above his superior officer's head. The officer was reading from a file on his desk. Rob's future was at stake.

As Rob waited, he sensed something in the air, an almost inexplicable feeling that somehow the axis of the earth had shifted, that things were different. When his superior officer spoke, the tone was somehow different from the tone officers normally used with privates. The officer told Rob that he was being offered an appointment to the United States Military Academy. Rob would report to West Point on July 2. Until then, he had several weeks of leave.

When Rob delivered the news to his parents, his mother began singing hymns as she worked around the house. Rob's father spent more time with his friends, and much of that time talking about his boy, Rob, who was going to West Point. And at church, the Scott family lingered after the service so Rob's mama could tell all who would listen that her boy would soon be a cadet at West Point. Her Rob would be a career Army officer, and one day he would be a famous pilot and a general.

"For the first time in my life, I could feel that my parents might even be proud of me," Rob later wrote. "The light in their eyes repaid me a thousand-fold for the long year of study."

In a town such as Macon, with its pervasive influence of Lanier High, there are fewer honors that can befall a young man greater than being admitted to West Point. But people had trouble believing Rob Scott actually had received one of the rare and coveted appointments.

"Rob is not much of a scholar, you know," they said, a layered Southern expression that at its worst means "That boy is dumb as a stump" and in its most gentle form means "Bless his heart. He did a lot with what the good Lord gave him."

And this business about becoming a fighter pilot? Rob Scott doesn't have what it takes to be a fighter pilot, they said.

Of course, Rob knew of the talk. And he was fearful. In his heart there festered a belief often found in the hearts of Southerners: the fear that stereotypes about Southerners may be right, that people from the South might not be as smart or as worldly or as cultured as people from other parts of the country. Rob feared that he did not have the educational background, the social skills and bearing, to be the material from which an officer is supposed to be made.

When Scott left for West Point, he wore a defensive air. He believed that West Point was waiting to humble him. He said he felt like a Spartan; he would return with his shield or on it.

# 3

## WEST POINT

WITHIN THE UNITED STATES ARMY, WEST POINT GRADUATES ARE THE chosen ones, the water-walkers. They are commissioned in the regular Army (as opposed to the Reserves), they receive better assignments, and they get promoted faster than their peers. They clank heavy West Point rings on their office desks and mess tables to signify their superior status as "ring knockers."

The history of West Point as a military post goes back to 1778. The massive buildings seem chiseled out of the stony ground. Everywhere are looming statues of past graduates, men of history and achievement, to remind the cadets of their duty and their potential. Ghosts of illustrious alumni hover over the parade ground in a palpable and weighty presence. This is holy ground.

But to Scott, West Point was simply the place he had to go in order to make a career of flying fighter aircraft.

Scott experienced little of the hazing—the physical and verbal abuse—that then was the lot of plebes, or freshmen, at West Point. First, he was older than most other plebes, and he let it be known that his wide range of accomplishments included being a pilot. Upperclassmen who hoped to go to flight school would often come to Scott's room, where he would line up two straight-backed chairs one in front of the other, and have the upperclassman sit in the front chair as if he were a student pilot while Scott sat in the rear chair as if he were the instructor. Scott would give the upperclassman a broom to represent the "stick" in the cockpit, describe the layout of an imaginary cockpit, and have the upperclassman visualize the instruments.

As the student moved the broom and "flew" the imaginary aircraft, Scott called out new compass headings, airspeed, and altitude, and issued commands such as "Keep the ball centered" or "Watch your airspeed" or "Get back on course."

Another reason Scott's plebe year was a good one was that he was charming and affable and he always had a big smile on his face. Scott's deep-fried voice and honey-baked manners caused him to stand out, and, when in his room, upperclassmen paid him the compliment of bestowing upon him a nickname: Scotty. He would wear that nickname the rest of his life.

Scott was from *down there*, and he had endless stories about building and crashing a glider, being a hobo, camping on a sandbar, shooting quail with a shotgun and killing cats with a bow and arrow, earning seventy-three merit badges as an Eagle Scout, meeting Billy Mitchell, flunking out of Mercer and the Citadel before winning a merit appointment to the Academy, and how someday he would walk the Great Wall of China. It was all so head-turning and Scott was such a *character*, and so likable, that—while he was called out on obvious breaches of discipline and good order—his plebe year was a good one.

Academically, Scotty's first year was also his best year. Cramming for the admission test at Fort McPherson had filled his head with much of the material taught to freshmen. At the end of the academic year, Scotty was in the top half of his class. His father was delighted but suggested in a letter that he hoped his son would move up to the top third of the class.

Because of his class standing, Scotty was granted Christmas leave. He went home and wore his white dress uniform to a Macon social event, almost certainly church-connected, and he was a dashing figure indeed. A uniform looked good on his tall slender frame and he took full advantage of it. His blue eyes danced. He had a mouth full of large gleaming white teeth. And he was cocky enough to be noticed, but not enough to offend.

Among those attending the event was Catharine Rix Green, a bouncy and vivacious little blonde from nearby Fort Valley. It would be another few years before *Gone with the Wind* was published, but Margaret Mitchell could have used Catharine as the model for Scarlett O'Hara. Catharine was the eldest of two daughters born to Glenmore Green and his wife, the former Sadie Hartley. Glenmore owned a peach orchard, and he was president of a company that sold orchard supplies. Soon he would be elected mayor of Fort Valley and he would hold that office for a decade.

Glenmore was also a deacon in the Baptist Church at the corner of College and Miller.

The Green family was one of the oldest and most prominent families in Fort Valley, and thus what passed for royalty in a small Southern town. It was said they were descendants of Revolutionary War hero Major General Nathanael Greene, but somewhere along the way had dropped the last "e" in the family name.

Catharine was self-absorbed, headstrong, and more than a little flighty. She had an outsized personality that dominated every room she walked into. She would date a boy once or twice and then toss him aside. She was five years younger than Scott, still in high school, but he had never known a girl such as this.

He introduced himself as "Scotty" and said, "I know everyone calls you Catharine. But I'm going to call you Kitty Rix."

Scotty and Kitty Rix would meet again.


During his "yearling," or sophomore, year, Scotty began a near-catastrophic academic slide. At the same time he began a round of extracurricular activities that made it seem as if he were trying to suck the marrow out of every extracurricular bone at the academy.

Scotty was circulation manager of *The Howitzer*, the West Point yearbook. He was on the committee that picked Christmas and Valentine cards for cadets. He played football, and on the track team he threw the javelin. He played intramural tennis and he was a cheerleader; and there is a picture taken of Scotty at an Army-Navy football game riding the Army team's mascot mule. He was rated an "expert" with the rifle. He was vice president of the Dialectic Society. (In one performance Scott played a role in blackface and was singled out by *The Howitzer* because he "made a big hit acting as others like to think he really is.")

*The Official Register of the Officers and Cadets at the United States Military Academy*, Scott's Cadet Service Record, and other West Point records for the years 1928–32 present a rounded—and sometimes incomplete—view of his time at the academy. Some of the records are simply wrong. For instance, Scott's Cadet Service Record reports that when he had been a student at Lanier High School, Scott played halfback in 1925–26, played center field on the baseball team from 1924 through 1926, and was assistant editor of the

*Lanerian* in 1926. All of this is baloney: Scott had falsified his West Point service record regarding his high school activities.

Perhaps the greatest intellectual gift West Point bestowed on Scott was an appreciation for the poems of Robert Service and Rudyard Kipling, and a book titled *The Travels of Marco Polo*. This is remarkable because West Point, at that time, buried the humanities inside other more practical courses, and subjects as frivolous as poetry were given short shrift indeed.

Modern academics say that Service and Kipling are poets for people who don't like poetry; that both men are racists, imperialists, and not worthy of being called poets. But to Scotty they wrote rollicking, boisterous poems that were perfect for declaiming loudly and at great length, especially during the long marches that cadets must endure during summer camp. Scott could read a poem three of four times and it was locked into his memory. It took little to remind Scott of a poem by either of these authors, and in conversation his eyes would suddenly widen, his head would tilt back, a finger would rise in the air, and off he would go, usually with more verses than anyone wanted to hear.

> *"Send not your foolish and feeble; send me your strong and your sane—*
> *Strong for the red rage of battle; sane, for I harry them sore;*
> *Send me men girt for the combat, men who are grit to the core;*
> *Swift as the panther in triumph, fierce as the bear in defeat,*
> *Sired of a bulldog parent, steeled in the furnace heat."*

Scott knew the standards, such as "The Cremation of Sam McGee" and "Gunga Din," but he also knew many of the more obscure poems by both men. Scott would later say that in his life he knew only one other person who could "say" as much Service or Kipling as he could. And that was his younger brother.

Service and Kipling were fun. They wrote poetry with hair on it. But it was Marco Polo who caused Scott to become truly obsessive.

If they are fortunate, every young person comes across a book that changes their life forever. *The Travels of Marco Polo* did that for Scott. He was truly stunned by the book.

Polo's book was a curious one to evoke such strong feelings. It tells of Polo's epic journey beginning in 1271 from Venice to Cambaluc—the name Polo gave to what is now Beijing. In his book the chronology is muddled, and it is difficult to understand the route that Polo followed. His revelations, while detailed, were so phantasmagorical that for centuries they were considered to be nothing more than a fabulist yarn. Few books have been deconstructed to the degree that Polo's book was, and, as would happen with any book under such prolonged scrutiny, the diggers found a few factual errors. But almost everything of significance was eventually proven to be true, so that today Polo's book stands in a category all its own as perhaps the greatest travel story ever written.

It was not so much what was *in* the book that intrigued Scott. It was what was *not* in the book that grabbed his attention: there was no reference to the Great Wall. How could Polo have traveled from Venice to Cambaluc and not mention the Great Wall? At first Scott thought the omission was a flaw in the translation, and he sought out every translation he could find. But in none of them was there even a tangential reference to the Great Wall. To Scott this was a serious omission, one that he should write about for an engineering class. He would title it "The Great Omission of Marco the Venetian."

It did not matter that in Polo's time the Great Wall was not thirty feet tall and topped by parapets as it would be during the Ming Dynasty some three centuries later. Rather it was a rough assemblage of earthen palisades. Polo was seventeen when he began his trek, and the book was dictated some thirty years later. Perhaps Polo's faded recollections were such that he did not think the palisades worthy of note. Whatever the reason, others had noted the omission and shrugged. But not Scott. And he wanted to reconcile this lapse; he wanted to know why the Great Wall had not captured the attention of the Venetian.

While Scott was interested, his instructor was not. The instructor vetoed the idea.

In September 1931, as Scott was entering his third year at the academy, events were taking place on the other side of the world that would later have a profound effect on his life: the Imperial Army of Japan, without the knowledge or consent of the emperor, invaded Manchuria and began a series of unbroken conquests.

To much of the world, this was a minor skirmish in a remote part of the world and hardly worthy of notice. But at West Point, career Army officers took a closer look at the highly trained Imperial Japanese army and its relentless aggression.

Scott's Delinquency Records and Efficiency Reports show that during his senior year, when he was about to graduate and was expected to have mastered the fundamentals of being an officer, he was still committing basic discipline offenses. He received demerits for not answering the telephone properly, talking in lecture room, shoes not shined, dirty floor in his room, dirty table in his room, dirt behind the radiator in his room, failing to wear spurs at a riding formation, soiled linen hidden in his full dress coat, and being late for class.

Scott's rebellion may have been caused in part by despair over his grades. Scott's father had ceased pushing him to be a scholastic success. He knew that Scott was near the bottom of his class, and now his only admonition was "Just hang on, son. Just hang on."

Another example of Scott's rebellion against Army authority can be seen in a story about his senior year, a time when cadets are given assignments to prepare them to be leaders. One such job was inspecting guard posts manned by plebes and yearlings. Scott found a yearling named Edward Sawyer asleep. This is such a serious offense that, if reported, it could have resulted in Sawyer's dismissal from the academy. Instead, Scott awakened the sleeping Sawyer and said, "Don't go back to sleep. And don't worry, I won't report you."

(Sawyer graduated, later became a major general, and had the opportunity to save the academic career of Scotty's nephew, Roland B. Scott Jr. Even when Robert L. Scott Jr. later became a polarizing and controversial figure, General Sawyer remained an unabashed admirer.)

At first blush, this story shows Scott's humanitarian side. But in truth he was violating a fundamental tenet of the U.S. military academy: it was his obligation to report any dereliction of duty, however slight.

In its mini biographical sketches of graduating cadets, *The Howitzer* for the class of 1932 reported that it was a daunting task to write of Scotty's experiences because those experiences "would occupy many volumes." The entry said that Scott could "recite reams upon reams of poetry" and that these poems, songs, and stories "brightened many of our hikes." The biography added that even though cadets learned many of Scott's favorites by heart, "we still like them all and like Scotty for making the Lord take down the darkness."

In a later oral history, classmate Hunter Harris (who became a four-star general and an Air Force commander in the Pacific) remembered Scott as a "very personable fellow and a great storyteller and one of our top English scholars."

But this was not a universally held belief. West Point records show that when the 262 cadets who graduated in 1932 were arranged according to general merit, Scott ranked 262.

Scott ranked 260 in engineering, 261 in ordnance and gunnery, 262 in law, 262 in economic and government, 240 in military hygiene, 252 in tactics, and 247 in conduct. He earned 117 demerits during his fourth year.

As he approached graduation, Scott knew that he was near the bottom of his class, and he sought to make it official: he wanted to be the class "goat"—the cadet who graduated at the bottom in every category—and he almost succeeded.

During Scotty's last year, most of his demerits—twenty-six in January and forty-one in February—came because of Marco Polo, the Great Wall, and insubordination. His Cadet Service Record shows that in class he submitted "facetious" and "argumentative" explanations on class subjects.

Here Scott's experience illustrates an unspoken part of West Point and Army culture: The school sets up conditions that invite students to break the rules, but severely punishes those who are caught doing it.

In one class, Scott was told to stand up and recite the details of a particular battle. He was not prepared and began "bugling," that is, talking in an assured manner to cover his lack of knowledge. Of course he was caught by the professor, received a zero, and was dropped to a lower section in the class.

In that lower section, Scotty tried to redeem himself by writing a paper on the Civil War battle of Bull Run, where he said his great-grandfather had fought and died. But cadets had written of Civil War battles for years, and professors wanted something else. So, again, Scott offered to write a paper on the travels of Marco Polo. By drawing in material from the logistics classes Scott had taken, he sought to reveal what a masterful logistician the Venetian had been. But his professor said Marco Polo was of no military interest and instead assigned Scott to write a paper on the Battle of Sandepu, which took place in the Russo-Japanese War of 1904–5.

Sandepu was a major battle with some thirty thousand casualties, and it was also a foreshadowing of what war was about to become with trenches, artillery barrages, and massed assaults against automatic weapons producing high casualty rates. But Scott thought the battle beneath his efforts. So he went big. He embellished the history of the battle to include fictional officers, pictures of New York City street cleaners whom he identified as Japanese soldiers, and engagements that never happened. Scott enlarged the story of the battle to make it comparable with more epic historical battles. He typed his work on heavy yellow paper, drew illustrations on many pages, and bound the opus with a red silk ribbon.

A few days later Scott found his classmates laughing loudly as they stood in front of the bulletin board where grades were posted. Scott had been "skinned," which was cadet jargon for an infraction of discipline.

Scott was charged with "submitting facetious monograph in military art, including imaginative and irrelevant matter in same, and casting demeaning reflections upon the Engineering Department."

Called before the Battalion Board—called the "Batt Board" by cadets—to explain his actions, Scott pleaded ignorance. . . . He told the two captains and the major who composed the board that after being dropped to a lower section, he realized he must be of inferior intelligence and could not write a worthy monograph on an actual battle. Therefore he had turned to fiction with the hope that when graded by the standards of the lower section—either pass or fail—his paper would be interesting enough that he would pass.

He was bugling, but members of the board were sympathetic. That is, until one of the officers asked Scott the purpose of the red ribbon binding his monograph.

"Sir, how long have you been in the Army?" Scott asked.

"Seventeen years," snapped the annoyed officer.

"Then, sir, you know about Army red tape."

That was it. Forty-one demerits.

It did not matter to Scott. He shrugged off his poor academic performance by saying, "I was not especially dumb. I was just saving my eyes for flying."

# 4

# BUGLING

During Scott's time at West Point, the Corps of Engineers had its pick of the top graduates from each class. The artillery branch had its choice of the next level of cadets, followed by the cavalry and—at the bottom—the infantry.

Scott would be commissioned in the infantry. But because he had splendid vision and met all the other criteria for becoming a pilot, he was selected for flight school.

By the spring of 1932, during his last weeks at the academy, Scott had lost all interest in academics. He was beginning to emerge as a performance artist who needed a big room for his productions, and he wanted to accomplish something important after his poor performance at West Point—something connected to Marco Polo, something people would remember.

Scott had a summer of leave, and rather than going home to Macon he decided to borrow enough money to go to France, and there buy a motorcycle. His intention was to spend that summer replicating the first part of Marco Polo's route to China. He would go to Venice, Polo's home, and then ride across Europe, maybe as far as Turkey, and perhaps somewhere along the way he might gain some understanding of why Marco Polo never mentioned the Great Wall of China.

Scott had absorbed enough of the military arts to know that all military operations depend upon detailed planning. Dry runs—that is, practicing the mission—are crucial, and they would enable him to anticipate most problems and to take steps to minimize them. On weekends before the journey he rented a motorcycle and rode it along narrow and winding roads surrounding the academy. But those routes were not sufficiently challenging, so Scott drove the motorcycle back to West Point and began ripping along the riding trails traditionally set aside for the sole use of academy officials and faculty. But putting a motorcycle on those bridle paths was not just illegal. It was sacrilegious.

The cavalry still had an almost mythic status in the Army. Americans had adopted the British feeling toward the cavalry; that is, skill in riding a horse well was the mark of a gentleman and cavalry charges were the stuff of legends and heroes, the most romantic side of the brutal business of war. Americans had nothing compared to the Charge of the Light Brigade in popular lore, but then there had been Colonel George Armstrong Custer and all those attacks made against savage Indians by officers on horseback, their sabers high, thundering into battle. Most West Point instructors rode horses and loved the smell of horse sweat on their boots, the rattle of spurs when they walked, and in their dreams they heard bugles sounding the call to charge.

To the cavalrymen, tanks were unreliable tin boxes, artillerymen were "cannon cockers," and infantrymen—while necessary—were little more than ciphers who walked into battle and who fought in the mud. But most heretical of all were those young men who wanted to be flyers, arrogant pups who tossed around phrases like "air power" and "air-mindedness" and who believed that airplanes would change the face of war.

West Point faculty may have sensed that horses were becoming a thing of the past, but many officers hung on with both hands. With the military, after all, the only thing more difficult than accepting a new idea is giving up an old one.

Scott said he put his motorcycle on the academy's bridle paths because those wooded dirt trails that followed the hillside down to the Hudson River were more realistic and would provide better training for his trip on the trail of the Venetian.

Nonsense. Scott was going into the Army Air Corps, which dismissed the cavalry and its horses as a laughably outmoded form of warfare. He was thumbing his nose at West Point officials and the cavalry.

So one Saturday morning in the late spring of 1932, Scott was on a red Indian Scout motorcycle, roaring along the wooded riding trails, leaning into the curves, as he imagined he was somewhere along Marco Polo's route when, suddenly, over the staccato splatting of his motorcycle exhaust, he heard another sound: the scream of a terrified horse. And there it was, eyes wide and ears flattened, riderless and plunging down the side of the hill, crossing a stream, and disappearing into the woods.

Into view hove an officer of the United States Army, brushing himself off and shouting for Scott to turn off his engine. Scott instantly recognized the officer: Lieutenant Colonel Robert C. Richardson, commandant of cadets, a man of patrician appearance and easy manner, but a godlike figure to cadets.

Scott, by riding a motorcycle on the riding trails, had violated the holy of holies. And he had done so in the presence of the commandant of West Point.

Scott was filled with trepidation as he followed the colonel down the hill. The two men waded the creek. The colonel caught his horse and was holding the reins, speaking soothingly to it and stroking its flanks, while Scott stood at rigid attention. As Scott later told the story, a few minutes thereafter the commandant turned to him and quietly said, "Don't you know, Mr. Scott, that the bridle paths are off-limits to you, much less motorcycles?"

Scott's offense had been so deliberate, so egregious, that the commandant could have levied a punishment that would have kept Scott from graduating. And if Scott were set back, he might wind up in the infantry instead of in a cockpit. His destiny was at stake, and there was nothing to do but bugle.

Scott talked of Marco Polo, how he wanted to retrace the steps of the Venetian, how his training was putting into practice the logistics lessons he had learned at West Point.

The commandant was fascinated. He had served as the military attaché at the American embassy in Rome, and he knew Europe well. He was interested in the route Scott would take. As would have been many other Army officers, he was also intrigued by the logistics of what was essentially a forced march: Scott had to push as far east as possible, but always looking over his shoulder back toward France, where, on a given date, he had to catch a boat to return to America and join his flight-training class in Texas. The commandant was so fascinated that not only did he forgo any punishment of this errant cadet, he asked Scott to drop by his office in the following week to further discuss the trip. He knew a few people in Europe should Scott have any trouble there.

On June 10, 1932, Scott attended his last parade, graduated from the United States Military Academy, and was commissioned as a second lieutenant in the United States Army. He received his heavy West Point ring.

If Scott's classmates had voted on the officer least likely to succeed, it surely would have been Scott. His record was deplorable, and his conduct often inexcusable. He was an affable fellow who talked endlessly of flying airplanes, and he knew more than what was worth knowing of Marco Polo. Although adventurous, Scott was not a military man and would not go far in this man's army. His greatest ability was bugling.

Scott had not learned that, in the military, facts are more important than storytelling. And the facts should be delivered straight and true with no embellishment. Being known as a bugler was no compliment.

Back in Macon, Scott's younger brother, Roland, graduated from Lanier as a cadet captain. He was an Eagle Scout with more merit badges than his older brother. The Lanier graduation fell on the same day as the West Point graduation. Scott's mama and his sister, Elizabeth, who had graduated from Wesleyan College, a small Methodist women's college in Macon, in 1930, attended the West Point graduation while Robert Senior attended Roland's graduation.

Elizabeth became a teacher and would marry an army officer. But she lived her life in the shadow of Rob and—to a lesser degree—Roland.

Scott was anxious to climb aboard the passenger liner *Europa*, cross the Atlantic, and chase Marco Polo across Europe. But first he had to spend a few days in Macon. His mama insisted. She also insisted on the family attending a social event and she insisted that Rob wear his Army uniform with the shiny gold bars of a newly minted second lieutenant.

Kitty Rix was at the party, and boys swarmed around her like bees around magnolia blossoms—heavy-breathing, scurrying, elbow-jostling boys trying to act grown-up and gentlemanly. But they were all so *anxious*. And she noticed the deference shown by Macon society toward Lieutenant Scott. Such things were important to a privileged young lady from Fort Valley.

But what really got her attention was the poetry coming through the smiling mouth of Lieutenant Scott. No one had ever courted her by quoting poetry.

*She's as light as any fairy; she's as pretty as a peach;*
*She's mistress of the witchcraft to beguile;*
*There's sunshine in her manner, there is music in her speech,*
*And there's concentrated honey in her smile.*

If Scott wanted to call upon her when he returned from Europe, she would be receptive.

Scott enjoyed the Atlantic passage. The weather was pleasant, the deck chairs were comfortable, and because he liked being paged as "Lieutenant Robert Scott" when telegrams were delivered, he sent numerous telegrams that required an answer.

Scott disembarked at Cherbourg and bought a Soyer *motocyclette*. Like most such machines of the day, it had no windscreen, and like most drivers of such machines, Scott bought goggles. "I needed both of my eyes for the rendezvous I had with my destiny of being a fighter pilot," he said.

He strapped his camera to his hip. On the front fender of the motorcycle he attached the American flag and the French flag. Later he would replace the French flag with the flag of whatever country he was traveling through. On the rear fender atop the baggage rack was a suitcase. On each side of the rear wheel was a can containing a gallon of emergency fuel.

In the midafternoon of June 14, 1932, Scott twisted the throttle of his machine and was off to Paris before departing on his quixotic Near Eastern adventure. The trip revealed much about Scott.

First, his observations were those of a small-town provincial man: the flies were pestilential, the villages were poor, sheep were blocking the roads. In short, the inconveniences were many.

The motorcycle trip across Europe is an example of how Scott dreamed big dreams and went after those dreams full bore, with nothing held back. "Obsessive" and "melodramatic" are good words to describe Scott. He was obsessed with becoming a fighter pilot, obsessed with the Great Wall, obsessed with Marco Polo, obsessed with the idea of going to West Point, obsessed with Service and Kipling, and obsessed with the idea of riding a motorcycle across Europe.

On the motorcycle trip there was more drama: every day the desire to drive farther than the previous day, a desire that basic math says will quickly end in frustration. And then there is the telegram Scott is supposed to have received from the U.S. Army in the far reaches of Turkey—a telegram canceling his leave and ordering him to Texas for flight training. Scott couldn't say that he had a steamship departure schedule to meet, but had to invent a dramatic message calling him back. He never said how he received the telegram while on the back roads of Turkey.

In later years when Scott would write again about his motorcycle trip, he would add many flourishes, including a Romanian princess.

He would tell many stories about this trip, and some of the stories were true.

But perhaps what is closest to the truth is found in the verses of Robert Service:

> There's a race of men that don't fit in,
> A race that can't stay still;
> So they break the hearts of kith and kin,
> And they roam the world at will.

In Cherbourg, Scott sold his motorcycle back to the shop where he bought it, boarded the ship, and was homeward bound. He would visit his mama in Macon and then drive to Texas.

During his trip he had sent postcards to his mama and to the commandant at West Point, but not to Kitty Rix. Now that he was headed back to Georgia, he found he thought of her often.

# 5

# FLYING AND DRIVING

BEFORE REPORTING TO FLIGHT TRAINING, SCOTT MADE A QUICK VISIT to Macon to tell his mama of his adventures in Europe. While in Macon he attended a party, and there he saw Kitty Rix.

She was by then a student at Shorter College, a small two-year Baptist college in the north Georgia hamlet of Rome. No matter its location, an all-girls school is a magnet for boys for a hundred miles in all directions. Kitty Rix said even boys from Georgia Tech came up from Atlanta on the weekends.

As usual, she was surrounded by multiple suitors. And she was wearing two fraternity pins, which meant she had *two* boys who were special to her: "Edwards of Cedartown" and "the Berryman guy." At the party, one stood on either side of Kitty Rix, and both stood entirely too close to her.

En route to Texas, all Scott could think about was those college boys and their fraternity pins. When he arrived, smoldering in his mind was a mental picture of Kitty Rix in her white dress wearing two fraternity pins, a well-dressed boy with slicked-back hair on each side, and her blond hair flouncing back and forth as she smiled at each in turn.

Scott reported for primary flight training at Randolph Field, located sixteen miles northeast of San Antonio. Randolph was called "the West Point of the Air."

After primary training, Scott would be assigned to advanced training at Kelly Field, sited just to the southwest of San Antonio. Schools were there because of the flat and sparsely populated terrain and the splendid weather; they combined to make this part of Texas an ideal place for young fledglings to gain flying skills that were almost commensurate with their self-confidence.

In addition to hundreds of flight students—both commissioned officers and cadets (the latter were enlisted flight students who would be commissioned when they received their wings)—there were thousands of young enlisted support personnel at these two bases. As a result, so many soldiers found wives in San Antonio that the town was called "the Mother-in-Law of the Air Corps."

The mating rituals of San Antonio were fueled in part by the Great Depression. It hit the southwest especially hard, and there was little opportunity for anyone in what had already been a poor corner of America. From miles around, young women left their homes on the flat mesquite-covered land and came to San Antonio to find a better life. For many that meant finding an Army husband. Military life might have been hard and transient, but it was dependable and offered benefits and security found in few other places.

For the men in flight school, dances and parties were held almost every Saturday. A pilot was considered a fine catch for a discerning and ambitious young woman. The roses of San Antonio attended such events by the dozens in their best dresses, high heels, and their most expensive perfume. They made it their business to know their business and their business was to marry a pilot. They knew military ranks and customs, they learned a bit about aviation, and they adopted the vernacular of pilots as they prepared.

Pilots are notorious womanizers. They boast that they will "screw a snake if somebody will hold the head"—and the patina of refinement and elegance could not entirely overcome the desire of these young men to mate, or the desire of the young women to become a wife. Scott attended these dances and by his account he made quite an impression with the young ladies. Without a trace of irony, he said that at these dances he was able to "temporarily shed my modesty" in accounting the adventures of his motorcycle ride across Europe.

"Why do you want to be a pilot?" was a common question from a dark-eyed beauty as she looked up at a man from Randolph.

Scott would tilt his head back like a wolf baying at the moon and he would declaim:

*Send me the best of your breeding, lend me your chosen ones;*
*Them will I take to my bosom, them will I call my sons.*

As the dark-eyed girl was rendered speechless, Scott would smile beatifically, say, "That's me. That's why I want to be a pilot." And then he would pull her close, and the dance would continue.

It was against this superheated backdrop that Scott went through flight training. In 1932, that training was relatively simple. The Army remained overwhelmingly a ground force and thus the Air Corps was still considered to be something of a nuisance to many traditional Army officers. One cavalry officer famously dismissed the Air Corps by asking what was the point of buying airplanes when they become obsolete so quickly and more had to be bought. To him—and to the entrenched Army hierarchy—it made no sense. Because of these views, and because of the minimal budgets authorized by Congress in that era, the Army Air Corps had only seventeen hundred aircraft in service, all of them outmoded and most worn out. The typical military cockpit of the period had only the basic instruments necessary to operate during daylight hours and in good weather. Few military aircraft had radios. Because of budget constraints, U.S. military aviation had not made significant advances since the end of World War I.

Scott was not a natural pilot. The few hours he had flown in the Jenny had given him only the barest fundamentals of handling an aircraft.

During primary training, Scott flew in the front seat of a low-powered and forgiving biplane called a Consolidated PT-3. Scott was too anxious to please and too anxious to show his flying skills, and that was a dangerous combination for a man with such limited experience.

He did all the inept things that students do—things that make an instructor's hair turn gray before its time, and that make him pray for the day when he is reassigned to a tactical unit.

Once, an instructor had ordered Scott to "Put it in a glide" and he heard "Put it in a dive." The results caused a few minutes of anxiety in the rear cockpit. And then there was the day Scott soloed—the biggest single moment in a pilot's flight training. The instructor told Scott to "Take it around and land as close to me as you can." Scott took off, climbed to pattern altitude, circled back to the base leg of his approach, and then straightened out, all the while keeping his eye on his instructor standing in the middle of the field. He made small adjustments to the throttle, worked his feet on the rudders, and made a near-perfect approach. He would have landed squarely atop the instructor had not the terrified man scurried out of the way.

Scott was so proud of his precision landing that he taxied across the field to the hangar, about a mile away, leaving his exasperated instructor—who was wearing a heavy parachute—to walk back in the hot Texas sun.

One day, after Scott had soloed, he was practicing his landings when he decided that rather than landing into the wind as expected, he would practice downwind landings, and crosswind landings. An instructor observed Scott landing from every point of the compass and concluded that his student had lost his mind. The instructor sent Scott to the base medical officer, who, after questioning Scott, filed a report saying Scott was mentally competent to be a pilot. Thereafter, Scott often showed a copy of the finding to others as proof that he was sane. "I got papers," he would say, as he flashed the physician's opinion.

Around 10 p.m. on July 20, 1933—at that point Scott was in advanced training and had 196 flying hours—he became lost on a night-navigation flight, landed in a pasture, and ripped through a farmer's wire fence and across two ditches before coming to a stop. The accident report said he wrecked the "landing gear, propeller and lower wings" and that the cause of the accident was "poor technique," or, put another way, pilot error.

Scott was making progress on fulfilling his destiny to become a fighter pilot. But he could not get Kitty Rix out of his mind. More and more he remembered her white dress and her blond hair and those two college boys hovering like raptors over her. And those *two* fraternity pins.

In those days, most Southern girls, like girls everywhere, wanted to find husbands. They were flouncy and flirty and eventually they would have a husband and children, but at parties they entered like mini blizzards, dressed in white, bouncy, eyelashes fluttering, vapid fluff balls all, who couldn't wait to be asked to dance.

Scott grew up in this environment and knew that for a Southern girl, a boy who was out of sight was out of mind. A Southern belle must be courted assiduously or else she would drift away to, if not a better prospect, then at least to a prospect who was present.

After about a month in Texas, Scott went into his obsessive mode and he began to court Kitty Rix with an ardor and a panache that few college boys could match.

Convertibles were de rigueur for pilots and Scott had bought a red Chevrolet convertible. He pulled out the rumble seat and replaced it with a fifty-five-gallon fuel tank, which, along with the usual twelve-gallon tank, gave his car considerable range. At the base exchange, he bought gas for a nickel a gallon.

One particular Friday afternoon, as soon as the duty day was over, Scott took off from San Antonio for Rome, Georgia. He drove out of the main gate and turned east on Highway 90, the Old Spanish Trail. The outbound route took him through Schertz to Seguin and then on to Gonzales to Halletsville, through Eagle Lake, Sugarland, Houston, and Beaumont. Soon he began angling north eastward through Louisiana, Alabama, and then northwest Georgia.

Scott had to be back at Randolph Field before 8 a.m. on Monday, and thus, like a pilot navigating his course, he was looking at his watch and doing mental calculations from the time he left San Antonio.

Today, on interstates I-10 and I-59, this is a trip of about 987 miles and, if one observes the speed limit, the trip takes about sixteen hours. But in the early 1930s there were no interstate highways, and the trip was more than twelve hundred miles each way.

Given the roads of the time, and the many small towns along the route, and the 55 mph speed limit, Scott would have been fortunate to average fifty miles an hour for the long trip to Georgia: that is twenty-four nonstop hours. And then the twenty-four-hour nonstop return trip to San Antonio.

Each trip was timed to the minute, and there was no allowance for flat tires, speeding tickets, traffic jams, meals, or other stops. Scott sometimes had only an hour or so in Rome before he had to turn around and aim for Texas.

If the trip to Rome was difficult, the return trip was brutal. He was driving west into the sun after two nights with no sleep, and fatigue sank into the marrow of his bones.

But more importantly, these trips were illegal. Flight students were ordered to go no farther from the base than the boundaries of San Antonio. Officers, especially West Point graduates, were honorable men, and their commanders wasted little time checking up on them. Had Scott been caught, he would have been charged with the offense of being absent without official leave (AWOL). If found guilty, he probably would have been dismissed from flight school and returned to the infantry. His destiny would have been thwarted.

But Scott believed that a man was not AWOL until he had been caught.

Or, as they would have said in Macon, "Hey, y'all. Hold my beer and watch this."

Unless it was raining, Scott drove with the top down, thinking that since he flew an open-cockpit aircraft, he should drive an open-cockpit car. It was a fighter-pilot thing.

Scott wore a flying suit on these trips. And as temperatures dropped, he began wearing a bulky winter flight suit and heavy boots. The flight suit had bronze zippers from top to bottom and big "U.S. Army Air Corps" insignia, and—to protect his eyes—helmet and goggles. And around his neck, streaming behind him, was a long white scarf.

State troopers, county sheriffs, and municipal police officers across the South were likely to give a uniformed military officer a bit of leeway if they stopped him for speeding. When Scott was stopped, it usually was because of his appearance. Scott would push up his goggles, flash his smile, and start bugling about being on a mission to protect his girl from pissant college boys. More often than not the laughing law-enforcement officer would caution Scott to be careful and wave him on his way. Scott would nod, pull down his goggles, and take off, flat out, belly to the ground, as he hurried the sundown.

Once he showed up late Saturday afternoon at Shorter College just as Kitty Rix was about to leave with her two boyfriends for a night football game at Georgia Tech in Atlanta. At Shorter, the proprieties had to be observed. In the dorm's living room were decorous and well-turned-out young ladies attended by mannered young men wearing coats and ties.

Then the door was flung open and there appeared an apparition in a flight suit, goggles, and boots. A tall man made large and bulky by his winter flight suit. To the fraternity boys, he was a Sasquatch-like figure both imposing and intimidating. Scott took off his headgear to reveal a face reddened by the wind and marked by the imprint of his helmet and goggles for the previous twenty-four hours. He was looking at his watch as he galumphed down the hall bellowing for Kitty Rix. To say he attracted considerable attention would be an understatement. But Scott knew that he had to trump the two fraternity pins.

And then there came Kitty Rix down the hall, her blond hair swishing, her heels making a staccato sound on the wood floor, and her green eyes flashing. She tried to look exasperated, but shining through was an expression that, to Scott, had made the trip entirely worthwhile.

Kitty Rix was shaking her head in a mixture of amusement and consternation. "Scotty, you just don't know the trouble you are causing around here," she said. "What am I going to do with you?"

The callow young men in the reception room stared openmouthed at Scott as he explained that he had just driven in from central Texas and must return within an hour or so, but would they mind if he spent that time with Kitty Rix? They gaped at Kitty Rix, who nodded in agreement, and, being mannered young Southerners, they acquiesced.

They were college boys, and Scott was a force of nature.

Scott says that when he left Rome bound for San Antonio, he always used different routes. He was following his training: a pilot should never be predictable. To confuse enemy gunners, always come off a target from different directions.

Scott made some two dozen of these weekend trips during his flight training. Toward the end of the program, he wanted to codify his existing practice; he asked his boss for permission to make a weekend trip to Atlanta so he could protect his girlfriend from college boys.

The captain looked at him in confusion. Scott remembered there was an Atlanta, Texas, and clarified his request by adding, "Atlanta, Georgia."

"Hell, no," said the captain.

And then as the captain realized the mileage involved and the short amount of available time to make the trip, he added, "Absolutely, hell no."

But Scott went anyway, returning to San Antonio in time to make Monday-morning roll call and another flying lesson, often after having had only two or three hours of sleep in the past three nights. On one trip he almost met with disaster.

Scott was westbound near Patterson, Louisiana, when his car began a terrible clanging, forcing him to pull off the road. It happened he was quite near a small airport, and when aircraft mechanics heard the noise, they came outside to investigate.

From Scott's appearance they knew he was an Army pilot and there was nothing they would not do for him, especially after he explained his dilemma. They quickly performed emergency repairs and put Scott back on the road, but it was midmorning on Monday when Scott rolled through the gate at Randolph Field. He expected to be met with orders to report to his superior officer. Instead he was met by his roommate, who said, "Scotty, you are the luckiest man alive."

San Antonio was going through a cold snap, and it was as severe as it was rare. The weather was so cold that morning that not only had training flights been suspended, but because the classroom pipes had frozen, all ground-school classes were canceled.

Scott nodded in appreciation. The Big Sky Boss was on the job.

As he approached graduation, Scott needed help from the Big Sky Boss more than ever. He knew the weekend trips to Rome were exciting to Kitty Rix and that she was the talk of the campus because she had a boyfriend in the Air Corps who drove in from Texas on the weekends just to spend a few minutes with her. But he also knew that Kitty Rix was not unlike an aircraft in flight: let your attention wander, and things can quickly get out of hand.

Scuttlebutt had it that most of Scott's class would be assigned to a pursuit squadron in the Philippines. Being in a pursuit squadron would be the culmination of all Scott's boyhood dreams, something he had striven for ever since he saw the wreckage of Eugene Ely's aircraft that day in Macon so long ago.

But Kitty Rix was not the sort of woman who would wait. One day in the early fall of 1933, as he neared graduation, Scott was in the officers' club and saw a visiting general having a cup of coffee.

Lieutenants do not interrupt a general to push a personal agenda. But Scott was not the normal lieutenant. He approached the general's table, stood at attention, and asked if he might make a request of the general. Sir. The general, almost certainly wondering what could be important enough to justify such a breach of protocol, nodded.

Scott began bugling along these lines: "Sir, I am in the Army and I will go wherever I am sent. But I want to get married. I may be sent to the Philippines. I've convinced my girlfriend that the Army life is a good life. If I could stay in America until she graduates from college next June, we can be married, and after that I will be glad to go anywhere the Army sends me. But I need to stay in America until she graduates."

The general stared at Scott. After a long moment, he asked Scott to write down his name, rank, and serial number. Scott quickly did so and passed the paper to the general, who said, "I will take it under advisement."

The general continued with his coffee and Scott went on his way.

A few days later Scott received his orders: he was to be a pilot assigned to the Ninety-ninth Observation Squadron at Mitchel Field on Long Island, New York. The two-seat aircraft he would be flying had an "O" designation, rather than a "P," for pursuit. Not exactly the fulfillment of his dreams of becoming a fighter pilot. But Georgia was only about nine hundred miles away—even shorter by air, and thus no distance at all for a pilot.

Scott graduated on October 13, 1933, and pinned on the silver wings of a pilot in the United States Army Air Corps. This achievement, he said, was "made possible by the faith and trust, and the drive, of my mother."

Scott was twenty-five years old. His base pay was $144 per month, with another $72 monthly in flight pay. Already he was planning cross-country flights or low-level-navigation flights that would take him to Georgia.

He did not know it, but the need to get back to Kitty Rix was greater than he imagined. The Berryman guy was about to write a letter to Catharine saying, "I love you so very, very much, darling."

As Scott prepared for his first tactical assignment, several people were emerging on the horizon who, in a few more years, would play a significant role not only in Scott's life, but in world affairs.

The first, and far and away the most important, was a dour, black-eyed, and hot-tempered man whose face was so roughly chiseled it looked like an unfinished piece of sculpture.

Claire Lee Chennault was born in Texas in 1893, the son of John Stonewall Jackson Chennault, and, according to family lore, a descendant of Robert E. Lee.

The Chennault family moved to Waterproof, Louisiana, where Chennault grew up hunting and fishing in the bayous and cypress swamps along the Mississippi River. After graduating from Louisiana State Normal College, he taught in one-room schoolhouses in Louisiana. Chennault married in 1911, and he and his wife Nell would have eight children. He joined the U.S. Army in 1917, and applied for flight training four times. Each time he was rejected. But in the end he was befriended by instructors and soon he had eighty hours of flying time, after which he was accepted for flight training.

Chennault was a brilliant pursuit pilot, and in the early 1930s he was selected to attend the Air Corps Tactical School, where he immediately clashed with one of the instructors, a Captain Clayton Bissell.

Chennault and Bissell had bad chemistry. They detested each other from their first meeting, and subsequent meetings only exacerbated their mutual dislike.

# 6

## LEARNING THE TRADE

SCOTT DID NOT LIKE BEING AN OBSERVATION PILOT, AND HE COULD NOT see how this fulfilled his destiny or fit into what he called "the Master Plan." But he believed the Big Sky Boss would sort it all out. In the meantime, he had a lot to observe, and a fine airplane from which to do the observing.

He flew the Curtiss O-1G Falcon, a biplane with wooden wings, fixed landing gear, a two-seat, open cockpit, and a twelve-cylinder, 435-horsepower inline engine that, when full power was applied, sounded like Judgment Day.

Long Island was Scott's area of operations; it extends eastward from Upper New York Bay and Manhattan for about 120 miles. Mitchel Field was east of Garden City, and when Scott took off, he turned southeast toward the Jones Beach lighthouse and then took up a due-east heading. By the time he reached Montauk Point he had settled into his cruising speed of around 110 miles per hour. Scott circled the magnificent hotel at the tip of Montauk Point, swung back toward Sag Harbor and Riverhead, turned right to overfly Orient Point, and then flew along the north shore until he was near the skyline of lower Manhattan. He overflew Queens and Brooklyn, and then back to Coney Island, where he turned north and returned to Mitchel Field. He had been in the air for about two hours.

These training flights were meant to increase Scott's confidence. Each flight was more or less the same, and a non-aviator might think that after a few such flights the routine would become boring. But Scott believed that one day he would be a fighter pilot, and in the meantime it was important to practice the more arcane facets of his profession. Scott considered each flight a combat sortie, and he made mental notes on various "targets" along the way: the best direction for an attack; the most probable location for anti-aircraft guns; major highway and rail intersections, and runway layouts; and the most likely buildings for command staffs at "enemy" airfields.

Scott had become a camera buff, and he often shot photographs along his route. He took numerous pictures of Montauk Manor, a large hotel at the eastern tip of Long Island, and was so pleased with his work that one day he drove to the hotel and presented a framed aerial photo of the property to the manager.

About two weeks after arriving at Mitchel Field, Scott was summoned to the office of his squadron commander, a former cavalry officer who wore spurs on his boots.

In late 1933 the Great Depression lay heavily on the military and funding was tight. Keeping airplanes in the air cost a lot of money. Ergo, a good way for the Air Corps to save money was to limit pilots to no more than four flying hours per month, the minimum required for them to receive flight pay.

Scott had violated the Eleventh Commandment of a young officer: "Thou shalt not embarrass thy boss." He had flown too many hours.

Scott believed differently. Many times in his life he would say that if professional musicians and professional ballerinas practiced ten hours each day to maintain their proficiency, then as a professional pilot he should fly as many hours a day as possible.

Scott stood at attention as the squadron commander laced into him about flying sixteen sorties, more than thirty-two hours, since he had arrived on base. Scott had flown all the hours allotted him for eight months. Therefore, for the next eight months, Scott was to be grounded. To fill his time and to teach him a lesson, Scott was now the squadron supply officer.

To a pilot, few jobs are more demeaning than the clerical, bean-counter job of keeping track of supplies—everything from uniforms and shoes to sheets and typewriter paper—and to make little marks on his clipboard about the status of each item.

But Scott was determined to be the best supply officer in the history of the squadron. He was energetic in filling out his paperwork and in offering new procedures to improve the always-cumbersome military supply system.

In the eyes of the squadron commander, such an attitude meant Scott had not been humbled enough. Scott's personnel file says he was given the additional job of transportation officer.

Lieutenant Scott was barely a month into his first tactical assignment, and he had been grounded, had been given two menial clerical jobs, and almost certainly was on his way to a poor efficiency report.

Efficiency reports are the military version of a schoolhouse report card. They are always awarded at the end of an assignment and they are of crucial importance when it comes to being promoted.

But if Scott feared for his future as an officer and as a pilot, he feared even more for his relationship with Kitty Rix. If he didn't get down to Georgia to see her soon, she might well wind up with one of those pipsqueak fraternity boys.

To add the final insult, his brother pilots began kidding Scott about being a "time hog," a man who wanted to do nothing but fly, and they teased him about his ground duties, his quoting poetry, his storytelling, his endless monologues about Marco Polo and walking the Great Wall of China, and being a Southerner. Scott's squadron mates believed his Georgia roots were the source of his oddities.

And then one day a notice appeared on the squadron bulletin board asking for volunteers to take a course in instrument flying—"blind flying," as it was called at the time—at Newark, New Jersey.

Scott's squadron mates snorted in derision. *Newark?* That meant the volunteers would have a three-hour commute by car every morning and another in the afternoon. And the training would not be in an aircraft but in a simulator—a tight little box mounted on a pedestal. The student would sit in the box for hours while looking at his instruments and trying to keep the "aircraft" in level flight while the instructor pressed buttons and pulled levers that caused the box to tilt back and forth, and to rock from side to side as it jerked up and down.

In the mid-1930s blind flying was still a novelty. As long as a pilot had a compass, an altimeter, and an airspeed indicator, why should he take special training that would allow him to fly in inclement weather?

The attitude of Scott's squadron mates was not an unusual mind-set among many pilots of the day. They had little interest in advancing strategy or tactics or equipment in their career as men-at-arms. These pilots would serve one tour in the Air Corps and then return to civilian life, often taking a well-paying job with one of the airlines. With a few notable exceptions, the cavalry-dominated Army officer corps did not have the vision to see the potential of aviation. Too many senior officers looked down on pilots as little boys playing with toys.

As a result, comparatively few pilots of the day had the heart of a fighter pilot. They had only the swagger. They liked the idea of flying four hours a month, tending to a few ground duties, and spending afternoons in the bar in the officers' club or on the polo grounds. It was a gentlemanly way to do things, and no one wanted to spend several weeks driving across town every day to Newark, and then only to sit in a box. It was so undignified.

Scott was the only volunteer from his squadron.

The squadron commander was pleased, and he readily signed off on Scott's taking the instrument-flying course. He had gotten rid of a trouble-maker and he believed that he had taught Scott a lesson in the process.

During the afternoons, while Scott was fighting his way through the traffic from Newark to Mitchel Field, his squadron mates were in the officers' club shaking their heads in amused condescension.

What Scott's squadron mates, his spurs-wearing commanding officer, and many others in the Air Corps did not realize was that the hell-for-leather seat-of-the-pants style of flying was coming to an end, and that military aviation was on the cusp of revolutionary change. Aircraft were becoming more sturdy and streamlined. Engines were becoming more reliable. Radio and navigation instruments were about to make significant advances, giving aircraft a modest all-weather capability. And to keep up with these changes, pilots would have to become far more proficient. They would have to become professionals.

The training at Newark was the first faltering step in that direction. It was the beginning of military pilots learning to hold a steady course and altitude at night, in the rain and snow, and in the clouds.

Volunteering for instrument training would be one of the most crucial decisions that Scott made during his flying career.

As Scott was returning to his squadron duties, the Department of Commerce began conducting weather research experiments out of Mitchel Field. The civilian meteorologists needed inclement weather for their research; they wanted clouds and rain, they wanted sleet and snow. These meteorologists also had to have planes and pilots capable of flying in such conditions.

Because of his training in New Jersey, Scott was the only pilot in his squadron fully qualified for the missions, thus forcing his commanding officer to lift the no-fly order. Within days, Scott was taking the researchers on cross-country trips, sometimes flying as many hours in a single day as his squadron mates would fly in a month.

With the advent of a new device called a barometrograph, the weather research grew more sophisticated. The device was attached to the strut of the aircraft, and every day at 2 a.m., weekends included, a research flight would take off, follow a precise rate of climb from the ground up to fifteen thousand feet, and then descend. The flights had to be made in the early morning because the daytime sun produced thermals that made the flights bouncy, and the flights had to take off no matter what the weather; in fact, the researchers preferred harsh weather.

The researchers' demands were such that some of Scott's less-qualified squadron mates were pressed into duty. They thought the whole thing ludicrous, and when they complained about having to get up in the middle of the night, Scott volunteered to fly their missions. Soon he was flying five, six, or even seven days a week.

And at the officers' club Scott remained the butt of other pilots' jokes. How could a man be so gullible as to volunteer to fly a little black box around every night? Truly, this fellow Scott was a time hog who cared about nothing but flying.

But Scott was happy to be thrown into this briar patch. He was honing his skills and building hours flying on instruments in the worst sort of weather. Again, he treated every flight as a combat mission. Take off and at every three hundred feet level off for a few minutes while the barometrograph did its mysterious work, climb another three hundred feet with his head on a swivel, constantly looking overhead, below, and astern, the latter being a fighter pilot's vulnerable six o'clock position. Hold the compass locked on course. Follow a precise rate of climb. Hold the altitude within several feet. Nail the numbers. Move the controls smoothly. Be professional.

And when Scott landed, usually before the sun came up, he was meticulous in keeping his logbook. The hours were building up.

By November, Scott had more flying hours than anyone else in the squadron, and he was a smooth pilot to whom night flying and instrument flying were second nature.

Scott's frequent letters to Kitty Rix were filled with stories of his flying experiences at night and in perilous weather. He boasted about being known as a "time hog." He had asked her to marry him, but she kept telling him to wait until she finished college and then to ask her. In the meantime, she was still seeing the Berryman guy and Edwards of Cedartown. They may have sensed that Scott had moved to the head of the line in Catharine's affections and they did not like being placeholders for her, mere amusements until she graduated and decided what she wanted to do. In November, both fraternity men wrote angry letters. (The intended recipients are unknown, but the letters came into Scott's possession.) Behind the anger are insights of both men regarding Kitty Rix.

Berryman wrote of her "contemptuous, long drawn-out Uuuugghh" and said he could not convey on paper her "sneery, disgusted, what-the-hell-do-I-care idea that it carries." He referred to her sarcastically as "the Great Green" when he said, "Who are we to dispute the right of the Great Green to rule and break our hearts at will? After all we are only the pawns on her field of play."

Edwards wrote to a friend of Kitty Rix's who had married and recently had her first baby. The friend sent Catharine a letter about the baby but Catharine did not respond. Now Edwards said he was writing on her behalf because "just recently her conscience (or whatever she has in place of a conscience) has been hurting her." He quoted Catharine, whom he said had told him, "I suppose I *should* write her and congratulate" (a burst of her well-known laughter was here interposed) her on her "little idiot." He ended the letter with what he said were Catharine's sentiments: "Hoping he doesn't bite you at meal time and with the greatest sympathy."

Shortly before Christmas, Scott took a few weeks of leave and went to Shorter College, where he found Kitty Rix surrounded by a triumvirate of adoring fraternity boys. "Oh, Scotty," she said. "Tell them about you being a time hog."

To her, knowing someone who was called a time hog was such a delightful and funny thing. Imagine calling a pilot a hog. A hog was a greedy and sloppy creature that would eat just about anything. How could a person eat time? How could Scotty be a time hog?

The fraternity men saw it differently. A twenty-five-year-old lieutenant in the Army Air Corps, waving his arms and demonstrating with his hands the perilous experiences of flying at night during violent storms, had trumped just about anything they might offer. And when he left Shorter, Scott noticed that Kitty Rix's friends were not quite as confident as they had been in the past. But they also had the advantage of propinquity, they could drop in and see Kitty Rix in the evening or on weekends whenever they wished.

Scott knew his battle was not yet won. He had proposed again, and again Kitty Rix had put him off.

Neither Kitty Rix nor Scott knew he was about to be assigned a job that would demand all of his flying skills, all of his instrument-flying ability, all of his passion about aviation, and more. And there would be times when he wondered if he would live through the night.

# 7

# DARK NIGHTS OF THE SOUL

DURING THE LATE WINTER OF 1934, SCOTT HAD THE MOST DANGEROUS job in the Air Corps: flying the U.S. mail.

This brief, deadly, and ill-remembered period in the history of U.S. military aviation came about because the U.S. Senate had investigated the conduct of commercial airlines, some of which were accused of committing fraud and bribery in acquiring their contracts to carry the mail. The allegations proved substantive enough that President Franklin D. Roosevelt signed an executive order directing the Air Corps to take over airmail service beginning on February 19.

Charles Lindbergh, world-famous since his 1927 trans atlantic flight and becoming *Time* magazine's first "Man of the Year," publicly opposed Roosevelt by saying the Air Corps did not have the experience, the aircraft, or the instruments to fly the mail in extreme winter weather. He was right.

The Air Corps had only ten days to prepare for a mission for which it was woefully ill prepared. But, as is the nature of the military when given a task, however hazardous, someone somewhere saluted, said, "Yes, sir," and set about to make things happen.

The call went out for pilots; single men were preferred. On February 16, Major General Benjamin D. Foulois, chief of the U.S. Army Air Corps and thus the officer responsible for the airmail operation, told a congressional committee, "We have assigned to this work the most experienced pilots in the Army Air Corps," a statement that ranks high among the greatest lies a senior military officer has ever uttered to Congress.

———

Like Scott, most of the 250 pilots assigned to the Army Air Corps Mail Operation (AACMO) were lieutenants with less than two years' flying experience. Only thirty-one of those pilots had more than fifty hours of experience in night flying. Most of the chosen pilots had been flying only four hours each month, and when they encountered bad weather they followed the usual procedure of either landing or getting below the clouds and "scud-running."

Scott was assigned to AACMO's First Section, Eastern Zone, where he served as an airmail pilot operating out of the municipal airport in Cleveland, Ohio.

Aircraft available for carrying the mail were open-cockpit observation aircraft. They did not have landing, navigation, or cockpit lights. Hastily installed radios were short-ranged and temperamental.

In 1934 there was no en route radar control, weather radar, approach control radar, distance-measuring equipment, GPS, or any of the sophisticated navigation systems available today. Pilots navigated largely by "dead reckoning" or "DR," a system based on a compass and a watch. The pilot picked a compass heading that would lead him to his destination, knowing that if his airplane cruised at one hundred miles an hour, an hour later he would be more or less one hundred miles farther along that compass heading. If the weather was clear, the pilot verified his DR by checking surface features such as rivers, lakes, railroad tracks, or towns.

This sounds simple, but in practice, DR was much more complicated, as the pilot had to compensate for winds aloft—they could affect both his course direction and the distance traveled. He also had to know how to get back on course if he flew around a weather system. But the pilots who flew the mail often never saw the ground during their flight. They flew a compass heading for a predetermined time and then they let down through "the soup" and hoped that when they broke out of the clouds they would be near their intended airport.

The mail was usually delivered at night. The winter of 1934 is remembered for having some of the worst and most prolonged bad weather in many years. In the beginning, pilots had no aviation charts. Instead they used road maps as they flew through fog, snowstorms, sleet, rain, terrible turbulence, and subzero temperatures, all while being lashed by winds of more than one hundred miles an hour.

Airmail pilots entered their cockpits as young men, but when they crawled out they were much older.

The only instruction Scott received was from a senior pilot who said, "Scotty, never be afraid to turn back. But if it is impossible to turn back, don't be afraid to go on. Just get some altitude and go on."

That advice would save Scott's life more than once.

Just four months out of flight training, Lieutenant Robert Scott was assigned to fly between Cleveland and Chicago—the worst of all routes: "the Hell Stretch."

Cleveland to Chicago was three hundred miles along the southern edge of Lake Erie and Lake Michigan, a route that had its own weather system, a system that in the winter consisted mostly of snow and ice, high winds, and subzero temperatures. That system was consistent only in its brutish and unforgiving nature.

That first night Scott was surprised to learn that most of the mail he carried consisted of letters for stamp collectors, people who wanted the U.S. Army Air Corps cachet stamped on their envelopes. When Scott landed, dozens of people were waiting, all asking him to autograph their mail.

He had flown the Hell Stretch for stamp collectors?


During the first two days the Air Corps carried the mail, there were two fatal crashes, there was one engine failure leading to a dead-stick landing, and one pilot had to bail out of his aircraft.

Scott was not only flying the missions assigned to him, but missions for other pilots as well. Any time a pilot wanted to take a break, even on a weekend and no matter how terrible the weather, he knew Scott would jump at the chance to fly the mission.

Scott flew sixty hours the first month.

One night Scott was blown far to the south of his course and lost his bearings. He was near Pittsburgh, and the turbulence was so rough he could not read his instruments. Scott was running low on fuel and he could not climb and motor on. Nor could he turn back. Scott performed the standard maneuver necessary to find the ground in such conditions: he reduced power, pulled back on the stick, kicked in full rudder, and entered a spin, hoping and praying he would break out of the overcast with enough altitude to recover and land. He did. He landed in a field, walked until he found a road, and then continued until he saw a sign saying MARS. In that suburb he made arrangements for refueling and pressing on.

That night, Scott's whereabouts were unknown for hours. Radio reports said he had crashed. Given the well-publicized accidents and deaths of so many Army mail pilots, some assumed he was dead. Kitty Rix heard the radio reports and cried herself to sleep vowing she would never marry a military pilot.

The next morning the weather cleared. Rested and refueled, Scott took off. Knowing that Kitty Rix might have heard the radio reports, he detoured some five hundred miles to Rome, Georgia, where Catharine was in her last year of school. Following the Coosa River, Scott found the campus of Shorter College, aimed his airplane toward the administration building, pushed the throttle forward, and lowered the nose to buzz the campus. Kitty Rix heard the snarling roar, and she knew immediately it was Scotty. Who else would buzz the campus in a military aircraft? Her Scotty was safe. She ran outside to see him make another pass and wave from the cockpit as he came in low and fast. Then he pulled up and away into a thundering climb as the noise echoed across the hills of north Georgia. Kitty Rix's girlfriends were envious of her dashing boyfriend who carried the mail. She looked at the airplane disappearing in the distance and thought, *That is all well and good and glamorous. But that wild man is not for me.*

# 8

# THE FORTRESS FALLS

By March 9, the AACMO death toll stood at ten, and the people of America were angry.

"Unwarranted and contrary to American principles," said Charles Lindbergh. The Lindbergh-Roosevelt fight made national headlines.

President Roosevelt called General Foulois to the White House and greeted him with a booming query: "General, when are these airmail killings going to stop?"

"Only when airplanes stop flying, Mr. President."

After what the general later described as the worst tongue-lashing of his military career, Roosevelt dismissed him and sent a letter to the secretary of war saying, "The continuation of deaths in the Army Air Corps must stop." He ordered that Army pilots undergo additional training both in night flying and instrument flying.

On June 1, the Air Corps flew its last mail flight, and the airlines resumed carrying the mail.

AACMO had suffered sixty-six crashes and twelve fatalities. What history remembers as "The air mail fiasco" was over, and the conventional wisdom said the whole thing was a terrible humiliation for the Air Corps.

As is often the case when the media sound off about military matters, they were wrong. The media concentrated on crashes and fatalities and largely overlooked that the Air Corps had flown more than 1.7 million miles in mail service and carried 629,150 pounds of mail. Not a single pound of mail was lost, compared with the average monthly loss of 172 pounds with the airlines. In every instance where an Army plane crashed, the mail was retrieved and sent on to its destination—sometimes by train or truck, but every letter eventually arrived. The Air Corps overcame terrible weather, mechanical troubles, improper aircraft, untrained pilots, and lack of familiarity with the airline routes.

This was no fiasco. The Air Corps performed in a magnificent fashion.

And while much of America fluttered over the number of fatalities, the Air Corps knew that the fifty-four aviation-related deaths in 1934 (a number that included the twelve deaths from AACMO) were not significantly greater than other years. Forty-six men had died in 1933 and forty-seven would die in 1935. In the mid-1930s, aviation remained a dangerous business.

But for the Air Corps and for Lieutenant Robert Scott, carrying the mail was a beneficial and—in retrospect—glorious experience.

The Air Corps benefited from the experience in several ways. Some of the men who flew the mail or were in charge of route segments would go on to fame and leadership roles in World War II: Curtis LeMay became a general who commanded bombing raids against Japan. Ira C. Eaker became a general and led the Eighth Air Force against Germany. And Henry H. "Hap" Arnold became the five-star general who led the Army Air Forces to victory.

The lives of Hap Arnold and Scott would soon become intermingled. Then-lieutenant Arnold had learned to fly from an employee of the Wright brothers, making him one of America's first military pilots. His passion for aviation and his disdain for cavalry officers were equal to Scott's. He was a hardheaded, impatient, and driven man whose passion for getting publicity for the Air Service was such that, while stationed in California in 1921, not only did he make numerous demonstration flights for the movies, he was the pilot in a goofy stunt to prove airplanes were faster than carrier pigeons. Arnold won the race from Portland, Oregon, to San Francisco, but only because the pigeons apparently landed somewhere en route to do whatever pigeons do when they are tired.

Arnold, far more than most officers, understood the connection between the romance of military aviation, the need for Hollywood stars to robe themselves in as much of that romance as possible, and the parallel need for the Air Corps to access the publicity machine that made Hollywood such a great cultural force. Beween 1931 and 1933, when Arnold commanded March Field—located about sixty miles east of Los Angeles—he frequently showed off his airplanes to the likes of Errol Flynn, Hedy Lamarr, and Clark Gable.

The winter of 1934 showed the American people that the Air Corps was only as good as Congress had made it. And it was not as large or as good as the air forces of England, France, or Japan.

Roosevelt wanted more money for new aircraft. The Air Corps appropriation jumped from $19 million in 1934 to $32 million in 1936.

When Army Air Corps leaders reflected on the airmail experience, one thing came through loud and clear: It was time to modernize military aviation, time to begin getting rid of cavalry officers whose spurs often got tangled up in the cockpit, time to get rid of officers who were content to fly only four hours per month. The successes and the failures of those months in the winter and spring of 1934 showed that it was time for the Air Corps to become more professional in training and outlook.

Scott gained great benefits by carrying the mail. The brutal flights had reinforced and cemented the skills he learned during the instrument-flying course he had taken at Newark, and the weather-research flights out of Mitchel Field. Now he had the special cachet of being not only a pilot who had flown the mail, but one who had survived the Hell Stretch.

For his rank, Scott had become one of the most experienced pilots in the Air Corps.

But when he returned to his old unit at Mitchel Field, his squadron commander was unimpressed. The squadron commander believed it was unbecoming for a pilot to fly as much as Scott had flown in the past few months. Scott resumed his duties as supply officer and transportation officer, and he also took on the additional duties of squadron adjutant and mess officer.

Pressure on the Air Corps relaxed. Scott had flown more airmail missions than anyone in his unit. But those harrowing flights had taken their toll, and even cavalry officers recognized pilot fatigue. Scott's boss knew that the young lieutenant's twenty-sixth birthday was approaching, and he knew that

Scott had given about all he had to give. He ordered Scott to take a few days off.

What he did not know was that Scott had already been planning such a trip. Scott had not seen Kitty Rix in several months. But he knew the panting Georgia Tech fraternity boys were still hanging around, and he was worried.

Scott's crew chief, who was a master mechanic and chief of the flight line, knew of Scott's aching desire to fly south. One morning when Scott and his crew chief were having breakfast, the crew chief leaned across the table and told Scott of a pursuit ship—pilots and crews then referred to their aircraft as "ships"—that had been flown in by an officer making a surprise inspection. Flying a Berliner Joyce P-16, the pilot had made a hard landing, twisted and bent the propeller, and caused so much structural damage that the aircraft had been towed to a distant corner of the flight line and written off as nonsalvageable.

"Lieutenant, if you can get me the parts, I can make that aircraft fly in less than ten days," the sergeant said. He passed Scott a list of the parts he needed.

Scott's eyes widened. The P-16 was a speed demon of an aircraft and so new that the Army Air Corps had only two squadrons of them. This was one of the fastest two-seater aircraft in the Air Corps inventory. It had a six-hundred-horsepower Conqueror engine that, at full power, bellowed like a moose in rut.

As an experienced supply officer, Scott knew all about the back-door way of doing things in the Army, and he managed to get the sergeant a new propeller and the needed parts without alerting anyone. The sergeant and a few of his men worked on the aircraft daily, and at the end of each day they shoveled snow over the wings to disguise their work. He hid the new propeller under the snow.

Scott wrote a letter to Kitty Rix and decided to deliver it himself. This would be a special-delivery airmail letter stuffed into an orange message bag to which Scott attached a long orange streamer.

"Hey, y'all. Hold my beer and watch this."

It was still dark that Sunday morning in April when Scott and the sergeant met on a back corner of the flight line. The weather was cold and the wind was biting. Attaching the twelve-foot propeller to the P-16 was a slow process. Not many squadron aircraft would be flying that morning, but enough were warming up their engines to cover the distinctive and powerful roar of the big Curtiss Conqueror V-12 engine. Scott radioed the tower, said he was making a test hop, and took off.

Scott had back-timed his flight, and it was crucial that he arrive at his destination within a minute or so of his planned time. It was barely dawn when Scott passed Sandy Hook, raced down the Jersey shore, and refueled at Pope Field near Fayetteville, North Carolina. The flight was made all the more cold by the P-16's open cockpit.

When Scott took off from North Carolina, he stayed at treetop level and pretended this was a combat mission, and that he was using DR to find his target.

Scott crossed the Savannah River exactly on time, then the Ocmulgee River, which flowed along the edge of his hometown of Macon, and moments later he saw the water tower reading FORT VALLEY. He had timed his arrival perfectly. The Sunday-morning church service at the Baptist church had just finished, and the good Baptists of Fort Valley were clustered in front of the church talking, catching up on the news, and thinking of the enormous Sunday dinner awaiting them at home.

Suddenly they heard the angry, high-pitched thunder of the Conqueror engine. And when they looked skyward, diving toward them was a bullet of an airplane, flying so fast and making such a loud noise that it had to be a military aircraft, one of those pursuit airplanes that only the most daring and skilled of pilots could fly.

Scott came in from the north, so when people looked up at him the sun would not be in their eyes. His first pass took him over the upturned faces in front of the church. He pulled the nose up and the engine sound deepened into a powerful growl. He turned the aircraft on its wingtip and circled, put the aircraft into a dive, and kept his eye on a patch of grass near the church. Out went the message bag trailing the bright orange streamer, and out from the church tumbled a half-dozen boys. They raced to the message bag, picked it up, and read a note that said, "Miss Catharine Green, College Street. Urgent! Rush it, please—and thank you. Lieutenant Scott, Army Air Corps."

The boys ran back to the church and presented the message bag to a beaming Kitty Rix, and it was clear from the faces of those at church that morning that they believed there would soon be a wedding in the Green family.

Scott waggled his wings, gunned the engine, and picked up a return course for the trip back to Mitchel Field. And as he ripped along at treetop level, crossing his checkpoints right on schedule, he smiled in contentment.

A few weeks later Scott was granted several weeks of leave, during which he drove to Fort Valley to pick up Kitty Rix for a tour of Mitchel Field. When they returned to Georgia, she was wearing a miniature of his West Point ring, and had agreed to marry Scott after she graduated from Shorter that summer. The fraternity pins were returned and the fraternity boys banished.

Scott later said, "I won because I had better transportation."

# 9

## WEDDING BELLS
## AND DISTANT TRUMPETS

AT HIGH NOON ON SEPTEMBER 1, 1934, LIEUTENANT ROBERT LEE SCOTT Jr. of the Army Air Corps and Miss Catharine Rix Green of the Fort Valley Greens were married in the chapel at West Point. Scott wore his dress uniform and Kitty Rix wore what Scott described as a suit of "high altitude blue." *The Macon Telegraph* called it an "Augusta-bernard creation of Glory Blue cloth which featured a blue fox cire cape." She carried roses and valley lilies.

The Macon paper said that Catharine was a graduate of Shorter College, where she majored in dramatic art, had "presented a number of recitals," and was a descendant of Robert E. Lee.

How her ancestry had evolved from Nathanael Greene to Robert E. Lee is not known, but it may be attributed to the passionate need of Southerners to lay familial claim to General Lee. If as many Southerners who claim to be descendants of Lee are in fact descendants, then it is Robert E. Lee and not George Washington who should be known as the Father of Our Country.

This we do know: Kitty Rix had decided that if she was going to be an army wife, she wanted her marriage to begin on the hallowed grounds of West Point, and she wanted to exit the chapel and walk under the crossed sabers of Scott's brother officers.

The couple spent their honeymoon at Montauk Manor. Scott had been so busy flying (in August he flew more than fifty hours) that he waited too long to make reservations for his honeymoon, and Labor Day weekend was booked. But when Scott called and spoke to the manager, a splendid room was found for the newlyweds. After all, the aerial photograph that Scott had presented to the manager now graced the hotel's stationery.

In September, Scott flew only eighteen hours.

Scott and Kitty Rix settled into a house at Mitchel Field. Scott had found an abandoned and run-down little house on base and the agreement was that he could have it if he fixed it up. Scott had spent untold hours scraping and cleaning and spreading twenty-two gallons of paint inside and outside. But even with the cleaning and painting, it remained a small and depressing place. Kitty Rix had brought in many of her "things," but even so the house was not much better than her dorm room at Shorter College, and certainly it was far from the luxury of the Green family house in Fort Valley.

Catharine found by total immersion what it was like to be the wife of a junior officer in the Army Air Corps of the mid-1930s. It was a hard and spartan life, and it speaks volumes about those who persevered. Living quarters were substandard, amenities were few, and airfields often were remote.

For the wives of junior officers, much depended on their social skills and the skills they manifested in their homes.

It did not help that Catharine could cook only two things. The first was called goldenrod egg; it consisted of a piece of toast over which was crumbled a hard-boiled egg mixed with a white sauce. The second was heavenly hash, which called for cutting up marshmallows with scissors, throwing in several teaspoons of lemon juice, adding chopped and toasted pecans, spooning the mixture into a sherbet glass, topping it all with a maraschino cherry, and then putting it into the refrigerator to chill before serving.

But Kitty Rix was determined to learn. One day not long after she and Scott moved in, she went into the kitchen to turn on the stovetop's gas burner. The burner had to be ignited with a match, but Kitty Rix had no match. It was several minutes before she could find one, and when she struck it, she caused a minor explosion. Kitty Rix was not injured and there was no fire, but thereafter Scott did all the cooking.

Catharine said later that she "cried in despair" upon finding that her husband was a splendid cook while she was taxed to boil water.

Scott had a bottomless curiosity about all things, which, when mixed with his ability to bring an intense focus to an issue, soon made him an accomplished cook—one of those men not bound by recipes, but who would strike out on his own and experiment with food, often with game birds, such as quail, pheasant, duck, and goose.

Kitty Rix, with little to do, found herself in the company of other officers' wives, many of whom also had little to do, and she soon took up two habits she had not learned in a Baptist household: drinking and smoking.

Unlike many pilots, Scott believed in moderation when it came to alcohol. This was not for religious reasons or because he was a prude, but simply because he believed alcohol dulled his edge as a pilot.

That said, Scott had discovered scotch and he considered it to be a far more classy drink than the bourbon consumed by the men of Macon. On Friday or Saturday night, he might have a couple of drinks, but no more.

As for smoking, he thought it a sign of weakness. Aviation gas and oil and hydraulic fluids and all the myriad smells of an airplane hangar he found ambrosial. But he could not abide the stench of a cigarette.

In the beginning the smoking and drinking caused only mild remonstrations from Scott. His marriage was fresh and green, both he and Kitty Rix were experiencing so many things for the first time. They were excited about their new life together, and they laughed often about his arduous pursuit of her with the weekend auto trips from Texas, and how he had buzzed the campus at Shorter and the Baptist church in Fort Valley.

Even though he had not yet received his new orders, he had been told that in early 1935 he would have his first overseas assignment. He was going to Albrook Field in the Panama Canal Zone, where he would be assigned to a pursuit squadron.

As a deckhand in his teens, Scott had seen some exotic ports of call. He had flown all over Texas and over much of the eastern seaboard. Kitty Rix had passed through Atlanta on the way to Shorter College in north Georgia, and that was it. She was excited about going to Panama, and Scott was excited about the two of them seeing this exotic place together. But most of all he was excited about his assignment. At long last he would be flying nimble little aircraft armed with machine guns.

He was about to become a fighter pilot, the culmination of what his mother had wished for him since he was about four years old. And now his prayer went from being "Dear Lord, please let me be a fighter pilot" to "Dear Lord, let me fly in combat and kill the enemies of my country."

Mama was happy for her son, of course, but she was not so happy about that Green girl. Catharine just didn't bring to the marriage the things a young woman should bring for her Rob.

Scott had two great loves in his life: his mama and himself. Mostly he loved himself.

Scott, in his fashion, loved Kitty Rix. But marriage is about compromise, and Scott was too selfish to modify his wishes and desires to accommodate his wife. Kitty Rix wanted a traditional marriage just like all the marriages seemed to be in middle Georgia. She wanted to be a good wife. But she was of no material significance to Scott's larger ambitions.

The immovable core in Scott's being was that it was his destiny to become a great fighter pilot. Whatever he did toward realizing that destiny, no matter who was hurt or what rules were broken, was okay. The goal was all that mattered.

Scott was one of those men T. E. Lawrence had in mind when he wrote, "All men dream: but not equally. Those who dream by night in the dusty recesses of their minds wake in the day to find that it was vanity: but the dreamers of the day are dangerous men, for they may act their dream with open eyes, to make it possible."

Throughout his life, Scott's ambitions set him apart from other men. He would come to have only one true friend, Claire Chennault.

Chennault was about to become a legendary historical figure. He would have more influence upon Scott than any other man.

The man from Waterproof, Louisiana, was not large or physically imposing. He stood five feet nine inches tall, was slender, blunt, and short-tempered. He rarely smiled. But Chennault was passionate about fighter aviation, and when he talked of fighter aircraft or fighter tactics, he seemed to grow much larger in size. If Scott reflected the character of William Tecumseh Sherman, Chennault was the physical double of U. S. Grant: same height, same wiry build, same commanding presence, same no-nonsense demeanor.

Chennault was making his presence felt in the Air Corps. At Maxwell Field, in Montgomery, Alabama, Chennault had formed "the Three Men on a Flying Trapeze," a group of three biplane fighters tied together loosely with a length of rope at the wingtips. They performed maneuvers at aerobatic shows so tight and precise and well coordinated that once after the group landed a doubting officer stalked out onto the field to make sure that Chennault's aircraft were indeed tied together. They were.

Chennault and Bissell, Chennault's old nemesis from Maxwell, continued to have their differences. Bissell believed that if fighters and bombers met in the air, the bombers would be omnipotent and would power through the fighters unmolested toward their target.

Such a belief was not uncommon at the time. Air Corps thinkers were searching for a doctrine, moving toward the belief that nothing could stop big bombers en route to enemy targets. Air power was the future and the man in the trenches was a thing of the past.

That is what most Air Corps thinkers believed in the 1930s, and that was what Captain Clayton Bissell taught.

Chennault became an instructor at the Air Corps Tactical School at Maxwell Field. By 1935 he had distilled his lectures into a book called *The Role of Defensive Pursuit*, in which he argued that a well-trained fighter force could stop enemy bomber attacks, or at least impose so many losses upon them as to make them unable to complete the mission.

Bissell, who was senior to Chennault, pooh-poohed the book. Bissell even argued that if bombers came under attack from pursuit aircraft, the bomber crews could throw chains out the doors to become entangled in the propellers of pursuit aircraft.

Chennault could not hide his contempt for such a ludicrous idea.

But he appeared to be losing the doctrinal battle. In those run-up years before the war, an idea was emerging that would soon become a bedrock belief in the Army Air Corps: Bombers will always get through.

Chennault came to be seen as a contrary man with contrary ideas; a man who would not listen to the wisdom of his superiors.

Chennault was a defensive man, in part because he was a Southerner who believed that his Louisiana education was inferior. He did not have the social graces possessed by many of his West Point–educated colleagues. He dismissed those men as "polo players" and believed they were promoted more for their social connections than for their accomplishments.

By 1936, Captain Claire Lee Chennault was an angry and frustrated man. He knew his time in the Army was limited.

# 10

# EXTRA DUTY

In April 1935, Lieutenant and Mrs. Scott arrived in Panama, where they soon found there were ants in the food, mildew on the clothes, and mosquitoes everywhere.

The U.S. Army had bases in Panama because, at the instigation of President Theodore Roosevelt, Panama had seceded from Colombia in 1903. Almost immediately the new Panamanian government gave the United States territorial control over the Canal Zone and permission to build the Panama Canal. Construction began in 1904, and the project was finished in 1914 at a cost of about $375 million.

During the early 1920s, the Army had installed heavy artillery at both oceanside entrances to protect the canal, but by the time Scott arrived, Army aviation provided the canal's chief defense.

Albrook Field was located on the east side—the Pacific side—of the Panama Canal just north of Balboa, where, because of a twist in the isthmus, the sun appeared to rise in the west and set in the east. The field had opened just three years earlier and it still lacked a paved runway. During the prolonged rainy season, flight operations were carried out at a high-ground runway at nearby Fort Clayton. The proximity to both the Caribbean and the Pacific, along with the uncharted jungle in between, fascinated Scott, and he delighted in the expeditionary feel of the small and remote outpost.

Living quarters for junior officers were new, but small and humid. Relief was found at the officers' club, where there were big windows, big fans, and a big supply of Atlas beer, a Panamanian brew that pilots considered inferior to American beer but that, if imbibed in sufficient quantities, would cause all the symptoms of intoxication.

Scott was assigned to the Seventy-eighth Pursuit Squadron, whose pilots flew the Boeing P-12, a muscular little short-coupled biplane with a five-hundred-horsepower radial engine. Painted on the fuselage of each aircraft was the squadron insignia depicting the head of "old yellow beard," the dreaded bushmaster snake, which has a yellow patch on the underside of its head.

On flying days, pilots took off around dawn before the stultifying heat set in, flew some sixty-five miles southwest to the gunnery range at Río Hato, and fired their machine guns into thirty-six-inch ground targets. Afterward the flight leader might take his formation of aircraft out over the Bay of Panama. Around noon the pilots returned to base and landed, their workday finished.

In those early-morning forays to the gunnery range or over the Bay of Panama, Scott's aerial gunnery skills flowered. He had an instinctive feel for leading airborne targets—pelicans were a favorite—and soon he was recognized as the best shooter in the squadron.

When he was not shooting from the air, he was shooting from the ground, frequently taking weekends to go on dove hunts in Central or South America.

In the beginning, Catharine liked the languid pace at Albrook. After flying, Scotty might have one obligatory beer with his commanding officer and his squadron mates at the officers' club, but then he came home and prepared a late lunch. Afterward there might be a nap, and perhaps a shopping trip into Panama City before dinner. Friday-afternoon parties at the officers' club were the highlight of the week: drinking, dancing, eating, telling stories. These parties extended far into the evening, and they were precursors of the infamous "happy hour" drinking parties that would remain common throughout the military until the post-Vietnam era.

For Scott, the leisurely pace lasted only a few weeks. There was work to be done. And with Scott, work came before all else. Part of that work was getting checked out in every aircraft he could get his hands on.

While he was being checked out in a new twin-engine Douglas OA-3 amphibian, he landed on Panama Bay, bounced, and in an effort to control the aircraft, pushed hard on the wheel. He pushed too hard and shoved the aircraft into the water nose-first at high speed. The accident buckled the hull of the flying boat, broke some of its windows, and caved in the wing surfaces. The aircraft had to have a major overhaul before it could be flown again. The accident report attributed the mishap to "Poor Technique."

But Scott was, at long last, a fighter pilot, and he wanted to acquire all the skills of a fighter pilot. He wanted more flying time, more time strafing ground targets, and more time shooting at targets in the air. He wanted to hone his navigation skills, along with his ability to fly in the heavy rains and thick cloud cover of Central America. Scott wanted to be the best fighter pilot in the Air Corps.

(The terms "fighter pilot" and "fighter aircraft" were creeping into the lexicon of the time, but that usage did not officially replace "pursuit pilot" and "pursuit aircraft" until the mid-1940s. Two of the most famous aircraft of World War II were "pursuit types"—the P-51 Mustang and the P-38 Lightning.)

Scott soon was rated as a "Fi Pilot 1 Eng" in his official records, meaning that he was an engineer and was fully qualified to operate a single-engine fighter aircraft in aerial combat. He was the most lethal creature in the skies.

Scott was promoted to first lieutenant and, in addition to flying, was assigned various ground duties, including those of communications officer, supply officer, assistant engineering officer, and acting armament officer. In that era, young officers were given numerous jobs for numerous reasons. America was mired in the Great Depression and the Air Corps had so few resources that it could barely garrison its widely scattered posts. Scott was a West Pointer; that meant he had engineering training, which dictated that he be assigned the jobs of engineering officer or armament officer. Finally, he was a new guy, and newbies always got the jobs that more senior people did not want.

But Scott saw these ground jobs as punishing and demeaning, more efforts by the Philistines to thwart his destiny. Anything that kept him out of the air, he saw as part of a giant free-floating conspiracy.

In his typical manner, Scott used one of the jobs to considerable personal advantage. It was a case of the finger-in-your-eye defiance that he would show many times in his career. As acting armament officer, Scott was in charge of the guns on every aircraft in the squadron, and he controlled the ammunition supply for those guns. After his morning mission, and while his brother pilots had retired to the officers' club, Scott would pick one of the squadron aircraft at random, refuel it, and take it back up to "test" the harmonics of the guns—the sweet spot in front of the aircraft where the bullets converge. This usually meant firing at pelicans in the air or at sharks basking near the surface of the water.

He was not just blazing away on these flights. In his mind's eye, he was on a combat mission. When he fired a few rounds at a pelican, he was firing at an enemy fighter. And when he put a long burst into a cruising shark, he was firing at an enemy soldier.

After Scott expended his ammunition, he returned to base and either said the guns were operating in good condition or ordered the crew chief to make certain adjustments. He looked around, picked another aircraft, and was off again. Sometimes Scott flew until time for dinner. He built up flying time rapidly. By October, six months after arriving in Panama, Scott had flown 302 hours and thirty minutes and had almost nine hundred hours total flying time, an extraordinary amount of flying time for a man who had been a pilot for only four years.

He flew so much that he was afraid some might question the hours he was logging. In July 1935, Scott asked his commanding officer to make a note in his flight records affirming that those records accurately reflected Scott's flying time.

And Scott worked on his gunnery until he became a master of the aerial snap shot—a quick burst during the split second a pelican came into his gun sights—and strafing ground targets or sharks.

"I was as good a machine gunner as there was in this world," Scott said later.

Once he shot three large sharks—he says they were in the twenty-foot range—and currents pushed the dead sharks ashore at La Venta Inn, a place Scott called a "fine hotel." An astute Danish businessman named Asger Kierulff owned the hotel and the land on which the Río Hato Gunnery Range was located. La Venta Inn was an easy walk from the gunnery range and the adjacent landing strip.

(An Air Force historian later wrote that the La Venta Inn was in reality a brothel "justly famous throughout Panama," and many young Army pilots landed there frequently for "rest stops.")

Asger Kierulff asked Scott to get rid of the decomposing sharks that were almost under the windows of the inn. Scott did so by flying an amphibian aircraft to the hotel, lashing airplane cables around the sharks' tails, and towing them out to sea with the airplane.


While Scott was building up his flying time, Catharine was building up her resentment. She did not like being home alone. There were occasional parties or lunches with other officers' wives, of course, and while she could have gone to the officers' club, she did not want to go alone. Nor did she want to go into Balboa or Panama City alone. She was not a reader, and thus there was not much for her to do but grow resentful at what it meant to be a pilot's wife.

If Catharine was angry at Scotty, his squadron mates were amused, even patronizing. Scott was again being ridiculed as a time hog. He was flying more than fifty hours a month.

And he was always declaiming loudly the many poems he had memorized, or going on and on about "the Venetian," or talking of the Great Wall of China and how one day he would walk the wall.

Scott's squadron commander soon discovered that the new guy had not only used up the squadron's ammunition that was supposed to last until the end of the year, but all of the ammunition for the entire Nineteenth Composite Wing, the parent organization of all the Air Corps units in Panama.

The enraged commander called Scott to his office, waved a piece of paper showing that more than fifty thousand rounds of ammunition had disappeared, and yelled, "You have expended all the goddamn ammunition in the whole Nineteenth Wing for the entire fiscal year." The colonel said that if he could have his way, he would order Scott to pay for every round, but given the pay of lieutenants that would take years.

He wanted Scott out of his squadron, and in November 1936 Scott was transferred to the Forty-fourth Observation Squadron, the only Air Corps unit in the Canal Zone equipped to conduct aerial reconnaissance.

Scott would continue flying more hours and making more long-range flights.

Brigadier General George Brett arrived to take over as commander of the Nineteenth Wing in the summer of 1936. Brett saw war in the future, as did many senior army officers. Hitler had occupied the Rhineland. Italy had invaded Ethiopia. Civil war was tearing Spain apart. And the Japanese were rampaging across Manchuria. If America became involved in the war, Brett wanted the Air Corps ready. There was already a Nazi presence in Latin America. (SCADTA, a German-operated airline, flew out of Colombia, a mere 250 miles east of Albrook, and it used passenger aircraft that Brett believed could be converted to bombers.)

President Franklin D. Roosevelt wanted the army to extend its "police power" from the Canal Zone to cover all of Central America; this was his corollary to the Monroe Doctrine.

Until then, Air Corps bases had been built along the coasts of Panama, but now they needed to be located inland. Newer and more modern aircraft, including a few amphibious aircraft, were beginning to arrive (the

cavalry officers called them "mounts"), and those aircraft were being fer-
ried by air to Panama rather than shipped, a radical innovation at the time.
The Army wanted emergency or auxiliary landing fields to extend from
Jaqué and Pito, near Colombia to the east, to the far end of the republic at
Bocas del Toro and Puerto Armuelles. Once those fields were built every
one of them would have to be inspected monthly.

General Brett designated Scott as the wing's engineering officer and "officer in charge, outlying landing fields." Scott's mandate included con-
structing emergency airstrips as far south as Tumaco, Colombia, and as far
north as Guatemala City. These fields would become well known to air crews
in World War II.

Scott was assigned his own personal airplane, given control of several
others, and given permission to use any of them at his discretion.

His job was big, important, and seemingly almost impossible. First he
had to locate suitable sites for landing strips. Second he had to convince the
local Indians who controlled the interior of Panama to allow him to build a
landing strip. Third he had to convince the Indians to hack the landing strip
out of the bush, build the strip by hand, and maintain the strip thereafter.
Finally, he had to inspect each field monthly to ensure that it remained ready
to receive aircraft.

In that climate, the jungle could quickly reclaim a runway, and ant hills
large enough to wreck an airplane could spring up in the middle of a landing field in a matter of days. And, to make things worse, the locals were steal-
ing the orange wind socks at each field and making clothing out of them.

Supervising the construction and maintenance of these fields and then
inspecting each of them was a demanding job. The obstacles appeared insurmountable in that the Indians were believed to have been headhunters
in the recent past, and they had always refused to allow airfields in the interior.

Scott saw it all as a dream job. Not only would he be flying even more
hours than he had in the fighter squadron, but he would be pretty much on
his own: he could fly whenever and wherever he wanted. It also meant that
the man who had, by car and aircraft, pursued Kitty Rix as arduously as
any young woman has ever been pursued would now be spending days, even
weeks, flying away from her. It was a pattern he would follow throughout
the rest of his Air Force career.

# 11

# ORCHIDS AND PIGS
# AND, OH MY,
# THE TRAINING COMMAND

FLYING IN CENTRAL AMERICA WAS ALMOST AS CHALLENGING AS FLYING the mail had been on the Hell Stretch. Ice, snow, and freezing weather were not a problem in Panama, of course, but the prodigious impetuosity of the rainfall was like nothing Scott had ever experienced. Navigation aids in Panama were primitive, and Scott's DR skills were tested to the maximum. Checkpoints over the Panamanian jungle, particularly in the unmapped and largely unexplored wilderness of Darién, in the south, were few and far between.

When scouting for new airfield sites, Scott flew a Boeing P-12, the same aircraft he had flown in the Seventy-eighth Fighter Squadron. When on construction, maintenance, or inspection flights, he either flew, or was accompanied by, a Bellanca C-27A, a single-engine transport that carried mechanics and a maintenance crew. At distant airfields, Scott and his men would often spend the night as guests of Chucunaque Indians. The tribe was named for the river that flowed through Darién. Scott later said that the Chucunaque were not only headhunters, they were the most aggressive of all the headhunting tribes in Central America. He said they used blowguns that could propel a curare-tipped dart some seventy-five feet.

On one trip Scott and his line chief had arrived to pay the Indians their monthly fee for use of the runway only to see a young boy lying on a mat, and clearly in great pain. Chanting locals circled the stricken boy, who, Scott was told, was the son of the chief.

The chief said the boy had a devil in his stomach and by morning his son would pass over to another land. The headhunters were engaged in an ages-old ritual of preparing the boy for death and burial.

Part of Scott's community-relations program included carrying basic medical supplies aboard his aircraft: aspirin, iodine, and bandages. He had treated boils, toothaches, and other minor illnesses, but this boy had what appeared to be appendicitis and Scott had neither the supplies and tools nor the medical training to help. Scott believed, however, that the boy's life might be saved by flying him back to the military hospital at Panama City. But it was risky. If the boy died, the Army would be blamed, and there would be no more landing strips built in Darién.

Scott claimed that he convinced the chief to let him take the boy to an Army doctor. A week later, when Scott returned, members of the tribe heard the sound of his engine and came to the runway. The healthy and smiling boy stepped out of the airplane, showing his appendectomy scar to all who might be interested.

The next day the Indians loaded Scott's Bellanca with hundreds of limes and avocados, oranges and pineapples, several parrots and parakeets, a 150-pound jaguar lashed to a pole, and a twelve-foot bushmaster in a gunnysack. Scott said he gave the fruit to personnel on the base, the jaguar to the local zoo, and the bushmaster to an Army doctor who was conducting antivenin research.

Thereafter, the Army built airfields anywhere it wanted in Panama (eventually there were forty-eight of them) and the Indians began bringing Scott fish or birds to eat. And in return for their gifts, Scott often brought them bolts of bright cloth.

A few of Scott's Panama stories may well be true. The problem is that in later years Scott changed some of the facts to make the stories more dramatic. For instance, he later wrote a story for *Reader's Digest* saying that on the trip involving the boy with appendicitis, he was accompanied by a young lieutenant who had attended a year of medical school, and who performed the appendectomy in the Indian village. It makes for a better story until you ask how a person with only a year of medical school could perform surgery, and why Scott just happened to be carrying the surgical tools and supplies necessary for such an unlikely procedure.

Scott would subsequently repeat this pattern again and again. In later years people would not know which stories were true, which were improved, and which were false. And this is why I have endeavored to, as much as possible, stick fast to historical records, Air Corps documents, and the relevant stories of those with greater credibility.

The unfortunate side to this strict protocol is that it screens out some experiences as unconfirmable, even though Scott might have had them.

By the late 1930s, Scott was a curious mixture of a man. He was one of the leading high-time pilots in the Air Corps and he had performed a sensitive job of strategic importance in an outstanding manner. On the other hand, while his brother pilots might be amused at his poetry spouting and his unending soliloquies about Marco Polo and walking the Great Wall of China, they also thought that he exaggerated every event in which he was a participant.

Showing still another aspect of his makeup, Scott's Southern-born appetite for wild game branched out in ways that surprised even Kitty Rix. Thanks to the appreciative offerings of Indians at various airfields, Scott obtained the meat of exotic fish, snakes, and birds, and he cooked whatever he brought home. Kitty Rix enjoyed it all and she and Scott congratulated themselves upon being so worldly.

Despite Scott's reputation as an independent sort who sometimes flouted regulations, General Brett saw something in Scott that he liked.

In January 1937, Scott transferred to the Nineteenth Wing, where his ground duties included serving as mess officer but, more importantly, as adjutant to General Brett. Now Scott was not only performing staff jobs at the wing level, but he was also performing jobs that presuppose certain virtues and abilities. As mess officer, Scott had considerable fiduciary responsibility. And as adjutant, he had to keep the paperwork flowing while exercising discretion in many sensitive matters.

At 12:40 p.m. on April 5, Scott had another accident. The report said the cause was 75 percent "Poor Technique" and 25 percent "Airport or terrain." Again, he was flying an amphibian, but this time he was landing on a dirt runway. Scott said that as he was landing, a gust of wind picked up the airplane's right wing just as the left landing gear hit a soft spot in the runway. The landing gear was ripped off.

Scott now had caused extensive damage to one aircraft while he was in flight training and damage to two other aircraft in Panama. In every instance the accident was attributed to "Poor Technique." When Scott later told the story of how, when he was twelve, he had crashed a home-made glider by trying to fly it off a neighbor's roof, he always ended by saying, "That was the only time I ever crashed."

Well . . . sort of.


If the accident board said that Scott's misadventures were due to "Poor Technique," the same might be said of his marriage.

Scott was gone for days, sometimes weeks, on end, leaving Kitty Rix cooped up in very tight, uncomfortable quarters. His being away meant she could not attend the Friday-night parties at the officers' club, and she missed those parties ever so much. They were the highlight of her week. She could dress up and engage in the banter and the repartee at which she excelled.

The parties also reminded her of the high school and college parties where she had been so popular. Now she was the wife of a mere lieutenant, and his rank dictated her rank among the wives. She was pretty close to being nobody. She was of the Fort Valley Greens and she was nobody.

Perhaps it was loneliness that turned her more toward the drinking and smoking. When Scotty came home, Kitty Rix wanted to talk of light and frivolous things just to release the tension from what felt like confinement. But first she had to listen to Scotty go on and on about the P-12 and what a great aircraft it was. Most of the time she simply lit another cigarette, made herself another drink, and passively listened. But once, when she had missed the Friday-night party, she was furious. And when Scotty came home and began preparing dinner and talking about his airplane, she stood in the middle of the kitchen to interrupt him with an angry rebellious shout: "Why don't you marry the P-12?" It was the first time she had ever raised her voice to Scotty.

Scott sat down, held Kitty Rix's hands, and looked into her eyes. "Catharine," he began. She knew that whatever he was about to say was important because he never called her Catharine unless the subject was important. "Catharine, flying is serious business. It is my profession. I would fly if I had to buy the gasoline. Flying is more than a profession, it is an art form." And then he used the analogy she would hear so many times over the coming years. "If Paderewski practices twelve hours a day, and a ballerina practices twelve hours a day, and they are the best, then I have to fly as many hours a day as I can if I am to be the best fighter pilot. All I need from you is understanding."

It was of some help to her when Scotty purloined a radio receiver and left it at his house so Catharine could hear the radio chatter when he was flying. He thought she would be less lonely if she could listen to him at work. And they devised private phrases that Scott could broadcast on the radio when his mission was over and he was about to return to Albrook Field. It was their little secret that he was talking to her while miles away.

But this was not enough. Catharine did not understand the fascination that flying and airplanes held for Scotty.

The difference in Scott the boy in Macon and Scott the man in Panama is only a matter of degree. He had the same catholic interests, the same drive to know distant places and different people. But the airplane had made the difference. The airplane separated the boy and the man. Scott the boy swam in the Ocmulgee River, hunted and fished, and was a deckhand aboard a tramp steamer. Scott the man had an airplane to take him into the most exotic places and among the most exotic people he had ever seen. He could fly from the Caribbean to the Pacific. He wanted to experience everything, and he could not get enough.

Few things show his willingness to experience everything as did eating the meat of a javelina. The javelina, the local name for a peccary, is a medium-sized mammal that belongs to the pig family. Another name for it is the skunk pig, so called because the animal has large musk glands that extrude a powerful odor. The aroma from a herd of javelinas can be detected from a considerable distance.

A large javelina may grow to ninety pounds, but most are in the fifty-pound range. The boars have straight tusks that they can click to warn would-be predators, and if the warning is not enough they do not hesitate to charge the hunter and use their tusks to devastating effect.

The Indians in Panama hunted javelina with everything from curare-tipped arrows to spears. Scott never went on a hunt, but he was sometimes present when the dead animals were brought into a village near one of the Army's airfields. Scott does not record his reaction to eating the meat of a musky javelina. Whether he liked it or not, he should be congratulated for cooking it, and for putting it on the table.


In later years, when Scott would write of his time in Panama, he would make a few tangential references to Catharine, but it is difficult to find her presence in his writings. The one place where he mentions her at length is, characteristically, during a story about himself. As he tells it, one day he returned from flying, saw a number of cars in front of his house, and knew that Kitty Rix was having a tea with the wives of his squadron mates. He was wearing a sweat-stained flight suit, the imprint of his oxygen mask was across his face, and he was sunburned from hours aloft. He entered the house by the back door intending to take a shower and make himself presentable before greeting the guests. But as he entered the house he could not help but overhear the conversation in the living room, where the other wives were taunting Kitty Rix.

He heard one wife say, "I hear that Scotty does all the cooking; that you never go into the kitchen."

Catharine laughed and said, "I go into the kitchen any time I want."

Another wife: "My husband says Scotty is flying sometimes eighty hours a month and is gone most of the time."

"Scotty tells me that someday when he has to fly in combat, he will be ready," Kitty Rix responded. And then she added, "You do know he won the gunnery trophy for his squadron and then for the wing. He is one of the best shots in the Air Corps."

The other wives laughed, and one said it was because Scotty had used a year's supply of ammunition and because the other pilots could not practice gunnery as much as they might have otherwise.

Another wife said her husband did not know what to make of Scott's flying hours, his shooting pelicans and sharks, and his dangerous sorties deep into the interior of Darién. "My dear," she sniffed, "you might as well be living with a stick of dynamite."

To that, Kitty Rix had no reply. Scott walked into the room, ignored the wives, leaned down and kissed Kitty Rix, and said, "You are the greatest wife any pilot ever had, honey, and I sure am happy to be home. I'm going to clean up and fix us dinner."

In June 1937, Scott was ordered from Panama to Randolph Field, where he would be a flight instructor. He was disconsolate. Being assigned to what would come to be called the Training Command removed him from the ranks of fighter pilots.

And this at a time when the military was keeping a close eye on Germany, where Adolph Hitler was growing in prominence, and on China, where some military thinkers believed the successful Japanese aggression was a prelude to an assault on American interests in the Pacific.

War was coming and thousands of new pilots needed to be trained. The Air Corps decreed that the job of instructing those young men was crucial. But Scott knew that when the call went out for young fighter pilots he would remain an instructor. He would stay at home while his students went off to war.

Scott saw it all as part of the conspiracy to keep him from becoming a combat fighter pilot. What Scott could not face was that, at twenty-nine, he was fast approaching the upper age limit for a fighter pilot.

# 12

# CALIFORNIA DREAMING

CLAIRE CHENNAULT WAS AN INDEPENDENT THINKER, AND INDEPENDENT thinkers do not fare well in a peacetime army. Military history has many examples of how some of the most brilliant and visionary men in uniform have been humiliated, minimized, or disgraced by their superiors. The military has uniformed personnel, and it likes them to have uniform ideas.

Fighter aviation was about the only subject that excited Chennault. He had the passion of the true believer, and when he talked of fighter aircraft, his black, unblinking eyes glinted with a powerful light, and he puffed on a cigarette and punctuated his arguments with dismissive snorts that blew puffs of smoke like a laboring locomotive.

His brother officers reacted to Chennault's passion by attempting to remove his pursuit-aviation course from the curriculum at the Air Corps Tactical School. Many of Chennault's superiors believed he was too one-dimensional, too skewed in his beliefs, and unworthy of promotion. Plus, he was a rough and abrasive man. Chennault had been in the Army almost twenty years, and he knew his enemies would soon force his retirement. In 1935, after one of his air shows, Chennault had met with a member of China's Commission on Aeronautical Affairs. The official offered Chennault a job as chief pursuit-aviation advisor to the Kuomintang Party leader, Generalissimo Chiang Kai-shek. If he accepted, Chennault's job would be to supervise the building of a Chinese air force.

Chennault did not say yes, but he did not say no. He wanted time to think. He loved Army aviation, and he wanted to continue his career.

The stress of waiting for his unwanted retirement papers sent Chennault hunting and fishing almost every weekend. He had always found solace in the woods of northern Louisiana and he took his accumulated leave there with his family. Chennault boarded a houseboat in the Tensas River and thereafter fed his children on fish and turtle so often that they cried when they saw them on the table.

In the meantime the Chinese air force was in trouble. Both the Soviets and the Italians had been brought in to train the Chinese, and both had gone home in frustration. The Chinese began pressing Chennault for an answer, and in July 1936 Chennault came to an agreement with his new employer. Chennault would take control of the Chinese air force's advanced pursuit-training program at an annual salary of $12,000. He would write training manuals and organize an aircraft warning system to alert the Chinese air force when Japanese air units were about to attack targets.

In early 1937, Chennault's fears became a reality. The Air Corps retirement board met and recommended that Captain Claire Lee Chennault be retired, ostensibly because his hearing was impaired. Chennault was forty-seven; the board considered him to be a washed-up old man.

Like many pilots who flew in open cockpits behind big radial engines, Chennault had suffered some hearing loss. But Chennault believed he had been kicked out of the Air Corps because of his book, because of his passion for fighter aviation, and because he had been opposed by brother officers, among them Captain Clayton Bissell.

Chennault installed his wife and eight children in a house on a lake near Waterproof, Louisiana, and then he was off to China. His passport listed his occupation as "farmer." The ship steamed away and so did Chennault. And when he left, Chennault was more defensive, more passionate, and more evangelical than ever about fighter aviation. He craved respect more than anything else. Perhaps in China he would find it.

Chennault arrived in China a few months before Scott arrived in Texas.

The American leadership certainly knew of Chennault's deal with China and did not object. In fact, Chennault's involvement with the Chinese air force fit in nicely with Roosevelt's growing urge to wage a clandestine war against Japan. Gradually, expanding economic and military aid to Chiang was leading toward setting up a "proprietary" American air force in China.

More and more, Japanese aggression in China was being linked with its German and Italian counterparts in Europe. America was beginning to gear up to support Generalissimo Chiang Kai-shek's fight against the Japanese, even as Chiang was gearing up to fight the Communists. The balance of power within China was, and would continue to be, precarious in the extreme.

American leaders did not realize it at the time, but as China descended into almost unimaginable chaos, America was cutting the template for future American policy toward the Chinese Communists.

In the meantime, Chiang was on the edge of despair.

Chiang smiled even less than Chennault. In viewing the man, it seemed as if Chiang had been wrapped in wire, thereby squeezing his body into the slight figure of a boy. Chiang was tendentious and angry about his lot in life, and more interested in preserving his leadership in the face of Communist opposition than in stopping the Japanese invaders. He needed help from America to achieve either goal. But Chiang insisted on controlling all foreign military personnel in China, that he have the last word on what equipment he would receive and how much money was needed to fund his requirements. In short, Chiang's demands were unrealistic. On top of everything else, he had a propensity toward intrigue, corruption, and recrimination.

Chiang knew all there was to know about skimming millions of dollars from China's treasury, and he knew everything necessary about giving jobs to his relatives and friends. Most of all, he knew to give his wife a big job to satisfy her lust for power.

Madame Chiang was in charge of China's air force, and she would have a close connection with Chennault and—later—Scott. She was born in Shanghai in 1898, the third daughter of Methodist minister Charlie Soong, a man who had made millions by selling Christian Bibles in China.

Because Soong was a devout Methodist, he sent his daughters to a college in America. As incredible as it sounds, that school was the Wesleyan College in Macon, Georgia.

In birth order, Soong's daughters were Ai-ling, followed by Ching-ling, and then May-ling. In 1908, when she was fifteen, Ching-ling was accepted at Wesleyan. She was accompanied by May-ling, then just ten years old. May-ling had special tutors at Wesleyan until, at fifteen, she, too, was admitted as a freshman.

Unlike her two older sisters, May-ling did not graduate from Wesleyan. Instead, after one year she transferred to Wellesley College, near Boston, Massachusetts, to be closer to her brother, T. V. Soong, who then was studying at Harvard University.

Because of her formative years in Georgia, May-ling spoke English with a Southern accent. And she understood and sometimes used idiomatic Southern expressions.

May-ling's ties to Macon, Georgia, were deep. People in Macon still love to tell the story, almost certainly apocryphal, about when then Wesleyan student May-ling was asked to recount the story of General Sherman's march through Georgia. Supposedly, she demurred, saying, "I am a Southerner and that topic is too painful for me."

In 1927, when she was thirty, May-ling married General Chiang Kai-shek, but only after he promised to convert to Methodism. It was a situational conversion, and there is little evidence to show that, as China's leader, he practiced his wife's Western religion.

Later it would be said that China had three daughters: one loved China, one loved money, and one loved power. Madame Chiang was the one who loved power.

Her diminutive size could barely contain her ambition, her leadership abilities, and her aggressive personality. Madame Chiang was the model for the original Dragon Lady; she was a self-centered, even megalomaniacal woman who talked often of democracy for her people but who lived an imperious lifestyle. She could make hard decisions quickly, and she never looked back. She knew what she wanted in her air force, and she knew that Claire Chennault could deliver.

Chennault was captivated by Madame Chiang. After their first long conversation, he paused, nodded, then smiled and said, "I reckon we will get along."

She smiled and said, "I reckon so."

Chennault was fond of Madame Chiang and referred to her affectionately as "the princess."

Madame Chiang was fond of Chennault and awarded him the rank of colonel, a rank she said was fitting for the man who ran her air force.

A year after Chennault arrived in China, he had under way a vast program of airfield construction—built without machinery by thousands of laborers—and was well under way in establishing his aircraft warning net. But Chennault was running into the same problems that had sent both the Soviets and the Italians away in frustration: The Chinese air force was crippled by a class system, corruption, and the unwillingness of pilots to train properly, as shown by how many crashed when they did fly.

Chiang had forbidden Chennault to fly in combat. But there is ample evidence that in order to inspire his students and to better know his enemy,

Chennault not only flew in combat but downed a significant number of Japanese aircraft.

In spite of all his efforts, when Chennault looked at his arrogant and incompetent young Chinese pilots, he knew it would take a hundred years to train them to fight and win against the Japanese. They had neither the aircraft-handling skills nor the aggressive mind-set needed in a fighter pilot.

In July 1937, the Japanese assaulted Shanghai, bombing civilians from the air and beheading them on the streets. It was a campaign that even military people thought brutal. Then came the Rape of Nanking, and Western military observers realized that Japan was seeking to destroy China's will to fight.

In December, coinciding with the fall of Nanking, the Japanese bombed and sank the USS *Panay*, a U.S. Navy patrol vessel, resulting in the deaths of two sailors and the wounding of thirty-eight more. The bombing took place at noon under a bright sun and upon a white ship with a large American flag painted topside. Although the Japanese government claimed the attack had been a mistake, and subsequently paid an indemnity of $2.2 million, many Americans took the attack as a direct challenge, and U.S. forces braced for orders. But Roosevelt chose forbearance and the incident faded.

But now the world knew that Imperial Japan waged war with brutality, ruthlessness, and treachery, and now the world was China-conscious. Generalissimo and Madame Chiang became the faces of China's great battle with Japan. A *Time* magazine cover story made them "Couple of the Year" for 1937.

That same year, the movie version of Pearl S. Buck's best-selling novel about life in rural China, *The Good Earth*, won two Oscars and was nominated for three more.

Clearly, China and its circumstances were on America's mind.

# 13

# WAR TOCSINS

On the other side of the world, Scott arrived at Randolph Field and found that life was easy and slow-paced and far outside the swirling eddies and high emotions that often precede a war.

Scott flew with students in the mornings. His "mount"—as cavalry officers continued to call airplanes—was a rugged Stearman PT-13, a fabric-covered biplane that was very stout and very forgiving, both necessary qualities in an aircraft flown by young men with heavy hands. As in Panama, the duty day more or less ended at lunch. Scott took up golf, and almost every afternoon he and his brother instructors played eighteen holes. Scott's golf swing was like his conversation: lots of power but little control.

He also found time to hunt birds and deer in Mexico and was considered a remarkable shooter.

When Scott had been a student at Randolph, life was exciting. He was learning to fly, dreaming of becoming a fighter pilot, and there were the weekend round-trips to Georgia to court Kitty Rix. But now he was a primary-stage flight instructor, a title that meant he took students up for their first flight.

Scott was a worker bee in the Training Command and he was living out his worst nightmare: a boring and repetitive life that moved at a torpid pace.

Catharine disliked Randolph even more than did Scott. The sunbaked base was as remote as if it were on the moon, and it held little promise for a young wife who continued to have trouble accepting an Air Corps wives' hierarchy in which her place was determined by her husband's junior rank.

She was, after all, of the Fort Valley Greens.

To pass the time, Catharine joined the dramatic club and was surrounded by all the thespian talent that one would expect to find on an Air Corps base in Texas.

But even as Scotty and Kitty Rix bemoaned their fates, in the background there was growing rumors of war.

Roosevelt wanted twenty thousand new pilots a year. And while Randolph was called the "West Point of the Air," it could only produce, at most, seven hundred pilots a year.

In 1938, General "Hap" Arnold became chief of the Army Air Corps. Blunt, acerbic, and messianic in his desire to build a respectable air force, he was the kind of man needed at the beginning of a great adventure, a man of drive and determination.

Arnold wanted more bombers and more trained pilots, and he had no compunction about going outside the chain of command, or, if need be, even ignoring military protocol altogether in order to prepare his country for war.

And if ever a country was unprepared for war, it was America in 1938.

But Arnold was not just preparing for war. He was looking beyond the war to the day when his air force would become a separate and independent military branch. In Arnold's view, the new air force must have a distinct philosophy, and it must be able to do something that none of the other armed services could do: drive heavy, multiengine bombers deep into the heartland of an enemy to destroy its ability to make war. Bombers that would always get through.

Arnold was as passionate about aviation as was Scott, and as passionate about his new job as Chennault. When these three men collided—as they inevitably would—there could be only one winner.

By 1938, Japan controlled all of China that was worth controlling. The Yangtze and Yellow Rivers were sealed off from commerce. Japan had taken over most of China's industrial factories and occupied all of China's major seaports.

That same year, Pearl Buck won the Nobel Prize in Literature for her novel *The Good Earth*. She was the first American woman to win the prize, and to many Americans that was the real significance of the award. But a few others saw it as a political statement toward Japan, now trampling China underfoot.

It was against this backdrop of an ever-hastening war that in September 1939 Scott was transferred from Texas to California. He was promoted to captain but, much to his disgust, he remained in the Training Command. Scott was assigned first to a flying school in Glendale and then to another school at Ontario and finally to a training base called Lemoore Field.

Hap Arnold had asked nine of the best flying schools in America to house, feed, and provide primary flight instruction to Air Corps cadets in aircraft to be provided by the Army. But Arnold admitted he could not immediately pay them. The best he could do was to promise that he would seek a congressional appropriation in the next year's budget to fund the project. In the meantime, Arnold said, they would just have to trust the Army.

It is a measure of the patriotism in America at that time that all nine of the flight school directors agreed to this most unorthodox approach.

Arnold also promised the private flight schools that he would assign West Point graduates to each of the schools to supervise the cadets, to discipline them when needed, and to instill West Point's code of honor in their behavior.

Cal-Aero Academy, near Ontario, California, would soon become the largest flight school in the Air Corps. Scott found himself both administrator and military supervisor of the 375-acre facility with three outlying auxiliary fields.

Scott was now caught up in the huge expansion of the Air Corps that resulted from Hitler taking over part of Czechoslovakia in September 1938, in response to which FDR called for American industry to begin producing ten thousand aircraft annually—an astounding demand, given that the Air Corps then had only thirteen four-engine bombers.

At Cal-Aero, Scott would grow more and more frustrated, convinced the Big Sky Boss had gone off duty and forgotten all about him. Scott had become a bureaucrat, in charge of a civilian flight school with military students.

The year Scott went to California was the year that General George C. Marshall was promoted over thirty-four men senior to him to become chief of staff of the U.S. Army. He presided over an army ranked nineteenth among the world's armed forces, after Portugal but slightly ahead of Bulgaria.

Marshall was a supremely gifted officer and a prescient leader. One of his first acts was to promote an obscure colonel named Joseph Stilwell to brigadier general.

Arnold, Marshall, and Stilwell are all important to Scott's story. They were all moving slowly toward a world stage where they, and Chennault and the Chiangs, would be in conflict with each other as well as with the Japanese.

There are those who contend that all wars are bad, that they result from the failures of men and governments; that the cost of war is too great, that there is always a better way to resolve differences. Most proponents of this theory are civilians; military people know better.

Evil and malevolent men do stalk the world. Men without conscience or scruple sometimes direct the fate of their countries and their people. Driven by self-aggrandizement and vainglory, these men will never sit down at the diplomats' table to resolve differences in good faith. They will use force to conquer new countries. They will seek to fly their flag over as much of the world as they can seize. And they will try to impress their evil and malignant ideas upon all they can reach.

Hitler was such a man. Tojo was such a man. Mussolini, Hitler's erratic caboose, was such a man, too.

These men dreamed of new empires, and if they had succeeded in their goals, America would have become isolated and forced to face disaster alone.

Roosevelt knew, and today all Americans should know, that sometimes war is necessary. The purpose of World War II was to insure that democratic government prevailed over tyranny, that America's way of life prevailed over the megalomaniacal cruelty of Hitler, the barbarity of Tojo, and the silly but dangerous dreams of Mussolini.

Had America and its allies lost World War II, the world today would be altogether different.

World War II was a good war. And most Americans have no idea how very close we came to losing it.

Until September 1939, many American civilians saw Hitler as irrelevant and the war in Europe of little interest or consequence to them. But then Hitler invaded Poland. Britain and France declared war on Germany. And almost overnight America was split into two bitter factions: isolationists who believed the affairs in Europe and China were none of America's business, and interventionists, who believed America must come to the aid of England and rid the world of Hitler.

Over the next few years, as Hitler conquered Europe and threatened the survival of England, the internal war in America ratcheted ever upward to become one of the most acrid periods in American history. Families and friends were torn apart. Today, those years are largely forgotten because they became so overshadowed by the surprise attack on Pearl Harbor and the subsequent events of World War II.

The bitterness in America was due not only to the intense feelings on both sides of the argument, but to the power and prestige of the two men who represented those two opposing views. President Roosevelt led the interventionists and Charles Lindbergh, who had bested Roosevelt over the issue of military pilots carrying the mail back in 1934, led the isolationists.

In 1939, Lindberg was thirty-seven, a formidable presence and the only man in America as famous as Roosevelt. Lindbergh was one of the first American celebrities to leverage his fame into political arguments. One writer said the battle between the two men was a battle "for the soul of America."

Perhaps Lindbergh's mother-in-law had a better picture of him than did the worshipful millions who knew him only as a daring aviator.

Elizabeth Morrow was the wife of Wall Street banker, diplomat, and former senator Dwight Morrow, and the mother of Anne Morrow Lindbergh, who would become one of the most felicitous writers of her time, or any other time. Elizabeth Morrow saw her son-in-law as a man devoid of social graces, a man who was wary and aloof, a college dropout who rarely read anything other than the dials in a cockpit. She believed that his ideas were ill formed, and that he was tone-deaf to the feelings of others. Lindbergh, said Mrs. Morrow, was "of a lower social stratum" and was in reality little more than a mechanic, who, had he not flown the Atlantic, would be running a gas station somewhere on the outskirts of St. Louis.

Mrs. Morrow stood with the interventionists, with Roosevelt, and with what she saw as the moral duty of all Americans to oppose the tyrannical forces moving across Europe and the Far East.


Throughout 1939 and 1940, Chennault sat under the trees at Chungking and watched Japanese bombers come over day after day. He studied and evaluated Japanese tactics in order to determine how his fighters could wreak havoc upon their bomber formations. And he developed an early-warning system that, while primitive, was becoming extraordinarily effective in providing his airmen with advance warning of Japanese air attacks.

While Chennault was studying Japanese air tactics in China, Scott was flying as many as twenty check rides a day in California, making sure his students were taught aviation as the military wanted it taught, and steaming and stewing over being "wasted" as an instructor. Scott did not hold the military axiom that the "good of the service" transcends all personal desires, and his feelings of frustration and paranoia about being locked in the Training Command were palpable. He moaned that when he was in Panama he had been told by his superiors that he was too young to lead an element (two aircraft), and now that he was thirty-two, they were saying he was too old to be a combat pilot—that flying fighters was for men ten years younger.

When was he ever the right age?

Sometimes it seemed that he, rather than Catharine, had majored in drama.

With hundreds of students rotating on a regular basis through Cal-Aero, it was inevitable that a few would draw Scott's attention. He would have favorites.

At the top of the list was Lieutenant Don Brown, the son of famed comedian and movie star Joe E. Brown. The comedian was as famous for his abnormally large and mobile mouth as he was for his gentle humor. It was through Lieutenant Brown and his well-connected father that Scott began to court Hollywood.

Don Brown was one of California's golden young men. He had been president of his class at UCLA, a football player, and by all accounts a man as well-mannered as he was handsome.

Joe E. Brown often drove the forty miles from Hollywood to Cal-Aero to visit his son. Brown and Scott became fast friends. Brown was devoted to his son and often put on free shows for students and staff at Cal-Aero.

By mid-1940, many of Scott's former students were showing up at Cal-Aero in Curtiss P-40 fighters and other warbirds. Ostensibly, these young men were on cross-country training flights and had stopped for fuel. Perhaps. But there is also a need for former students to show their old instructor what they are doing and to thank him. Scott was not the sort to accept such an attitude, and while these young men were filling out paperwork at base operations, he would jump into their warbirds and take off on what he called an "engineering flight." Afterward he would park the airplane, look around at all the students waiting on him to give them a check ride, and go to his office, where he wanted to eat his own entrails.

Scott's fears of missing his chance at war were not unfounded. While wars have been common throughout history, the probability of combat at a given location is low and the chances of an individual being in a position to influence that combat are even lower.

Because William Tecumseh Sherman was on duty in California in 1846, he missed the Mexican-American War and all the chances for glory and fast promotion that it afforded. Clausewitz, by all accounts a brilliant officer, never reached sufficient rank to put his theories into practice.

Chance and accident and coincidence play major roles in war. Opportunities are limited and easily missed. But Scott felt he could achieve his destiny only in war.

Many Southerners in the Civil War had experienced the euphoric highs and abject terrors of combat. Men who had fought hand-to-hand in blood and gore, those men who had killed and who had narrowly escaped death themselves, defined their experience by saying, "I have seen the elephant."

Scott wanted to see the elephant.

While he waited, he prepared.

He packed what he called a "war bag." It was a regulation army B-4 bag, a soft-sided and commodious suitcase, and he filled it with everything he would need when the call came: toiletries, underwear, extra socks, one dress uniform, spare flight suits, extra shoes. He parked the bag in the living room beside the front door. When the call came, and he knew it would come, he would kiss Kitty Rix good-bye, grab the bag, and be gone.

Kitty Rix looked at the war bag and looked at Scott. He quoted poetry:

*Women all, hear the call,*
*The pitiless call of War!*
*Look your last on your dearest ones,*
*Brothers and husbands, fathers, sons:*
*Swift they go to the ravenous guns,*
*The gluttonous guns of War.*

———————

After the last check ride of the day, when his fellow instructors headed for the bar at the officers' club, Scott climbed into whatever aircraft was on the ramp and flew out over the nearby Chino Valley, where hundreds of acres of melons grew. Crenshaw melons, Scott always pointed out. He landed in a field and loaded the culls—those melons too big for commercial use—into his cockpit. He jammed them wherever they would fit, even putting a few in his lap. And then he took off for a nearby auxiliary field where a fifty-foot circle had been laid out on the ground with lime and could be seen for miles.

Scott imagined the center of the circle to be an enemy tank or a truck-load of enemy soldiers or an enemy gun emplacement. He adjusted the throttle and dove on the target. He calculated the complex equations of aircraft speed and altitude and dive angle and threw out a "bomb." He bent the aircraft around, looked at where the melon had landed, and then lined up for another bomb run.

It was not in Scott's nature to keep silent about such matters, and he talked to anyone who would listen about how he could put melon after melon into the center of the circle. He could do it from various altitudes, various dive angles, and various speeds. And now he had proven, at least to himself, that he was one hell of a bomber pilot as well.

"I've got to be ready when they call me," he said.

Scott believed. Even when, intellectually, he knew that his age and his duty assignment would in all probability keep him out of the war, he continued to believe. Scott believed that when the time was right the Big Sky Boss would open the way for him to achieve his destiny. The Master Plan would be fulfilled. His destiny to become a combat fighter pilot would be realized. He would fly in combat against the enemies of his country and he would be victorious.

Oh, yes. He believed.

Of course, Scott's fellow instructors, all younger than he, laughed at him behind his back. A thirty-two-year-old captain throwing melons out of an airplane and bragging about his bombing skills? It was ludicrous. It was embarrassing.

Scott ignored the jokes. In his later books he wrote that he began calling generals and writing congressmen asking that he be transferred to a fighter squadron.

In May 1940, Germany launched a blitzkrieg attack and its troops quickly overran the Low Countries and slashed across France. In June, Paris fell and the unthinkable happened: the sharp synchronized thunk of German boots echoed through the streets in the City of Lights.

Now, Britain was in peril. And for Americans, the war in Europe had suddenly become much more real.

For the next eighteen months—until Pearl Harbor—the battle between the interventionists and the isolationists tore America apart. The animosity between Lindbergh and Roosevelt became even sharper and more personal. Lindbergh accepted the Service Cross of the German Eagle from the Nazi reichsminister of aviation, Hermann Göring; declared that the Luftwaffe was invincible; and proposed that Britain and France should appease Hitler.

Lindbergh had only a superficial knowledge of Germany and the Germans. As his mother-in-law had implied, he was a shallow and rather one-dimensional man. But he was the Lone Eagle, and because of that fame his comments were assigned far more gravitas than they deserved.

That same summer, Madame Chiang came to the conclusion that the Japanese military was unstoppable. The Japanese air force was so confident that oftentimes it did not bother to have any protective fighter cover for its bombers. China was losing the war.

On November 11, 1940, after six years of trying, Scotty and Kitty Rix had their first child: a daughter named Robin Lee Scott.

More and more it seemed the closest Scott could get to war was through the movies. In December he became technical advisor to a Warner Brothers short feature called "Wings of Steel," about a football hero who joins the Air Corps.

Scott's paranoia about a conspiracy to keep him in the Training

Command segued into the depression that he would battle for much of his life. While younger men were dancing off to fly in combat squadrons, he was relegated to a role worse than that of a wallflower; he was like the chaperon at the dance—he could only watch.

One day Scott was demonstrating to a cadet the correct and safe way to "prop" an airplane, to pull the propeller through a rotation with enough force to start the engine. Somehow the propeller dinged Scott's West Point ring and broke the stone. The hole in the top of the gold ring was like the hole in his life, and he did not bother to have it repaired.

He did not know then that he was on the leading edge of what would soon become an incestuous but mutually profitable relationship between the military and Hollywood, a relationship that would continue until the Vietnam War. And he did not then know that the hole in the West Point ring, and the hole in his life, would soon be filled.

# 14

# "YOU ARE NOT BLOODED"

THE RELATIONSHIP BETWEEN HOLLYWOOD AND THE U.S. MILITARY took a giant leap forward on February 1, 1940, when Scott hosted a grand ball at Cal-Aero Academy.

Scott appointed Lieutenant Don Brown as chairman of the ball. Young lieutenants want to impress their superiors, and Brown, as Scott knew he would, called on his famous father for help. Joe E. Brown, of course, wanted to make his son look good.

Thus it was that Mickey Rooney, Andy Devine, Linda Darnell, and Betty Grable were among the Hollywood nobility who attended the ball.

While the ostensible purpose of the ball was to celebrate the graduation of a new group of pilots, the real purpose was to harness the star power of Hollywood for the Air Corps. Scott, by now besotted by the glamour of Hollywood and the beautiful women he was meeting, was in full accord with this mission, and he threw himself into the role as had none of his predecessors. And, as so often happened in his life, his timing could not have been better.

By now there was little doubt that America would eventually become involved in the war in Europe. While the interventionists and the isolationists still squabbled, a great spirit of patriotism was bubbling up in America, and Hollywood wanted to be a part of the nation's growing love affair with the military.

Brown opened many Hollywood doors for Scott. The Army Air Corps was about to become the Army Air Forces, a significant step toward becoming an independent military department, and a Hollywood benediction would help that process along.

Along with the Hollywood stars attending the ball was a somewhat mysterious but well-connected man named Merian Cooper. He was a colonel in the Air Corps but somehow divided his time between Washington and Hollywood. Cooper was a former movie producer who had made *King Kong*. He had been on the board of Pan American Airways and thus he had learned a lot about airline logistics, management, and planning. Now he was an intelligence officer who reported directly to General Arnold. Or at least that was what people said about him. No one seemed quite sure of exactly what Colonel Merian Cooper did when he was in Washington.

Scott gave Cooper his spiel about being the best fighter pilot in the Air Corps, the best shot in the Air Corps, a man with many hours of flying in heavy weather, and a man who could navigate uncharted territories with ease. And by the way, few men in the Air Corps had as many hours in the air as he did. "I would rather fly in combat than be a general," he told Cooper.

He was ready to assume command of a fighter squadron and go to war. Could the colonel help?

Colonel Cooper was bemused. "You lack the greatest qualification of all for a fighter pilot," the colonel said. He looked Scott in the eye, said, "You haven't been blooded," and walked off.

For one of the few times in his life, Scott was speechless. He remembered stories of Confederate war veterans who had seen the elephant. Scott figured that being blooded and seeing the elephant meant the same thing. He wanted nothing more than to see the elephant. But how in the hell could he do that?

How could he be blooded when he was in the grip of the Training Command? That was the point of the whole thing. He wanted to see the elephant. It was all part of the Master Plan. Why couldn't anyone understand that?

The pilots who graduated from Cal-Aero in early 1941 would remember that ball for the rest of their lives. And even though Scott danced that night with some of the most glamorous women in America, to him the evening was a failure.

A colonel who worked for Hap Arnold had dismissed him because he had not been blooded.

In 1941, the stories of Scott and Chennault began to overlap.

Chennault was making no progress in building the Chinese air force and thus no progress in stopping the Japanese advance. And he was enough of a strategist to know the situation could only grow worse.

Training accidents, incompetence, and poor spirit bedeviled his Chinese pilots. They did not have the calling.

Chennault went to the Princess, and the two agreed that to depend upon the Chinese air force was to lean upon a frail reed. It was time to bring in the professionals. China would hire American military pilots. Roosevelt quietly approved the effort to recruit U.S. military pilots—reserve officers who were preferably single men and willing to resign their commissions. When their contracts expired, they would be allowed to resume their careers at their former rank. In the meantime they would be mercenaries fighting against a country with which America still had diplomatic relations.

Arnold was opposed to the idea. He wanted those pilots available for the Air Corps when America went to war. He was so incensed at the idea of what would be called "the American Volunteer Group" (AVG) and to FDR's desire to help Great Britain that he leaked to the press one of America's most highly classified military secrets: the plan for war against Germany.

And the revered, almost saintly, General George C. Marshall, while he did not openly oppose Roosevelt's plan, supported and protected those on his staff who did.

But Roosevelt had spoken, and his will would be done. Recruiting for the AVG was done more or less in secret, but of course word got out that retired Captain Claire Chennault was looking for mercenaries to fly P-40s against the Japanese in China. The AVG was America's first-ever adventurism into a covert war with a country that, at least on paper, was friendly to America.

Scott wired Chennault and volunteered his services. He received no answer.

On July 10, Chennault's volunteers boarded the Dutch liner *Jagersfontein* in San Francisco: destination Rangoon. They were booked as missionaries, salesmen, preachers, laborers, athletes, every craft and profession imaginable. They were fit young men, lean and wiry, and they often turned their gaze to the skies as if searching for distant aircraft.

The Japanese had superb intelligence sources in California and knew all about the AVG.

As the ships carrying the AVG passed Hawaii, a Navy cruiser joined as escort and followed the ship to Rangoon. There the AVG men hopped aboard trains and made their way upcountry through Kipling country to

Chennault's base. He wasted no time in putting them to work. Mornings were for classroom work, an idea that rankled the young pilots, many of whom already had considerable flying experience. But Chennault told them to forget everything that they thought they knew about aerial combat. The old ways were a path to certain death.

The AVG flew the Curtiss P-40, an obsolete aircraft but the only one available. It was a heavy and capricious aircraft. On takeoff, one wheel usually retracted before the other. In a dive the pilot had to stand on the right rudder to keep the aircraft flying in a straight line. Powered by an Allison V-12 engine of 1160 horsepower, each P-40 cost the Chinese government $60,562.00. The P-40 had six .50-caliber guns, three in each wing, and a two-second burst could put some twenty pounds of lead into a target.

Never turn with a Japanese fighter, Chennault taught. Those nimble little aircraft can outturn and outclimb you. Use your skills and the strengths of the P-40 to fly against the weaknesses of the Japanese aircraft. Get up high and make slashing high-speed attacks, then disengage, climb back to altitude, and do it again.

The P-40 is big and heavy and the enemy can never catch it in a dive. Unlike its opponent, the P-40 has armor to protect the pilot and it has self-sealing fuel tanks.

You can defeat the Jap, but you must do it the way I teach you.

I will teach you how to kill the enemy. And I will teach you how to stay alive.

The Japanese have been fighting in Manchuria since 1931 and they have never been bested, Chennault said. Japanese bombers have always gotten through. Their bomber crews are as arrogant as they are experienced. When the Japanese aircraft approach their targets in a big open formation, pounce on them from above and take out the lead aircraft. Japanese officers do not have the individuality of American officers, and if their lead ship—usually carrying the senior officer—is shot down, the entire group loses its focus and flounders about.

In the afternoons Chennault sent his pilots aloft to practice the maneuvers he had taught them that morning. He watched through binoculars, used his radio to correct them, and then, when they landed, debriefed them on every maneuver of the flight.

Always fly in pairs, he taught. The lead aircraft is the shooter and the wingman protects his six-o'clock position. Fighter combat is like a boxer's hands: You need two to win the fight.

Know the capability of the enemy aircraft and know your own aircraft. If you get into a turning fight you will die.

When you attack a bomber, aim for the fuel tanks or the engines. When you attack a fighter, aim at the wing root. Gunnery skills are crucial.

The young pilots knew Chennault's background and reputation. They knew how he had been shafted by his superiors in the regular Army and of his disdain for the Army's bureaucracy and its meaningless regulations. The old man rarely smiled and he was not one for small talk. But he had a command presence and his pilots felt his passion and absorbed his knowledge.

Few aircraft before or since have evoked such devotion, ambition, and pride in the hearts of preteen boys in America as did the P-40 flown by the AVG. No plane has been drawn by a pencil more than the P-40. No plane has been modeled more than the P-40. No plane has caused so many young men to yearn to fly as did the P-40.

A big part of the reason was the shark mouth painted on the front. Under the engine of the P-40 is a gaping scoop containing radiators for the engine and oil coolants. One of the AVG pilots had seen pictures of how British pilots in North Africa had painted a shark mouth on the noses of their P-40s, and he asked Chennault for permission to do the same. Chennault agreed, and soon his P-40s were adorned with shark mouths. But the Americans, as Americans are wont to do, carried the idea even further. The Chinese believed that the aircraft's personal devil should be able to see, so the AVG painted flat impassive eyes above the mouth. And then they added a lolling and salacious red tongue inside the shark mouth. The overall appearance—bright red tongue, black eyes, white teeth—was malevolent, slightly obscene, and absolutely terrifying.

The AVG made the shark mouth their own. They made it world-famous. And they made it such a talismanic insignia that decades later it would be painted on the noses of Army helicopters in Vietnam and on the noses of A-10 attack aircraft in Afghanistan. It was even painted on the nose of Air Force rockets launched from California and on the bow of small Navy assault boats. And it all goes back to the Flying Tigers in China during World War II.

On the aft fuselage was the squadron insignia of a winged tiger with a shredded Japanese flag in his mouth. The tiger was picked as the squadron insignia because in Chinese mythology the tiger is a fearful and rapacious creature.

---

Chennault and his men lived in conditions beyond primitive. Because Chennault was at the far end of a slender logistical pipeline, he and his men had few creature comforts and none of the amenities usually enjoyed by pilots. Their quarters were spartan. They ate Chinese food, drank Chinese beer, and were troubled by malaria and dysentery. They lived on hope and broken promises.

They knew they would soon be in combat and they celebrated in the way of fighter pilots. They drank themselves into a stupor, drove their jeeps into bars, frequented whorehouses, and more than once shot out the lights of a bar as they departed for the evening. Once a few of the pilots attended a Chinese play and were so taken with the star that they jumped on stage. One of the men threw the star over his shoulder, and the men fled the theater. They lived big because they knew that soon they would be going up against the might of the Japanese air force.

If a man could fly, and if he wanted to kill the enemies of America, Chennault did not care if he wore cowboy boots and mismatched clothing and was devoid of most military courtesies. But the respect his men gave Chennault was genuine. They did call him "sir." They stood up when he entered a room, and sometimes they even saluted him.

How the AVG morphed into the Flying Tigers is a story of various versions. The most likely version is that Madame Chiang sat with Chennault, watched the AVG practicing its tactics, and said, "These are my flying tigers."

Chennault formed his men into three squadrons, two operating out of Kunming to protect the vital Burma Road—the vertiginous and twisting seven-hundred-mile road that linked Lashio in British Burma to Kunming, China—and the third at Mingaladon to cover the vital port of Rangoon.

By now he had perfected a primitive but effective air warning system. He had Chinese eyes and ears everywhere, and his observers passed the word whenever the hangar doors opened on a Japanese field. When Japanese aircraft were within one hundred kilometers, a ball was raised on a flagpole at Chennault's fighter base. When the Japanese were within fifty kilometers, a second ball was hoisted up the pole. Once their training was finished, raising the second ball would be the signal for Chennault's pilots to take off and climb high into the sun, and when Japanese bombers came overhead, they would pounce.

August and September and October and November passed, and still the AVG trained in the ways of Claire Chennault.

# 15

# HOLD MY BEER . . .

IN JULY 1941, SCOTT WAS PROMOTED TO MAJOR. HIS SUPERIORS LIKED the way he was bringing the Army Air Forces to the attention of Hollywood, and they liked the number and caliber of the pilots he was turning out.

What they did not know was that Scott was taking the Hollywood part of his job quite seriously. He was spending a great deal of time with beautiful Hollywood stars.

On August 15, the *Los Angeles Times* carried a story that Scott had appointed Lieutenant Don Brown as public-relations officer for Cal-Aero Academy.

Scott was learning the political side of being a military officer.

But despite the time he spent in Hollywood, Scott was not neglecting his flying duties. He continued to fly every type of airplane he could, believing that being qualified in many aircraft would help him go to war. He even went to aircraft manufacturers in southern California and flew aircraft fresh off the assembly line. His logbook shows that on August 25, he had flown enough flights and had enough hours in a big four-engine bomber to be qualified as aircraft commander.

To be rated an "aircraft commander" means that a pilot was not only checked out to fly the aircraft, but that he knew a great deal about the electrical, mechanical, and hydraulic systems of the aircraft. He knew the job of every man on the crew.

In the mid-1930s, Boeing developed a bomber for the war that many knew was coming. The highly classified airplane project was called the

Model 299 and it was of a size and complexity never before known in a production airplane. The wings stretched a hundred and four feet, and on each wing were two big radial engines, each putting out a thousand horsepower and pulling the big lumbering aircraft along at a stately 220 mph. Takeoff weight for the aircraft was fifty-seven thousand pounds, at the time a monstrous weight for an aircraft. To fly such an aircraft took a large crew: four officers and six enlisted men.

During an early demonstration flight before top Air Corps officials at Wright Field, the ponderous aircraft lumbered down the runway, lifted off, and, at about three hundred feet, stalled and crashed. A newspaper story said the aircraft was "too much airplane for one man to fly." After all, there were four of everything: throttles, oil pressure gauges, manifold pressure gauges, and cowl flaps and a host of others. Plus, synchronizing four engines was like directing a symphony orchestra. Getting the aircraft off the ground and up to cruising altitude called for dozens of tasks by crew members. Take-offs and landings could be particularly stressful, and it seemed at the time that it was almost impossible for pilot and crew to remember the tasks in the proper sequence.

But the Army had bought Boeing's Model 299, by then designated the B-17 Flying Fortress, and began improving it. By late 1941, B-17s were beginning to roll down the assembly line by the hundreds.

Pilots were ordered to make this ship safe. The safety issue, as is often the case with complex issues, was resolved by the simple expedient of something called a "checklist." Now pilots had a book with page after page listing every task: the preignition checklist, ignition checklist, taxi checklist, pre-takeoff checklist, checklists for every possible in-flight emergency, and the all-important landing checklist.

Thereafter the checklist became a mandatory and indispensable part of every aircraft, from single-engine training aircraft to four-engine bombers and later to jets and spacecraft.

Another fascinating and seemingly contradictory behavioral trait of the Model 299 was that once it was at altitude, trimmed out, and the props were synchronized, flying the aircraft—what pilots call the "stick and rudder" part of aviation—was simple. The elephantine aircraft might be a bit slow in the turns, but once aloft she was as easy to fly as a single-engine training aircraft.

The army bought some thirteen thousand B-17s during World War II, and many of them would become the backbone of the air war against Germany, the heart of the famous Eighth Air Force.

Scott was qualified to command a B-17.

By now Scott's life was divided between building flying hours in every aircraft he could find, and socializing with every Hollywood actress he could find. He continued to fly several hours almost every afternoon after work, still practicing bombing with crenshaw melons. By the time he got home, Robin was usually asleep and Kitty Rix was having a cocktail and smoking one cigarette after the other. The sight of Kitty Rix smoking cigarettes, and the sight of his war bag by the door, did not improve his mood.

Kitty Rix promised to reduce the number of cigarettes she was smoking.

But then, as the couple went to bed, Kitty Rix deployed all the paraphernalia necessary to trim her cuticles and polish her nails, the little scissors that went clickety-clack, the acetone-based nail-polish remover, the nail polish with its own sharp smell, the repeated whoosh of Kitty Rix's breath as she blew on her nails to dry them.

To Scott, the oil and gas and grease and leather and hydraulic fuel smells of the flight line were divine. The high-pitched thunder of radial aircraft engines, the thousands of squeaks and thunks in an aircraft, all were a heavenly symphony. But the smells and the sounds of going to bed were an ordeal.

In late 1941, Universal Studios filmed a movie called *Keep 'Em Flying*—the title was the unofficial motto of the Army Air Forces—at Cal-Aero. Starring the zany comedy team of Bud Abbott and Lou Costello, it revolved around the antics of a cadet going through flight training.

The film crew brought along a masseuse, who made her services available to Scott. The news that the commander of Cal-Aero was receiving massages from a movie masseuse did not sit well with Scott's superiors.

Scott was not only the military consultant to the movie; he took an active role in the filming and the flying.

The script called for an aircraft to be flown through four open aircraft hangars. The dangerous maneuver was to be flown by Paul Mantz, a famed stunt pilot, who was paid $500 per minute for his flying time. But the Air Forces saw a liability problem in letting a civilian pilot fly through Cal-Aero's hangars, and it denied Mantz permission.

"Hell, Paul," Scott said. "I'll fly through the hangars for you."

And he did. Mantz was amazed that a regular military pilot could jump into an airplane and perform such a dangerous stunt. In gratitude, Mantz gave Scott a set of expensive golf clubs.

That the commander of Cal-Aero was accepting expensive gifts from Hollywood people was something else that did not sit well with Scott's superiors.

Scott's involvement with Hollywood naturally brought him to the attention of local newspapers. He was always ready with a quote or a story idea, especially if the story revolved around him.

On October 19, 1941, the *Home* magazine of the *Los Angeles Times* devoted almost a full page to Scott's recipes for roast goose, wild rice dressing, roast duck, and steamed doves. Although the paper made much of how the commander of Cal-Aero was a hunter and a cook, the recipes were simple and only a half step up from cooking around a campfire. For instance, Scott's recipe for steamed doves involved Worcestershire sauce and canned mushrooms.

Scott says he continued to write to generals asking for a transfer. It is more likely that he wrote to one general whom he knew well.

There was only one general who knew Scott well, and had the opportunity and connections to help him. That was now-major-general George Brett, the officer who had been Scott's wing commander in Panama. Brett was moving between Java, Australia, China, and India, and he had the rank to assist Scott.

By now the fight between the interventionists and the isolationists was boiling over in the bitterest internal dispute in America since the Civil War. The fight was not just between Roosevelt and Lindbergh and their determined followers; now it involved the U.S. military.

Both Arnold and Marshall continued to oppose the idea of American pilots in American aircraft flying and fighting for the Chinese. They believed those pilots and those aircraft were needed for the expansion of the Army Air Forces.

In late October, Thomas G. Lanphier Jr. was one of Scott's graduating pilots. During the war Lanphier would become famous as one of the P-38 pilots on the mission that shot down Admiral Isoroku Yamamoto, Japan's senior commander in the Pacific. Lanphier later was asked to record an oral history of his career. Part of his interview revolved around famous officers he had known. He remembered Scott as a "loquacious, lanky guy" who "never let a fear of overstatement inhibit his exhortations."

At a Cal-Aero graduation dinner, Scott told Lanphier's class, "You are fortune's fools, because you are to serve your country with wings on."

The next day the students lined up to watch Scott demonstrate his flying abilities. Scott put his aircraft through a series of aerobatic maneuvers, and then came in for what the students thought would be a routine landing. But then Scott gunned the motor and flew the aircraft through the open doors of two aircraft hangars, reprising his movie stunt and leaving his students wide-eyed.

On Sunday morning, December 7, when Scott heard the news of Pearl Harbor, he sat by the phone for hours, war bag at his feet, fully expecting that someone who knew his background would say, "Get Scott and put him in charge of a fighter squadron." But the phone did not ring. Finally, after several agonizing hours, Scott grabbed his war bag, kissed Robin and Kitty Rix good-bye, and said he might never see them again because he was going off to war. Or so he thought. Scott jumped into his car and drove some 150 miles north to Moffett Field on San Francisco Bay, where he presented himself to his boss, General Henry Harms, and said, in effect, "General, I am reporting for duty. I'm ready to go to war."

Harms looked at Scott as if the man had taken leave of his senses. Here was a thirty-three-year-old major acting as if he were a young lieutenant. Most unseemly behavior for a West Pointer who was being promoted rapidly and likely destined for much higher rank.

"You are not going anywhere except back to your present duty station," the general said. "Scott, you are too old. You are thirty-three, a decade older than fighter pilots."

A chastened Scott returned to the Training Command, to his wife and baby, and there he wondered what had happened to the Big Sky Boss and the Master Plan. Why wasn't he being allowed to fulfill his destiny?

He was *too old.*

Nothing can be said to a fighter pilot that is more painful.

America and her allies—well, *most* of her allies—were devastated by the attack on Pearl Harbor. But Chiang was so exultant that he walked around singing an opera aria all day. Now America was at war with Japan, and China's strategic importance blossomed overnight. American money and equipment would begin flowing, by the hundreds of millions of dollars. America would *have* to support Chiang.

America was hoping to use China's almost endless reserves of manpower against Japan. But Chiang wanted America's money and weapons to suppress the Communists and to cement his power just as much as he wanted them to fight Japan.

More than seventy years have passed since the end of World War II. Yet, the American people retain a deep and abiding interest in that conflict. There are, however, some matters relating to World War II that most people get wrong. Many people believe that Chennault's Flying Tigers were fighting the Japanese before Pearl Harbor, when, in fact, the AVG first flew in combat twelve days *after* Pearl Harbor. They were fighter pilots, and their mood, disposition, and every fiber of their being was to attack, attack, attack. At last the training was over, and they were doing what they had come to China to do. And now, after Pearl Harbor, they had a new and powerful incentive: They were flying against the enemies of their country.

On December 19, Chennault's air-raid warning net gave him notice that ten Japanese bombers were bound for Kunming, terminus of the vital Burma Road that linked China with the outside world. Chennault ordered his Tigers up high, into the sun, to wait. The bombers came in a broad open formation with no fighter escorts, the pilots arrogant in their presumption that they could bomb Chinese soil with impunity.

Above them were Chennault's men. He watched the Japanese bombers and he waited and then, when his pilots were tense and anxious and wondering when the Old Man would give the order, he leaned into the microphone and in his intense voice growled, "Take 'em. Take 'em."

And all at once the Japanese bombers were shaking from the impact of .50-caliber machine-gun bullets, and the Japanese pilots watched in fear as P-40s slashed through their formation, P-40s with a shark mouth on the nose. The P-40s were a blur as they roared past and then they continued diving before converting their speed to altitude, and then they were coming back in again, flown by highly disciplined pilots who waited until the last moment before firing, and then slammed bullets into the most vulnerable place on the bombers: the engines.

Six Japanese bombers were shot down the first time the Flying Tigers rose in combat.

From then on, the bombers would not always get through.

On Christmas Day, the Flying Tigers and a few British aircraft climbed high over Rangoon against a force of 108 Japanese bombers and fighters. Thirteen enemy bombers and ten fighters were shot down.

As *Time* magazine put it in a December 29 story, one of the first written about the AVG, "The Flying Tigers swooped, let the Japanese have it."

The AVG was flying aircraft that had been rejected by Britain as inadequate, aircraft for which there were few replacement parts, rarely enough gasoline, at the end of one of the longest logistical pipelines in the world. The pilots were short of everything but courage.

That the AVG provided about the only good news for the Allies in the Far East was emphasized when on February 15, 1942, the British fortress at Singapore, the "Gibraltar of the Far East" with its ninety-thousand-man garrison, surrendered to the Japanese. It was an event Winston Churchill called the "worst disaster" in British history. The British had assumed that any attack would come from the sea, and all their weapons and defenses were oriented toward the ocean. The Japanese simply marched up the Malay Peninsula—the back door, as it were—and took the city in a matter of hours.

That same week, the Japanese army surrounded one hundred thousand American troops in the Philippines.

The March 30, 1942, issue of *Life* had what the magazine called "the first full-length portrait of the Flying Tigers in action," a series of dramatic photographs and superheated verbiage: "one American flier is equal to two or three Japs," the pilots are "always looking for a fight," the Flying Tigers were a "holocaust" to the Japanese, the Japanese interfered with the plans of the pilots and now the Japanese "must be eliminated," the story of the pilots' "skill, courage and fighting spirit has swept Free China."

It was what the people back home in America needed.

(Rarely has an enemy been so dehumanized as were the Japanese in

World War II. The surprise attack on Pearl Harbor put the American people in a blazing rage toward the Japanese. In newspapers, in magazines, on the radio, in official military reports, they were "Japs." The word "Japanese" was rarely heard or seen. And then-stereotypical images of the Japanese prevailed. Thus, when *Life* or *Time* referred to "the Jap," they were only reflecting the tenor of the time.)

Chennault's tactics might have been ridiculed by his old colleagues back in America, but now those tactics were proven sound in the most unforgiving cauldron of all—combat.

And while Chennault's old colleagues thought him cranky and opinionated and cold and aloof, he gained from his young hell-raising pilots a gift rarely bestowed on a combat leader: he was loved as much as he was respected.

The legend of the Fei Hu—Chinese for Flying Tigers—had begun. The Chinese looked upon the American pilots as the saviors of their country. An English-speaking Japanese broadcaster was almost frothing at the mouth as she sputtered about the American "outlaws" and "renegades." And America looked upon them as the most heroic, romantic, and devastating group of fighter pilots the world had ever seen. That belief has only strengthened with the passage of more than seventy years.

It must be remembered that in the weeks after Pearl Harbor, indeed through the spring and early summer of 1942, the Japanese juggernaut seemed unstoppable. At that time, it appeared to be one of the most formidable military machines the world had ever seen. Today we think of our World War II victory as inevitable. But it was not. After Pearl Harbor and the fall of the Philippines, America was reeling. The Pacific was a Japanese lake. America was losing the war, and it would be some six months before the Marines began to take the initiative on postage-stamp-sized islands that no one back home had ever heard of. But even after the Marines took Guadalcanal, there remained numerous other islands where, had the Marines been defeated, the war could easily have gone either way.

Most Americans thought of the coming war in terms of England and Europe and Hitler and Mussolini. Sure, they knew of the fighting in China, but that was a sideshow. And now as Americans were still shaking off the initial shock of Pearl Harbor and America's entry into the war against the Japanese, from out of nowhere—well, out of China, which was the same thing as nowhere—came news that a small group of young American pilots flying old P-40s with big shark mouths on the nose were giving the Japanese the first thrashing they had known since they invaded Manchuria in 1931. In China, a crusty and taciturn Southerner by the name of Claire Lee Chennault was leading his Flying Tigers to victory.

Chennault and his fighters were proving the fallacy inherent in what now had become the driving imperative in the Army Air Forces: The bombers always get through. Within the Army Air Forces, the idea that bombers were omnipotent—now codified in the doctrine of strategic bombing—was growing stronger.

By January 1942, the Flying Tigers had sixty confirmed kills. A Japanese radio broadcaster said, "We warn the American aviators that they must cease their unorthodox tactics immediately, or they will be treated like guerrillas and shown no mercy whatsoever."

The Flying Tigers knew little of this. They were at the end of the world and did not even know they were famous. All they knew was that they worked for a great man, and that they were killing their country's enemies.

The euphoria Americans felt toward the Flying Tigers has not since been replicated in any war. No other group has achieved such mythic stature. That the exploits of the AVG took place in the China-Burma-India theater, that far-off, unknown, and mysterious place on the other side of the world, only added to their mystique.

The year 1942 was the pivotal year of Scott's life. Beginning in January, events came at him furiously.

He was promoted to lieutenant colonel, given the title of "Director of Training," and transferred two hundred miles north of Los Angeles to Lemoore Field, a dry-weather field about as far out in the boondocks as it was possible to go. Scott said being sent to Lemoore "was one of the low periods of my life."

Kitty Rix would have said the same thing.

On February 1, 1942, Scott became one of the first in his West Point class to be promoted to colonel, a distinction not without irony. After all, Scott had barely graduated.

A few days later the American public learned that Chennault's pilots had conducted a raid over Rangoon and destroyed forty-three enemy aircraft without the loss of a single P-40. And a few weeks later they shot down eighteen Japanese aircraft.

Scott fired off his second wire to Chennault volunteering his services but again got no response. He knew he was the best fighter pilot in the Air Forces, the best shooter, and a splendid bomber. He had some five thousand hours of flying time, as much if not more than any other pilot in the Air Forces.

But everyone kept saying to him, "You are too senior, and you are too old."

One day Scott arrived home around eight p.m. after a long day of giving check rides. He was tired and dispirited, and he was wondering if he would ever see the elephant.

His mood was bleak. Scott was edging up against the depression that would hound him all his life. He opened the door of his house and heard the phone ringing. He called out for Kitty Rix but heard nothing.

Exasperated, Scott strode across the room, picked up the phone, and said, "Colonel Scott's quarters. Colonel Scott speaking."

That phone call changed Scott's life.

# 16

## THE FLIGHT TO DESTINY

KITTY RIX CAME INTO THE ROOM JUST AS SCOTT ANSWERED THE PHONE. He smiled and nodded. When he saw she had a drink in one hand and a cigarette in the other, his smile changed to a grimace.

"Good evening, sir," he said into the telephone. "Good to talk with you again." He went silent, and as he listened his eyes widened and he stared at Kitty Rix. He had said "sir," so she knew the caller was senior to Scott. She looked at her watch. Who could be calling at this hour?

The voice belonged to Colonel Merian Cooper, the shadowy military-intelligence figure on Hap Arnold's staff whom Scott had met at a Cal-Aero party.

"Colonel Scott, how many flying hours do you have?"

"More than five thousand hours, sir."

"Are you checked out in the B-17?"

"Yes, sir."

"How many hours?"

Scott reached out a hand to Kitty Rix, who put her drink on the table and held Scott's hand.

Scott had been checked out as aircraft commander in the B-17 back in August 1941, and he had occasionally flown the B-17s that stopped at Cal-Aero. He had enough hours in the aircraft to be proficient. But he was not current.

Scott sensed that Merian Cooper was not making idle conversation; that much depended on how he answered the colonel's question.

He squeezed Kitty Rix's hand.

Cooper's impatient voice came over the telephone. "Colonel Scott, how many hours do you have in the B-17?"

Deep breath.

"Sir, I am current in the B-17, and have more than a thousand hours in the aircraft."

Cooper advised Scott that their conversation now was classified and what to expect in the next few days.

Scott listened, occasionally nodding and saying, "Yes, sir," then said, "Thank you, sir. Good night, sir." He placed the phone on the cradle, looked at Kitty Rix, then turned and stared at his war bag.

He could tell Kitty Rix only that he was leaving and did not know when he would return.

She had lived in dread of this day. But after so many months in the Training Command, and after so many rebuffs to Scotty, she had begun to believe her family might remain intact, that the war would pass them by. But now the war was here.

Kitty Rix lifted her glass and fortified herself for what was ahead.

Scott continued to stare at his war bag. He had lied about his flying hours to a senior officer and it was likely that if anyone discovered his lie, Scott would be in the Training Command for the rest of the war.

A few days later, on March 14, 1942, Scott received orders sending him to Fairfield Air Depot in Ohio for a preliminary briefing on something called Task Force Aquila. After the briefing he was to ferry a new B-17 to McDill Field in Tampa, Florida, for more briefings and more training.

The March 30 issue of *Life* contained an eleven-page photo spread titled "Flying Tigers in Burma." The romantic piece told how Flying Tigers in their P-40s were wreaking hell, death, and destruction upon the Japanese. The pilots pictured were so very young, had such boyish smiles, and were clad in such an array of cowboy boots and scarves and Chinese air force hats and piratical garb that they seemed almost like college boys playing a colossal prank. But when the story detailed the number of Japanese aircraft shot down, the number of bombs dropped, the number of enemy troops killed in strafing runs, it was readily apparent that, while they might be boys, they were also—like all fighter pilots—stone killers.

———

Task Force Aquila was a group of twelve B-17s that, upon completion of their training at McDill, would fly to Karachi for final orders.

On the flight to Tampa, Scott detoured to the east. As he approached Aiken, he dropped down to an altitude of about a hundred feet and flew over the cemetery at the Millbrook Baptist Church where his grandfather was buried, and then down the Whiskey Road until he came to the home place. He circled the farm, dropped his landing gear, and pushed the nose of the B-17 down until the landing gear was dragging through the tops of row crops. He looked out the cockpit, and later he said that he saw his long-dead grandfather Burckhalter standing there, wearing his faded overalls, waving his Confederate hat, and that in his mind he heard his grandfather repeat the words he had uttered to Scott so many years earlier: "You just keep your heart in the heavens, son, and you'll fly back here someday in your own airship and you'll light in that field out there and I'll be waiting for you."

There was no doubt in Scotty's mind that he saw his grandfather waving to him.

At Tampa, Scott and his crew met the commander of Task Force Aquila: Colonel Caleb V. Haynes, a big, gruff, bearlike man from Mount Airy, North Carolina, and a legend in the Army Air Forces. Haynes had set several distance records in multiengine aircraft, and he had opened up the early aircraft ferry routes from America to South America and Europe. He was considered one of the most experienced bomber men in the service.

Colonel Merian Cooper was also present. He would be flying with Haynes as the executive officer of Task Force Aquila. Cooper had organized this top-secret mission and was traveling under orders signed by General Arnold. Only Cooper knew the ultimate target of the task force. To maintain operational security, he would not tell the crews what that mission was until they reached Karachi.

The mission was not hard to figure out. Twelve B-17s meant the target was big and important. The jumping-off point was Karachi. The target could only be Japan. Task Force Aquila was going to bomb Japan. Beyond that, the very name of the task force gave away its purpose: "*aquila*" is the Latin word for eagle and represents the bird that carried aloft the thunderbolts of Zeus.

But in case there was any lingering doubt anywhere, Scott had his crew chief paint a red map of Japan on the nose of his B-17 and inscribe under the map the phrase "*Hades ab Altar,*" which roughly translates to "Hell from on high."

Scott liked drama when he went to war.

Training in Tampa was intense. Simulated bombing missions, high-altitude flights, navigation training.

The training flights also were shakedown flights. Big bombers are notoriously temperamental, especially new ones, and all the systems had to be checked and rechecked for the long flight ahead.

All the time Scott was in full paranoia mode. He feared that *they*, whoever *they* were, would find out about what he was now calling his "big lie" and send him back to Cal-Aero. From the frequency and the passion with which he would later write of this fear, you would have thought the Army Air Forces was about to track him down and return him to the Training Command.

Perhaps it was this paranoia and tension about the upcoming mission that informed Scott's March 27 letter to Kitty Rix. "I cried tonight for the way I fussed at you yesterday," he wrote of their recent telephone conversation. He said his querulous mood was because he had been flying at thirty-five thousand feet, and his head ached.

Kitty Rix was in Macon in a rented house near Scott's parents. He wrote detailed instructions to her saying she should pay only for the new stove, refrigerator, and washing machine and Robin's books. If other creditors contacted her, let them know he would be cabling money to them. He hectored Kitty Rix about her smoking and drinking.

And he told her he would not have to write many letters because "I'll be in all the papers anyway and you can always tell where I'll be or at least where I've been."

He said, "Someday, perhaps very soon when all this is over, I'll swear I'll never leave you again."

He meant it at the time.

Much has been made over the years of how and why a man whose flying career was based on single-engine fighter aircraft would have been picked to participate in a top-secret mission involving heavy bombers. George Cully, a retired Air Force historian who has reviewed some of Scott's assignment records, suggests that Scott was recommended by General George Brett, the officer who had previously been Scott's wing commander in the Canal Zone. Brett knew Scott was a first-rate navigator and had gained considerable experience in building and expanding expeditionary airfields in Panama, skills that would be needed where he was going.

Another possibility is that the B-17 was so new and so big and coming off assembly lines in such numbers that there was no ready reservoir of B-17 pilots to draw upon, and that Scott was picked simply because he was a high-time pilot who was checked out in the B-17.

Whatever the reason, there is little chance that Scott's flying background was not known in detail. But talking about his "big lie" and raising the bogeyman specter of the Training Command made such a great story. So much drama.

Scott did overstate the hours he had in the B-17. But once Scott's orders were issued, no one was going to reach out and tell a highly qualified pilot to return to running a flight school.

Merian Cooper kept a close eye on the calendar. He knew that Lieutenant Colonel James Doolittle and his force of sixteen B-25s were aboard the USS *Hornet* bound for Japan with an assignment to bomb Tokyo, and then to fly on to China and set up a base there. Cooper had to get his twelve B-17s to Karachi, some twelve thousand miles away, and then to air bases inside China, before he could attack Japan. Cooper was determined to beat Doolittle and organize the first bombing mission against Japan.

Because the Japanese owned the Pacific, Task Force Aquila would have to fly the long way around to reach Karachi: Florida to Puerto Rico, Trinidad, Natal, Liberia, Ghana, Nigeria, Khartoum, Aden, and finally to Karachi.

Colonels Haynes and Cooper took off from Tampa in a Consolidated B-24 Liberator, a heavy bomber like the B-17, but slightly faster, to lead the way. They flew to West Palm Beach and then took off for Puerto Rico. One by one the B-17s followed. To avoid attention, the takeoffs were spaced several hours apart.

Scott was delayed for two days waiting on engine repairs and it was not until March 31, in a driving rain, that he finally took off from West Palm Beach. He was the tail-end Charlie, and he was not happy. He might have been the last to take off from Florida but there was no way in hell he would be the last to land in Karachi.

Later Scott would write that when he climbed into the left seat—the aircraft commander's seat—he turned to the copilot, one of his former students, and said, "How about showing me how to fly this ship—I want to see how to work these turbos and such."

Nonsense. At Tampa he had logged eleven hours and twenty-five minutes on the B-17. And of course Colonel Haynes would never have let Scott occupy the left seat of a B-17 if he had not been qualified to fly the aircraft.

As Scott finally took off, the wheels lifted off the ground and tucked into the wells with a satisfying thunk. When he heard the sound, Scott cried out, "They can't get me now." His crew members looked at each other in bewilderment. Who was chasing the tall, slightly gawky, and visibly agitated colonel?

The stately B-17 soon reached its assigned altitude and settled into the monotony of a long over-water flight. The four engines were synchronized, the cowl flaps closed, the fuel mixture leaned, the aircraft trimmed out. The crew settled into its routine.

At long last, Colonel Robert Lee Scott Jr. of Macon, Georgia, was going to war, and he was a happy man. Finally, he would see the elephant.

Two things about that long flight are worthy of note.

First, Scott had a great fear that *they* might recall the last plane. In Puerto Rico he found that two of the B-17s that had taken off before him were grounded as they awaited engine parts. He roused his crew before dawn the next day and took off hours before the other two B-17s could be repaired. On each subsequent takeoff, he expressed exultation that now "they" could not recall him to the Training Command. Once Scott even unplugged his radio so no messages could come through.

He also told the crew he was about to celebrate his thirty-fourth birthday. The average age of the enlisted crew was nineteen, and to them Scott was an old man.

The second thing worthy of note is the nineteen-hundred-mile flight across the Atlantic from Natal to Liberia. As the aircraft approached the equator, Scott saw that huge thunderstorms with magnificent displays of lightning were astride his course. He expected them, as thunderstorms are usually present along what pilots call the intertropical convergence zone (ITCZ), the area where northeast and southeast trade winds converge. The accepted method to penetrate the ITCZ was to get in close to the bad weather, make a hard turn directly into the storm, and penetrate the system in the shortest possible distance. Once in clear air on the other side of the storm, the pilot resumed his course.

The turbulence inside those storms was horrendous, and, even as large as it was, Scott's aircraft was tossed about as if it were a toy. Stress caused the skin of the wings to wrinkle, and the blue light of Saint Elmo's fire to play around the propeller tips, all as jagged lightning lit up the night sky.

Perhaps the violent display and the turbulent air rattled the confidence of the young lieutenant serving as Scott's navigator. The aircraft had been flying on a course of eighty-one degrees—slightly north of due east—for much of the night. All at once the navigator told Scott to turn to a heading of 135 degrees—southeast. Scott was puzzled but did not want to second-guess his young navigator, so he turned to the new course. Then the navigator ordered another change, to 145 degrees.

Scott went down to the navigator's compartment, where the sheepish navigator said he had set his watches wrong, that the error threw off his navigation, and now he was lost over the Atlantic.

Scott patted the lieutenant on the shoulder and expressed confidence that the young navigator could get them back on course, that they would make landfall at the designated place, and that all would be well.

He returned to the cockpit, and a few minutes later the navigator called up another change of direction. Now every member of the crew knew there was a good chance they were going to ditch. Scott decided to take charge of the navigation.

He looked at the chart of the Atlantic and the bulge of West Africa, and everything he had learned about dead reckoning came surging back, everything he had learned during those long nights of flying the mail, everything he had learned flying over the uncharted jungles of Central America. All of his flying hours coalesced into this one moment when his experience mattered more than the navigator's training.

Scott knew that when a pilot is lost, he can't go blundering about and poking the nose of the aircraft here and there as he searches for his destination. The only way to get anywhere is to pick a course and fly it. Scott did a few quick mental calculations, set up a new course, throttled back the engines to conserve fuel, and waited. An hour later he reduced power even more. Now the B-17 was flying at only 165 miles an hour. Scott and the engineer computed their time in the air, and the fuel consumption rate, and calculated that the fuel tanks would be dry in less than an hour.

Among the crew members, apprehension was high. Scott sought to alleviate the fears of his young crew by announcing that he was on course, and Africa was straight ahead.

Then through the rain clouds Scott saw trees atop a big hill and the crew let out a shout of relief.

Scott again consulted the chart and saw only two big hills on the part of the coast where he hoped to make landfall. One was near Freetown about a hundred miles north of their destination and according to the chart rose 835 feet above sea level. The other was near Fisher's Lake in Liberia, minutes from their planned destination, and was four hundred feet above sea level.

Scott dove, skimmed the top of the hill, and checked his altimeter. He was slightly above four hundred feet.

He had made landfall only a few miles from where his flight plan called for. Scott pushed up the throttles and a few minutes later buzzed the landing field at more than two hundred miles an hour, chandelled up and around, and—after a flight of thirteen hours and five minutes—landed the B-17.

The navigator was as well trained as the Air Forces could make him. He knew the latest techniques of celestial navigation, shooting sun sights, and parsing an infinite number of arcane details regarding compass headings, magnetic deviation, ground speed, and other things. But he did not have Scott's practical experience in dead reckoning. And more importantly, the lieutenant did not have the sixth sense that comes with the accumulation of many flying hours alone, with surviving nights of flying blind in snowstorms along the Hell Stretch, the settled reasoning that comes with crossing trackless jungles in blinding rains, and the self-confidence to think the situation through, pick a course, and stick to it.

Scott had proved that age has its advantages. He had saved his crew from what might have been a fatal error by a young navigator.

Scott knew what every experienced pilot knows: No matter how skilled a pilot may be, there will come moments when he needs to put into use everything he has ever learned, everything he has ever heard, everything he has ever experienced. And if he makes the right decision, he will live.

Scott was a fighter pilot. He was used to making every decision that was made in the cockpit. He was used to having no one to consult. It was figure it out or die.

The remainder of the flight was uneventful. And on April 11 he took off from Aden on the last leg of his trip: eight hours and twenty minutes to Karachi.

He again told his crew he was now safe, that "they" could no longer reach him.

Scott had pushed his crew hard, and he knew he had passed most of the other eleven B-17s. Now he would land and learn the mission of Task Force Aquila.

Scott looked out of the cockpit to see the runway at Karachi, an airport that almost overnight had become one of the most crucial airports in the world. Karachi was then in western India and was a city of about 400,000; a city of few motorized vehicles but lots of camels, horses, donkeys, and a famous performing bear that roamed the streets with his handler. To remove themselves from the multilayered aromas of the city, British colonial types often went down to Lady Lloyd Pier to breathe the fresh air from the Indian Ocean. Karachi was then, and remains today, something of a cloaca for the subcontinent.

As the B-17 slowed to its approach speed, Scott opened his side window a crack and the smell of Karachi flooded the cockpit. It was not a pleasant smell.

It is said that the most confusing and dangerous times in a war are at the beginning and in the end. The beginning is dangerous because personalities are in conflict, roles and duties are vague, and everything is in a rapid state of change. Uncertainty prevails, confusion reigns, and chaos is the order of the day. Needs are many and largely unfilled. One is not sure of the enemy's location, capability, or tactics. Boundaries of the battlespace may be uncertain and the rhythm of battle has not yet been established. All is jangled. Danger and death lurk in unexpected places.

All that and more, Scott was about to find in Karachi.

# 17

# AT THE END OF THE WORLD

THE MAGNETIC PULL OF WORLD WAR II REMAINS STRONG IN THE American psyche. Every year there are more books, more movies, more television shows, and more Internet sites about World War II. We venerate the men who fought in that war and call them "the Greatest Generation," an appellation that is romantic claptrap but, nevertheless, codified in our collective memory.

But when Americans think of World War II, it is usually Europe and D-day, Churchill and Eisenhower. We know how Ike breached Fortress Europa and how his men marched across France, the Low Countries, and Germany and down into Austria to end the menace of Hitler and the Third Reich and, to use the saying of the time, make the world safe for democracy.

U.S. Marines, of course, think of the Pacific, where they fought the Japanese for almost two years before D-day.

Not many Americans know of the China-Burma-India theater (the CBI), and if they do, they don't know much. And what they do know is often wrong.

The CBI was an obscure place, a roiling backwater. But Roosevelt believed it was also a place where the Japanese army must be held in place; else three divisions from that army would go to the Pacific to fight U.S. Marines.

By the time Scott arrived in the CBI, the Chinese had been fighting Japan for five years, not winning but at least holding on when none of Japan's other enemies could do so.

Some mark the beginning of World War II as July 1937, when Japanese and Chinese troops clashed at the Marco Polo Bridge near Peking. But a better date is 1931, when Japan invaded Manchuria and began using the country as a training ground.

Now, in April 1942, China was fighting for its very existence, well along on the way to the loss of fourteen million of its citizens and the destruction of its embryonic modernization.

The CBI was vast, the weather was horrendous, and living conditions were abysmal. And things were in a mess. They were in a mess when Scott landed and would descend into an ever greater mess over the next few months.

Military people assigned to remote theaters are often quirky. Some are quirky before they arrive, and others are made quirky by the place and the circumstances. Sometimes these people are also mediocre, even incompetent. But both the mediocre and the incompetent sometimes grow to become great men. And the CBI was a place where giants would walk the earth.

Combat in the CBI took place in the vast reaches of eastern China, in the skies over Burma (now Myanmar), and in Indochina.

In China the battlefront stretched some five thousand miles, from Chengtu in the northwest to Chungking on the Yangtze and south to the Red River.


Burma was a tight little country that is flanked on three sides by mountains, obstacles that have always discouraged both trade and travel. Rain is heavy much of the year and the water drains off through the Irrawaddy and Chindwin Rivers on the west, and the Salween and Sittang on the east.

Burma was then a British colony, but the British had made few preparations to defend it from the Japanese.

And when Japan began rampaging through Burma, the AVG and then the U.S. Army Air Forces had to support Great Britain.

And that country needed a lot of support.

Even though the CBI was a backwater, the wartime stakes could not have been higher. China, America, and Britain all had competing and conflicting national interests.

Boiled down to the basics and free of all the high-minded rhetoric, China wanted to survive, to become an equal among the Allies, and to take her rightful place among the great nations of the world. To do this, China needed

America's money and matériel, both to fight the Japanese and to quell the rising threat of communism.

Nationalist leader Chiang Kai-shek once famously said that the Japanese were a skin disease while communism was a heart disease.

The British wanted America to defend Burma because that country was a buffer protecting India, the jewel of the British Empire. The British were having a bloody rough go of it, what with the fall of Hong Kong and Singapore, and now the Japanese were about to seize Burma. While the British might have had stiff upper lips, they did not have stiff spines, and they wanted America to protect India and the empire. Military leaders in the CBI were hardheaded and intractable men who were wrong about many things most of the time.

To know why these men are important, consider the words of Erich von Manstein, Germany's most brilliant general in World War II. He said that historians do not find truth in files and documents and official records, but *"The essential thing to know is how the main personalities thought and reacted to events."* (Italics added.)

Historians rarely agree on either the interpretation of events or the importance of main personalities. And if they do agree, along comes a generation of revisionists to change it all. The result is that history is a deep, murky, and slow-moving river in which certainties are few and last only a year or so before being replaced with newer certainties.

This is especially true regarding World War II, about which so much has been written and is still being written.

Most of what has been written about military leaders in the CBI is contradictory and conflicting. Then there is Scott, who wrote much of his own history, and whose story has been muddled by both hero worship and animosity.

The main personalities in the CBI were a contentious lot.

Scott is about to make a grand entrance, to begin chewing on the scenery and become one of the legends he is about to join.

The sulky Chiang Kai-shek was a man who made up for his shortcomings as a leader and strategist with his skill at corruption. (In America some said the proper pronunciation of Chiang's name was "Cash My Check.")

By now China is on the razor's edge of losing the war to Japan, and its people are about to be cut off from the world. Chiang is desperate, lashing out in the most demanding and intemperate fashion. Were it not for the leadership skills of Chiang's ambitious wife, his hold on power would have been tenuous in the extreme.

Madame Chiang would soon become the first foreign woman ever to address a joint session of Congress. She was immensely popular in America and, early in the war, held great sway with Roosevelt. Her favorite American was Claire Chennault.

General Joseph "Vinegar Joe" Stilwell came to Burma in early 1942 as the senior American officer in the CBI, and Chiang's chief of staff. Stilwell was known for his blunt language and prickly disposition, neither of which improved upon arrival in-theater. Stilwell had served in China in the 1930s as a military attaché, spoke fluent Chinese, and understood the Chinese military and Chinese culture as well as any American officer. On paper he was the perfect man to send to China.

But Stilwell believed that wars are won on the ground, and he was disappointed that he had been sent to China when he had hoped to lead the invasion of North Africa.

Stilwell was a great soldier, but in the CBI he was a disaster. He was contemptuous of Chiang and referred to the man as "Peanut." He fought with Chennault on everything from the role of air power to Chennault's close relationship with Generalissimo and Madame Chiang.

Stilwell was contemptuous of the British, and he referred to them as "bastardly hypocrites" and "pig fuckers." Using a nickname as distasteful as it was unpolitic, he referred to the polio-crippled Roosevelt as "Rubber Legs."

Stilwell had been sent to a part of the world where dreams go to die, and he quickly found himself mired in a Chinese bog where his knowledge of the country and its people would be of little use. He would be rendered almost impotent by Chennault, a man far junior to him who believed in air power as strongly as Stilwell believed in the infantry.

The differences between Chennault and Stilwell are best shown in an exchange the two men had in one of their early meetings. Chennault was elaborating on his ideas about air power when Stilwell snapped, "It is the ground soldier slogging through the mud and fighting in the trenches who will win the war."

"Goddammit, Stilwell," Chennault said, "there aren't any men in the trenches."

Then there were the British. In considering British military officers in the CBI, it is difficult to avoid the conclusion that Prime Minister Winston

Churchill was blessed with such an abundance of greatness that there was little left over for his military leaders. After General Archibald Percival Wavell was defeated by Rommel in North Africa, Churchill would send him to India with the hope he would kill more Japanese than British. Wavell would lose Burma, resign in disgrace, be promoted to field marshal, and return to the CBI with a mandate to take back Burma. He would fail, and in 1943 he would be created a viscount and named Viceroy of Burma.

Such is the way of empire.

The quixotic Louis Mountbatten followed Wavell as supreme allied commander in Southeast Asia. A great-grandson of Queen Victoria and called "Dickie" by family and close friends, Lord Mountbatten had banged up so many navy ships that he was called the "Master of Disaster." He would be the mastermind of the disastrous Dieppe Raid in August 1942, in which thousands of Canadians were killed—the Canadians said needlessly—and came to the CBI with the idea of conducting an amphibious landing at Rangoon. Churchill squashed the idea.

Mountbatten shared with Scott a gift for telling stories that had little or no connection with the truth. He liked wearing his formal uniforms and he loved the medals and decorations and ribbons of his rank, along with the formalities and entitlements that came with his being a cousin to the queen.

And, of course, there was the enemy. In the spring of 1942 the Japanese were about to chase the British, Stilwell, and Chennault out of Burma. They had overrun numerous air bases in China, cut the railroad from Hanoi to Kunming, and then seized the Burma Road. More than 100,000 workers had toiled for two years to build that road, and now it was being used by the Japanese. China was cut off from the world.

When Scott landed in Karachi, Japan had already achieved most of its major wartime goals—and in the process had virtually destroyed what remained of the White Man's Empires between Hong Kong in the north, almost to Port Darwin in Australia, and Calcutta in the west.

The Dutch homeland was conquered, making moot its losses in Indonesia. And of course, England had endured the Battle of Britain and was used to the feeling of looming defeat.

But Americans were restive and wanted to know when we were going to strike back against the Japanese. When was America going to start winning battles? When were we going to get revenge for Pearl Harbor?

Chennault's Flying Tigers were the only warriors anywhere winning against the Japanese.

But now the very existence of the Flying Tigers was threatened. Not by the Japanese, but by the U.S. military.

Senior AAF officers were gathering like flies in the luxury hotels of Karachi, and they all wanted to control something, to command anything, to be in charge of whatever would give them a chance to play a big part in the war.

One of those men was Colonel Clayton Bissell, Chennault's nemesis from his days at Maxwell Field in Alabama. Bissell was the man who had believed bomber crews could stop attacking fighters by throwing chains out the doors and entangling the propellers of the fighters. And that Bissell, of all the officers in the AAF, would be assigned to Stilwell's staff as his principal aviation officer is just one more example of how jangled things were in the CBI.

Every success of the Flying Tigers made Chennault's fighter force more attractive to the AAF. Plus, now that America was in the war, the AAF's newly formed Tenth Air Force could not allow an independent group of fighter pilots to operate in its theater of operations.

Bissell tried to subsume the Flying Tigers into the new China Air Task Force. But Chennault said his pilots were under contract to the Chinese government and those contracts did not expire until the end of June. Wait until then, he said.

Chennault faced opposition from almost every direction, but especially from Bissell, already acting as if he were Chennault's boss in Delhi. Bissell was a colonel, the same rank Chennault held in the Chinese air force, and his enmity toward Chennault had festered through the years. Bissell was the ultimate bureaucrat, a man who went by the book in all matters, and he was personally and professionally offended when he heard about the ragtag and undisciplined Flying Tigers. He was about to be promoted to brigadier general and he was aching to teach those unkempt young officers a thing or two about military discipline.

Many academics, especially historians, are patronizing toward journalists. But historian Barbara Tuchman said that the best source of information about the early years of World War II was the journalists who became war correspondents.

Most American reporters were waiting for D-day and the invasion of Europe. That was the big show. That was the part of the war where young reporters and old generals could make their bones—where they could see the elephant.

But there were a handful of reporters who went to the CBI in the late 1930s and early 1940s. They had created the legend of Chennault and the Flying Tigers, and they were looking for more big stories. People back home craved good news about the war, because there had been so little of it.

The war correspondents in the CBI were some of the most talented reporters and writers ever gathered in a combat theater. Several of them would write books that even today—more than seventy years later—remain fundamental reference works to anyone wanting to understand China.

Henry Luce was not in China, but he was the most important news presence in the country. Luce was owner and publisher of *Time* and *Life*, and he was very much a hands-on publisher. In the pretelevision days of the early 1940s, Luce's magazines were among the most important news outlets in America. There are no periodicals today in the same universe those publications occupied in the early 1940s. Both had upward of five million subscribers and were influential to a degree almost impossible to imagine by today's lights.

Luce was a "mishkid"—the child of missionaries who had served in China—and he spoke fluent Chinese. He had a passionate interest in China, in Chiang, and in America's policy toward Chiang and toward the growing Communist party led by Mao Tse-tung.

Luce believed that America would have to make a choice between Chiang and the Communists, and he wanted to make sure America made the right choice. He was passionate in his support of Chiang and sixteen times put the generalissimo on the cover of *Time*.

Among the writers in the CBI, Clare Boothe must be mentioned first. (She had married Luce in 1935.) She was a famous correspondent for *Life*, and she had been in Brussels in May 1940, when that city was bombed by the Germans. Her articles about France and England had been published in book form. In 1941 she covered the brutal Japanese bombing of Chungking, and she knew Generalissimo and Madame Chiang. In April 1942, about the time Scott landed in Karachi, she was landing in Lashio, Burma, a few minutes after the Gissimo and Madame Chiang had arrived to confer with Stilwell about the fate of Burma. She left ten days later and wrote two splendid pieces for *Life* about her visit.

Henry Luce's protégé Theodore "Teddy" White was first among equals among the reporters on the China beat. A short, plump, bespectacled young man of boundless energy, White had majored in Chinese studies at Harvard and then gone to China, where he had a menial job with the Chinese government until Luce brought him on as a stringer, or part-time correspondent. In White's heart burned twin beliefs that nothing in the world was as important as China and that his passionate desire to get a big story would result in a full-time correspondent's job.

White became the first Westerner to venture deep into China and to report on a devastating famine. The story was a sensation, and White's brilliant career was launched.

Edgar Snow was there also, and he wrote numerous stories for both *Time* and *Life*. He, too, would become a famous writer. Later, much of his work would be discredited because of its pro-Communist slant.

Jack Belden was a young correspondent who had more nerve than all the other correspondents combined. He had a knack for being the only writer at the scene of a great developing story. When the Japanese overran Burma, Belden was the only correspondent at Stilwell's headquarters.

White, Snow, and Belden would all meet Scott and write of his adventures in the most widely circulated publications in America.

As Scott stepped down from the aircraft in Karachi, he was six feet tall, weighed 168 pounds, and had dark brown hair, blue eyes, and a spirit that thirsted for adventure.

Merian Cooper told Scott what the mission of Task Force Aquila was to have been: fly to bases in China, load up with bombs, and then take off to bomb the Japanese homeland. But now the mission was scrubbed. The Japanese had captured the airfields that were to have been used by the B-17s. And the Tenth Air Force, the Air Forces' high command in the CBI, had commandeered the force of B-17s.

Scott had no airplane and no mission. He was adrift on the backside of the world.

On April 18, he wrote Kitty Rix and said, "Honey, will you promise me one thing—it's not to stop smoking or drinking—it's not to stop being away from home every time I get there—off playing bridge—but it's this: take care of yourself."

Catharine was having a hard time being on her own and taking care of a baby. Checks bounced and bills were not paid, and creditors were writing threatening letters.

Even though he had been in the theater only a few weeks, Scott was anxious over not receiving any mail from Kitty Rix.

His mood was not improved when he learned that Doolittle and his sixteen B-25s had launched from the deck of the USS *Hornet* and bombed Tokyo.

Today, the Doolittle Raiders are legends. Few people have ever heard of Task Force Aquila.

During the third week of April the Assam-Burma-China (ABC) Ferry Command was created to get supplies into China. The idea was to use Douglas C-47s—known as the DC-3 to civilians—to ferry supplies over the Himalayas to the beleaguered forces of Chennault and Chiang.

Haynes was named commanding officer of the new organization, and Scott was assigned to be his executive officer. Now Scott at least had a job, even if it was flying a transport.

In addition to several weary C-47s, the ABC Ferry Command owned four fighter aircraft: two P-43s that leaked so much gas the Chinese air force refused to fly them, and two P-40s. Like so many other things in the CBI, the provenance of the P-40s was uncertain. In his history of the ABC Ferry Command, Haynes said that all four aircraft were donated by Chennault to protect the C-47s, and for "offensive reconnaissance" in Burma. Scott makes it sound as if Chennault personally gave him a new P-40.

However they came to the Ferry Command, the important thing is that Scott was the only fighter pilot in the command, and he had the rank to make the aircraft his own.

On April 30 he flew an hour in one of the P-43s and an hour in a P-40, checking them out, luxuriating in flying a fighter aircraft after the long trip in the B-17.

But before he could go gallivanting around the CBI in a fighter aircraft, he had to remember that his job was to fly the C-47 across the Himalayas.

To a fighter pilot, the C-47 was the most ignoble of aircraft. Called "the Gooney Bird," often shortened to "the Goon," the C-47 was a slow and awkward aircraft that maneuvered with the deliberate nature of a Burgundian snail. The aircraft had a wide wing and two engines that—on a good day—could pull it along at about 160 mph. Within the military the Goon's primary use was as a "trash hauler," a cargo airplane. In the hierarchy of aircraft that fighter pilots wanted to fly, it was somewhere south of the bottom. Many of the early C-47s had been commandeered from U.S. commercial airlines, and they were not powered for cargo work at high altitudes. The published maximum altitude of the C-47 was twenty thousand feet.

The Goon was the most unsuitable aircraft imaginable for the job at hand, but in the beginning it was all that was available.

Scott and Haynes operated out of an RAF base in the insalubrious region of Assam, located in the extreme northeastern corner of India near the borders of Burma, China, and Tibet. The great curve of the Brahmaputra River was close, and the crocodile-dotted riverbanks were surrounded by dense jungle filled with tigers, elephants, jackals, and cobras.

Scott and Haynes lived in a basha—a mud and bamboo hut—and for much of each night both men were kept awake by jungle noises and by the burden of their new mission.

Geography matters, and nowhere does it matter more than in war. The five-hundred-mile air route from Dinjan, India to Kunming was across the Himalayas: the Roof of the World, the most foreboding terrain in the CBI. The route was unmapped, there were few charts and no navigation devices, and the weather was known for blinding rain, high winds, and extreme turbulence. Japanese fighters patrolled the route.

With Haynes, Scott flew the first flights, and they developed techniques for flying the route that soon would become legendary as "the Hump"—one of the most dangerous flying jobs in the world.

But Scott had a high heart, and his blood was up. He would be flying supplies to Chennault and the Flying Tigers. His destiny was about to be fulfilled.

April was a good month for Scott. He flew eighty-two hours and fifty minutes, splitting the time between the B-17 and the C-47 with a few hours of fighter time.

On May 1, Scotty and Haynes flew a C-47 to Kunming and unloaded their cargo. Scott tried without success to convince an AVG squadron commander to let him accompany the Flying Tigers on a raid. The squadron commander did not think much of regular army colonels and he had no desire to be a mother hen to a pilot who had not been trained in Chennault's way of victory.

The conversation ended when Haynes motioned for Scott to get aboard the C-47. Haynes had received an urgent radio message ordering him to "proceed immediately vicinity Shwebo effect evacuation Stilwell and staff most urgent."

The Japanese had crossed the Irrawaddy River and advanced to within twenty miles of Shwebo. Stilwell and many staff members of the American Military Mission to China were in imminent danger of being captured.

Scott ran to the C-47, pulled out a map, and began searching for Shwebo. Where the hell was Shwebo? Eventually he located it in lower Burma: about fifty miles north of Mandalay, a remote little nothing place that only Stilwell would have chosen for a headquarters. The chart did not show an airfield anywhere near the town.

Haynes and Scott flew through black clouds and blinding rain all the way to the Mekong River. There they found clearing skies that were controlled by the Japanese.

The two men landed in Myitkyina and topped off their fuel tanks. Now they could take Stilwell to just about anywhere that he and his staff would be safe. Before they left, Scott talked to a British pilot who told him that there was a small dirt strip southeast of Shwebo.

Now Haynes and Scott were deep inside Japanese territory in the slow, lumbering Goon—an easy target if ever there was one. Everywhere were the burning towns of central Burma. The Japanese had been here. And they were still close by.

Scotty and Haynes flew at treetop level. They were expecting trouble, and both had their heads on a swivel, looking in every direction for Japanese fighters. The Allies had fled, which meant that any aircraft Haynes and Scott saw would be Japanese. Behind them the crew chief and radio operator stood by open cargo doors, tommy guns at the ready. A tommy gun is no defense against the guns of a Japanese fighter, but tommy guns were the only offensive weapons available for a Goon.

Flying at low altitude caused bugs to smash against the windshield, and every new speck seemed like a Japanese fighter.

Haynes bent the lumbering C-47 around as if it were a fighter aircraft and landed on the small dusty airstrip.

Jack Belden was there, and he told Scott that when Stilwell's staff saw the approaching C-47 with the big white star of the Army Air Forces on the fuselage, they threw their helmets into the air and began singing "God Bless America." They could hear the artillery of the advancing Japanese army, and they never thought an American aircraft would come so close to the front lines to rescue them.

The accounts of what happened next vary according to who is doing the telling. Barbara Tuchman in *Stilwell and the American Experience in China* has her version. Jack Belden in *Retreat with Stilwell* has his. Of course, Scott has his own version. And there are official Army histories as well. It is a comment on the nature of history, or the confused state of affairs in the CBI, that none of these accounts agree on the particulars.

But it seems that a rather agitated Scott burst into Stilwell's office and said, "General, we are here to rescue you. General Arnold sent us."

All the stories do agree that Stilwell, sitting behind his desk wearing a battered old campaign hat, was not overjoyed to see a couple of flyboy colonels who wanted to rescue him. He was an infantryman. He had marched into Shwebo, and by God he was going to march out. No matter what Hap Arnold said, he did not need rescuing. He could take care of himself.

And he did.

Haynes and Scott were feeling considerable distress at being caught between their boss—the hardheaded and dictatorial Arnold—and the senior American officer in the CBI. But unless they roped and hog-tied Stilwell and forcibly rescued him, he was walking, and they were flying.

Scott and Haynes loaded part of Stilwell's staff on the C-47 and took off for Calcutta. They were barely ahead of the Japanese.

That day Scott flew seven hours and thirty-five minutes in the C-47.


As Scott and Haynes took off, Stilwell began walking.

Stilwell was angry. He was America's senior officer in the CBI, and the Japanese had forced him out of Burma. Another defeat for America. Burma was about to belong to the Japanese. American prestige had never been lower. When would the fortunes of war swing in America's favor?

The fifty-nine-year-old Stilwell gathered 114 people, including American and British soldiers, Burmese nurses, a British Quaker ambulance unit, nine cooks and porters, correspondent Jack Belden, and various stragglers, and off he went. Stilwell walked north along the Myitkyina railroad, walked west and overland by trail to a tributary of the Chindwin, rafted downstream to Homalin, and then walked over the mountains toward India. He hiked through jungles, swamps, heavy rain, and muddy terrain. Stilwell led the column some 140 miles in twenty days, pressing on at 105 steps to the minute, and with tongue-lashings and by iron-willed example he led the tatterdemalion group to Imphal, India, arriving on May 20.

When he got there, Stilwell was as blunt-spoken as ever: "We got a hell of a beating," he told reporters. "We got run out of Burma and it is humiliating as hell."

Evading capture and suffering no losses was a minor miracle. Now "Vinegar Joe" Stilwell had become "Walking Joe" Stilwell.

But to Scotty, and Haynes and their AAF bosses, Stilwell's refusal to get on an airplane was an insult; proof that he was not a proponent of air power, proof that his orientation remained solely toward the men with muddy boots.

While Stilwell and his band were marching toward India, Scott twice dropped food and supplies to them. So did the RAF and other pilots of the ABC Ferry Command.

Given Stilwell's antipathy toward the AAF, it is a small wonder that he did not ignore their deliveries and try to forage off the land. Had he not been accompanied by so many women and civilians, he probably would have.

Scott's family always contended that he was fortune's child. One measure of that can be seen in the fact that weather was often so bad over the Hump that the Goons could not fly. This meant that Scott had time to fly the fighter aircraft under his command.

He was in the right time at the right place. He was a fighter pilot and a colonel and when he saw a window of opportunity, he jumped through it.

Scott first gained notice flying the Republic P-43.

On a whim, Scott had a maintenance crew replace numerous parts, repair the fuel leak, and tune up the aircraft. The Republic P-43 Lancer had a turbo supercharger that gave it the ability to reach high altitudes. But how high would it go? Were that tired old engine and supercharger strong enough to enable him to reach the windswept heights above Mount Everest?

On May 4, Scott took off on what he called a "test hop" to determine the capability of the aircraft. Just for fun, he would fly high above Mount Everest.

*Hey, y'all. Hold my beer and watch this.*

His later account of that flight is one of the most lyrical pieces he ever wrote. Scott climbed beyond Burma and over Tibet, naming the river and mountain peaks and describing the jungles and valleys in what his chart describes as "unexplored and unadministered."

He circled above Lhasa, the city of the Dalai Lama, to take pictures of the Dalai Lama's palace, and then he continued north, where he identified the lake of Tengri-Nor, near which arise the five great rivers of Asia: the Irrawaddy, Salween, Mekong, Yangtze, and Yellow.

Scott continued climbing, and one can almost hear him rolling off the names of the great mountains: Makalu, Chamo Lhan, Kamet, and finally Everest, which he calls by the Tibetan name, Chomolungma—the Goddess Mother of the World.

He was flying over some of the most inaccessible land on earth, and he knew the name of every peak, the source of every river, the location of every hidden valley.

His altimeter registered thirty-seven thousand feet, which, corrected for temperature and barometric pressure, means he was above forty thousand feet.

Scott had topped Mount Everest, but there must always be more. So he did what every experienced pilot knows not to do: He flew through the "plume" of Everest, the cloud on the lee side of the peak where dangerous downdrafts can slam an aircraft into the ground.

The plume grabbed him and shook him and he thought the wings were going to break off as the mountain hammered him more than five thousand feet downward and spit him out miles away.

When Scott landed, he contacted the United Press writer in that part of the world and announced that he had climbed above Everest.

That was still not enough. He pointed out that several years earlier the British had performed a similar flight, but they had spent hundreds of thousands of pounds and planned for months, while he was merely conducting a test hop.

The AAF was not amused by all this. Nor were Tibetan officials, who sent a polite reminder that it was forbidden to fly over the sacred city of Lhasa.

Scott was all innocence. He was just doing a little old test flight, and what was all the fuss about?

But he enjoyed the newspaper coverage.

On May 5, flying a P-40, Scott strafed a Japanese convoy on the Burma Road, flying in and out of heavy monsoon rains, dark clouds pressing him dangerously close to the ground, scud-running at high speed while hundreds of soldiers on the ground fired at him.

He refueled, swung over a Japanese air base, saw a bomber on the ground being refueled, and destroyed it with gunfire.

When Scott returned from a mission, he had his ground crew paint the spinner another color, entered Burma from another direction, and attacked more Japanese targets.

Scott was now flying two and three missions every day.

He had no wingman, no one to cover his six-o'clock position, and he had not been trained in Chennault's way of victory. He was flying alone, deep in enemy territory against an enemy whose efficacy in battle had been proven again and again.

On May 6 he flew ten hours and forty-five minutes.

He strafed troop-carrying barges on the Chindwin River, returned to base and had bombs attached to his aircraft, and then returned and blew more barges out of the water. He killed so many Japanese soldiers that he named his airplane "Old Exterminator."

Scott was in the air eight to ten hours a day and wanted more. Enough was never enough.

During early and middle May, Scott's logbook is filled with entries such as "strafe convoy," "Recon," "food dropping," "strafe," "convoy."

His paranoia was in full bloom. He believed that if he did not put the P-40 to good use, it would be taken away and he would spend the war flying Goons.

Scott fueled up, charged his guns, and flew into Burma spouting Kipling:

*On the road to Mandalay,*
*Where the flyin'-fishes play,*
*An' the dawn comes up like thunder outer China 'crost the Bay!*

A Japanese radio broadcaster announced that a new American squadron had entered the battle, and that the pilots were guilty of illegal and unorthodox tactics and would be severely punished if caught.

AVG pilots looked at each other in disbelief. What new squadron?

War correspondents flocked to Colonel Scott, who said, "Call me Scotty." He told them in great detail of his missions. He was a regular quote machine.

Of course the correspondents loved him. He was good copy. He had an accent like cane syrup on a cold morning. He was daring and brave and flew into combat alone. This guy took a P-40 he called "Old Exterminator" deep into Japanese-held territory. Alone. He referred to himself as "the Lone Wolf of the Chindwin" and "the One-Man Air Force." The correspondents loved these names and used them often.

*Time* and *Life* and the *Saturday Evening Post* and United Press International wrote stories about Scott.


It was difficult to keep pace with Scott. One day he was shooting up a Japanese convoy in the Salween Gorge, the next day he was flying the Hump.

Edgar Snow, writing for the *Saturday Evening Post*, was aboard one of Scott's early flights across the Hump.

Snow said that Scott was the first Army pilot to fly a fighter aircraft over Burma, where he "shot up a Jap bomber." He told how, on the flight across the Hump, when Scott's Goon was threatened by a Japanese fighter, Scott somehow nursed the overloaded C-47 up to seventeen thousand feet, that no one was wearing oxygen masks, and that it was a struggle to remain conscious as the aircraft flew for more than an hour through heavy clouds. Scott had no charts, and once the clouds broke for a moment, off to the side Snow saw a mountain peak "a good couple of thousand feet above us." The aircraft was slowed by high winds, clawing the air to maintain altitude, flying in instrument conditions, and running low on gas. The crew was preparing to bail out when Scott found a hole in the clouds, descended rapidly, located the airfield, and landed safely.

People in America read these stories and nodded in appreciation. At last, America was in the war. At last, America had a hero who was killing Japanese soldiers.

# 18

## THE HUMP

CHINA WOULD HAVE FALLEN HAD IT NOT BEEN FOR THE ABC FERRY Command. Scott's flights over the Hump demonstrated a casual courage that cut the template for the dozens of brave men who followed him in carrying vital supplies over the most dangerous flying route in the world.

Scott would never forget the details: Dinjan to Kunming was more than five hundred miles on a compass heading of one one eight. Two hundred and seventy-five miles of the flight were over Japanese-occupied territory. The flight path went within twenty-five miles of a big Japanese airfield at Myitkyina. To avoid uncharted mountain peaks, all flights were at the very top of the C-47's maximum operating altitude. Icing conditions on most flights. Instrument flight conditions for most of every year. Aircraft were always over gross weight, sometimes by two or three thousand pounds.

Aeronautical charts were unreliable and weather information was sparse. The passes were at fourteen thousand feet and they were flanked by peaks rising above sixteen thousand. The Hump was a mountain range between the Salween and the Mekong Rivers. Flying time on a good day was four hours; on most days, six hours. Winds as high as 100 mph created updrafts over the ridges and downdrafts over the valleys. Turbulence could flip an aircraft on its back without warning. Icing was a problem above twelve thousand feet and sometimes wings were bulgy from the buildup of ice, causing the aircraft to lose lift and approach stalling conditions.

In the beginning, when Scott and Haynes were pioneering the route, AAF leaders did not fully realize the dangers of the Hump. It was the beginning of the supply missions into China and everyone was feeling his way, making up the rules as he went.

Some crews flew the route for months and never saw the ground from takeoff to touchdown. So many aircraft crashed, either from Japanese fighter attacks or from the weather, that the route was called "the aluminum trail." And dozens of brave men died, or, in the phrase of pilots, "went west."

On his supply runs, Scott sometimes carried goods for Chiang, and sometimes for Chennault and the Flying Tigers. For Chiang he carried bales of Chinese currency printed in New York, typewriters, file cabinets, and luxury goods. For Chennault he carried gasoline and bombs and ammunition. If he landed at an AVG base he often left a carton of Camel cigarettes or a bottle of scotch to be delivered to Chennault.

When Scott first met one of the Flying Tigers, he did not fare well. After all, he was the antithesis of those men: West Point graduate, regular Army, a senior officer. And they dismissed his boyish enthusiasm about flying with them. Plus, he was flying silly and frivolous materials to Chiang when they needed fuel, spare parts, bullets, and bombs.

Scott has a dramatic account of his first meeting with Chennault. Scott's version does not square with the history of the ABC Ferry Command written by Caleb Haynes. Nor does his version square with accounts written by Martin Caidin, who wrote more than fifty books and a thousand magazine articles—most of which were devoted to aviation. Scott's version does not even square with his own flight log. But the important thing is what Scott never wrote about, and that is the chemistry that must have flashed between them at their first meeting.

The similarities between the two men and their common interests would have come out quickly. Both men were from easily ridiculed Southern towns. Both men had Lee as a middle name. Both men were unreconstructed Southerners for whom the Glorious Cause was still alive. Both men were hunters and fishermen and at home in the outdoors. Both men were more rural than urban in their outlooks; they liked simple uncomplicated foods, an occasional drink of scotch, and the company of their own kind. Both loved bird hunting. They liked to tell the stories that bind Southerners together. Both men were mavericks who felt betrayed by their superiors—Chennault because he had been forced to retire over his ideas about the role of fighter aircraft, Scott because he had been stuck in the Training Command until everyone told him he was too old to fly fighters. Both men were mistrustful to the point of paranoia about their superiors and inclined to take the bit in their teeth, thumb their noses at Army regulations, and do what they wanted. Both men—and this is the most important similarity of all—believed in fighter aviation and had what a World War I pilot called "the spirit of attack planted in brave hearts." Political correctness did not exist. Collateral damage was not a concern. Subtleties of war were for others to ponder. The only thing Chennault and Scott wanted was to kill Japanese pilots.

Chennault was fifteen years older than Scott, but his dour and preoccupied demeanor made him a father figure to the talkative, impetuous, and worshipful Scott. At another level the two men were like brothers, and from the very beginning melded into a seamless friendship that, for each man, would become one of the most important relationships of his life.

It is likely that from the first time the two men met, Chennault had something special in mind for Scott. Bissell was leaning on Chennault to fold the AVG into the Tenth Air Force and re-form it as a new and larger organization to be called the Twenty-third Fighter Group. Chennault knew he could hold off the merger until July when the AVG contracts expired, but after that he would lose control.

It seemed every colonel in Karachi and Delhi was flying into AVG landing fields on vague "inspection trips." Chennault knew that each man was laying the groundwork to become the commanding officer of the Twenty-third, even though it did not yet exist, a job that promised to be the most glamorous flying billet in the CBI.

Bissell was flying in and out wanting to know why AVG pilots did not shave, shine their shoes, and jump to attention when he walked into their presence. He wanted to know why they played poker in their rooms rather than spending that time practicing basic military courtesies. He wanted to know why they drove vehicles on the sidewalks of nearby towns, why they tipped over honey buckets being pulled down the roads, why they shot out the lights of bars when they left.

Bissell and Chennault had both been promoted to brigadier general in mid-April. Chennault had asked Hap Arnold that their date of rank be the same, but out of a desire to bring the Flying Tigers firmly under control of the AAF—and perhaps out of spite—he promoted Bissell one day before he promoted Chennault. In the military that one day of seniority made Bissell the senior and Chennault the subordinate.

Chennault knew that if he could not present a compelling case for choosing his own man to lead the Twenty-third Fighter Group, Bissell would choose one of the sycophants flocking around him. And that man would be loyal to Bissell rather than to Chennault. The spirit of the Flying Tigers would end right there.

Perhaps Scott could be Chennault's man.

But Scott had been an instructor for the past five years. Would the Flying Tigers follow him into combat?

Even garden-variety fighter pilots are difficult men to lead. The Flying Tigers were not garden-variety fighter pilots. They had learned their tactics from a maverick genius. The men who forced Chennault to retire had been men like Scott, regular Army officers, many of them ring knockers.

A bigger problem was the Chiangs. If Madame Chiang and the Gissimo did not approve of Scott, he could *not* command the Twenty-third.

Chennault arranged a meeting.

No account of that meeting has surfaced. But it is easy to imagine the synergistic explosion of delight that must have occurred when a boy from Macon met the First Lady of China, who had spent six years of her life in that same town; a woman who knew many of the same places in Macon that Scott knew, a woman who spoke English with a Macon accent, and who often used Southern idiomatic expressions. Madame Chiang was the original steel magnolia.

A cultural and professional divide separated Chennault and Scott from many of their contemporaries. This is not unusual for Southerners. But what is uncommon is that one of the most powerful forces in the CBI—Madame Chiang—moved to the same side of the fence as these two men. Her position and the authority of her husband gave her access to Roosevelt. For strategic and political reasons, the president wanted to please her. And this gave her, and by extension Chennault, extraordinary power.

Chennault's closeness to Madame Chiang and her influence in Washington became the biggest source of military friction in the CBI.

Chennault must have sensed that, as the war developed, he would stand a good chance of being neutralized by his Washington superiors. It had happened before. But he knew how the war in China should be fought and he was determined to whisper in the ears of the Chiangs in order to hang on as long as he could.

Madame Chiang missed nothing. At her first meeting with Scott, she noticed that the stone in his West Point ring was missing and the hole had been filled with sealing wax.

After Scott met Madame Chiang it was clear that not only did Madame Chiang approve of him, she was simply delighted to be dealing with a fellow Maconite.

Now Scott had to prove himself with the AVG.

# 19

## FLYING TIGER

THE PILOTS OF THE AVG DID NOT KNOW WHAT TO MAKE OF SCOTT. He was a bird colonel, regular Army, whose job was flying supplies in the Goon. They smiled about his scooting around in a P-40 with a shark mouth painted on the nose—that is, until they learned that he was the "new squadron" that the Japanese radio broadcaster had been griping about. He was everywhere—dropping bombs, strafing troops, raising hell all over Burma, and killing Japanese soldiers as if afraid the season might soon end.

But he had not been trained in the Chennault way, and if he was attacked by a Jap pilot he was going to get his ass waxed.

Scott's paranoia was in overdrive. In May, he flew 213 hours and forty-five minutes. Pilots know that to achieve and maintain a high level of proficiency they should fly the same type aircraft all the time. Switching from a fighter to a cargo aircraft or a bomber, especially in combat, calls for skills possessed by few pilots. Yet in May Scott flew the P-40, the C-47, the twin-engine B-25 medium bomber, and the P-43.

And never was his Kipling more appropriate:

*He shot at the strong and he slashed at the weak*
*From the Salween scrub to the Chindwin teak.*

But it was not enough. Each time he met members of the AVG, Scott was like a member of the junior varsity trying to prove himself good enough to be on the varsity team.

Chennault granted Scott permission to fly "guest missions" with the AVG.

Scott quickly flew nine missions with the AVG. On these missions, he did not pull rank. That is, he did not assert the prerogatives of a colonel and take command over officers far junior to him. Instead he flew as a wingman, telling the Flying Tigers that he had much to learn from them. He sought their advice on technique, and learned Chennault's tactics. His willingness to strafe low and tight—the most dangerous of missions—earned him the respect of the Flying Tigers.

But his superiors in Delhi were raising hell. Not only was Colonel Scott flying combat missions that should have been assigned to a second lieutenant, he was flying too many hours.

The criticism from the big brass only endeared Scott to the AVG, especially when Scott ignored the criticism and kept flying combat missions.

Back home in Georgia, the *Macon Telegraph* of May 25 had a front-page story that said that Scott was blasting enemy trains and ships and had received "international tribute" from various war correspondents.

On June 15, Scott was grounded for a week. The offense: flying too much. It was unbecoming for a senior officer to be out strafing Japanese convoys and dropping bombs on Japanese installations.

Nevertheless, Scott flew seventy-nine hours and ten minutes in June, bringing his total flying time for the first half of the year to 749 hours and thirty-five minutes.

The late spring of 1942 was, for the AVG, the best of times and the worst of times. They were winning big in the air, setting combat records unmatched by any other Allied flying unit in World War II. But they were short of bullets, bombs, gas, and aircraft parts, and Bissell said the shortage would continue until the AVG became the Twenty-third Fighter Group. The AVG kept going, short of everything. They sometimes were on alert for ten consecutive days. They had only fifty airplanes to hold back the full fury of the Imperial Japanese air force. They were exhausted and needed rest. They lived on hope.

Then one day Brigadier General Clayton Bissell flew in to tell AVG pilots they were about to be inducted into the Army Air Forces. He said that any man who didn't return to the bosom of the American military would find a draft notice waiting for him when he returned to America. He would come back into the Army as a private and not as an officer.

Bissell ranted and raved and pounded on the table and talked to these young warriors as if they were errant schoolchildren.

Most of the AVG pilots got up and walked out. They would not fly and fight for Bissell, not after flying and fighting for Chennault.

Afterward the AVG pilots taught the Chinese driver of a gas truck the phrase "Piss on Bissell." It was the only English the worker knew. Proud of his language skills, the truck driver raced to meet every transport aircraft that landed. As the door opened and officers began descending the steps, he smiled and bowed and said, "Piss on Bissell. Piss on Bissell."

The June 26 issue of the *Abilene Reporter-News* announced Scott's pending assignment as commander of the Twenty-third Fighter Group with a headline that read:

## DAREDEVIL FIGHTER PILOT FROM GEORGIA
## HEADS ARMY SQUADRON TO ABSORB AVG

The headline was wrong in that the AVG had not been absorbed into the Army. It was dissolved. But if the headline writer got it wrong, so did most of America.

After about three months in the CBI, Scott was now one of the best-known figures of the war, a daring young colonel who flew solo missions against the Japanese, a bold pilot who strafed Japanese troops on the Burma Road, blew up barges on the Chindwin, briefly stopped the Japanese advance at the Salween Gorge, and, by the way, was also flying Goons over the Hump.

Scott became the symbol that America needed so badly.

He received the Distinguished Service Cross. The citation noted his "continuous bravery and exceptional gallantry."

At the bottom of the citation it was noted that his next of kin was his mother, and that his home address was also the address of his parents. It was as if Catharine did not exist.

# 20

# GLORY

THE CHINESE GOVERNMENT DISBANDED THE AVG ON JULY 3. THE NEXT day, the anniversary of American independence, the Tenth Air Force activated the Twenty-third Fighter Group and named Scott as its first commanding officer.

Scott knew the Master Plan was falling into place. He considered twenty-three his lucky number. After all, his old Boy Scout troop was Troop 23. And now the new organization was the Twenty-third.

The bitter irony of it was that Bissell, who for months had scorned Chennault, his leadership, and his doctrine for fighter aviation, now piggybacked onto Chennault's fame by keeping the old shark-mouth P-40s, painting the shark-mouth on new P-40s, and calling the Twenty-third the Flying Tigers. The change to the group insignia was small: the addition of a top hat with red and white stripes atop the head of the tiger.

Most Americans then and now did not notice the difference. American pilots were flying shark-mouth P-40s and they were called the Flying Tigers. It was, and remains, to untold thousands, a continuum.

But it was not.

The AVG flew from December 19, 1941, until July 3, 1942—a little more than six months—and in that time they wrote history large. Their value was twofold. Officially credited with destroying 299 Japanese aircraft (with an equal number of probables) and killing some fifteen hundred enemy crewmen, the AVG lost eight pilots in combat. It was then and remains today a record without parallel in aerial warfare. In the years since the war, revisionists have tried to nibble away at that record. But Martin Caidin says that the chaos of the CBI was such that, if anything, the number of enemy aircraft shot down is probably greater than that reported.

In any event, the number of shootdowns by the AVG is not as important as the morale boost that the AVG gave to America. In that terrible winter and spring of 1942, the Flying Tigers were the only Americans winning in the war against the Axis.

They came along in one of those rare moments, one of those eyeblinks of history, when a small group of brave men was willing to take a stand and say to an implacable and seemingly unstoppable enemy: thus far and no farther. They were a gallant band flying outmoded aircraft, but they stopped, and began to push back, a powerful air force that until then had never been defeated in battle. Rarely in history do such groups come along. When they do, like the Spartans at Thermopylae, they are memorialized in the halls of valor, and their stories will be told until the end of time.

Not even famed Jimmy Doolittle and his raiders—today acknowledged by many historians to have been a short-term American morale boost that imparted no real military damage on Japan while having terrible consequences for China—can stand up to the undying legend of the AVG, whose pilots flew those satanically beautiful P-40s.


As the disbanding of the AVG approached, Scott had two immediate problems. First, the contracts for the AVG pilots were about to expire, and most of the pilots would quit because they did not want to fly for Bissell. Scott had to convince as many of those men as possible to stay on and to use their experience to teach the new pilots. He succeeded in convincing five pilots to stay and fight. They would become commissioned officers in the AAF, and they would lead the Twenty-third Group's new squadrons into battle. These men already were legends, and their fame was further burnished when they agreed to fly under Scott's command: David Lee "Tex" Hill, Ed Rector, Frank Schiel, J. Gilpin Bright, and Charles Sawyer.

In addition to these five who agreed to stay, another several dozen said they would hang around for several weeks to teach the new group Chennault's way of victory.

As Scott prepared to take over the Twenty-third, he needed to make nice to the Gissimo and Madame Chiang. At their meeting, Madame Chiang handed Scott a small package, and in a voice that resonated of Macon, Georgia, she said, "The commander of my fighters should have a proper stone for his West Point ring."

Scott opened the package and found an incomparable piece of jade. A luminous stone, translucent but yet opaque, it embodied the green of China's hills, the bluish whiteness of her skies, and all the depth and mystery of eternal China.

Madame Chiang's gift was of such a size that Scott visualized not only a piece cut for his ring, but a necklace and earrings for Catharine.

Scott later took the jade to Tiffany's in New York City, where he said the jeweler at first refused to cut it, saying it was priceless and that mines producing such jade had been closed. But Scott persuaded him to make the pieces he had in mind.

Forever afterward, when Scott walked into a room, his ring drew the eye of everyone in the room. When people commented on his ring, he would twist it and say, "Madame Chiang Kai-shek gave me the jade."

Yes, Madame Chiang and the Gissimo approved of Colonel Robert Lee Scott Jr. as the first commanding officer of the Twenty-third Fighter Group. It would take a few weeks for Scott to wrap up his business with the ABC Ferry Command, where he had accomplished much to be proud of. In the first months of the command's existence, the Hump pilots had brought an estimated five thousand wounded British soldiers and refugees out of Burma and dropped two million pounds of rice to the Chinese army. For his leadership and participation in that effort, Scott received his second Silver Star.

On July 3, a Japanese broadcaster took to the air to say that the new fighter group, under the leadership of "Hollywood Playboy" Colonel Scott, was about to be annihilated. The broadcaster said that the original Flying Tigers were all going home and that the new and untrained young replacements would be blasted out of the sky.

It was important to the Japanese to regain air superiority over China. The Japanese needed to achieve psychological superiority over the flood of Americans about to arrive in the theater and take to the air. The Japanese knew that there is always a lag between the formation of a new fighting unit and the day when that unit becomes combat-ready. Finally, the Japanese assumed that on such a significant U.S. holiday as July 4, most of the American pilots would be celebrating instead of flying.

What the Japanese did not know was that the transition from the AVG to the Twenty-third had been seamless. The spirit of the AVG, sustained and imbued by the spirit of Chennault, Scott, and the former AVG pilots, forged a new group that was strong at the broken place. In those days, air combat usually boiled down to who was the best trained and the best led. What the Japanese could not know was that Scott and Chennault had planned their July 4 celebration as if they were planning a hunting trip.

When the warning system advised that Japanese aircraft were inbound on July 4, members of the Twenty-third launched and climbed to a high perch at twenty-one thousand feet, moved into position up-sun, as they had been trained, and waited. On the ground Chennault watched through his binoculars as the Japanese approached, so confident and so arrogant that some of the Japanese fighter pilots were performing aerobatics. Chennault watched, jaw clenched, as the Japanese developed their attack. High overhead the P-40s prowled, their pilots watching the Japanese and anxious to fight.

Finally, Chennault growled, "Tigers, take 'em," and the P-40s roared out of the sun. They slashed through the Japanese formation, and when the fight was over, eight Japanese aircraft littered the landscape.


On July 13, Scott landed at Kweilin to take charge of all fighter operations.

No matter how many times a pilot flew into the single runway at Kweilin, the approach was sobering. On each side of the runway were two-thousand-foot stalagmite-like mountains that were honeycombed with caves. Summer temperatures above one hundred degrees and a powdery gagging dust settled over everything.

Little wonder the operations office and the radio and medical facilities were hidden in the cool caves inside the mountains.

Scott moved into what was called the "headquarters building," an L-shaped house near the runway. In the room next door was Chennault. Down the hall was the flight surgeon.

Out back was a tiny garden where Chennault grew the beloved hot peppers that are a food staple of rural Louisiana. If he had a good crop, he ate heartily. If he had a bad crop, friends from Louisiana would send him replacements. At dinner Chennault would munch on the peppers as if they were candy. Most guests who sought to emulate him coughed, and mumbled curses, and searched desperately for water to assuage the fire. Chennault would appear not to notice.

Scott believed that commanding the Twenty-third was the best job in the theater. But what he did not like was all the paperwork that must be handled by a group commander. And rather than going up and flying whenever the urge struck, he had to frequently visit every squadron under his command to review their performance and see to their needs.

On the morning of July 31, Scott was frustrated when he took off from Kunming to fly to Kweilin, five hundred miles over mountainous terrain. He climbed atop a blinding white overcast of clouds that—even from twenty thousand feet—stretched out to the horizon and beyond. He was a tiny speck of an aircraft, outlined against the white clouds, and he flew solo through hostile skies . . . a fighter pilot's dream.

His account of what happened on that flight is sketchy and lacking important details. But the results cannot be contested.

He had been in the air for more than two hours and was about to begin his letdown through the clouds when the radio crackled with news that Japanese aircraft had been sighted in the sector where Scott was flying.

Scott scanned his instruments. He had about twenty gallons of fuel remaining, not much for a thirsty Allison engine. But by the time other P-40s could be diverted to Scott's area, the Japanese might be gone. Yet, if Scott engaged, there was a good chance he could run out of fuel and become an easy target. Fuel calculations for the Allison, the probable distance of his squadron mates, altitude, a dozen calculations flashed through Scott's head in a millisecond. And in the back of his mind was the inescapable fact that he had not yet seen the elephant. He had not yet engaged in the purest of all blood sports: air-to-air combat. And thus, at this moment, deep in enemy territory and with only twenty gallons of fuel remaining, there was only one thing to do: attack.

Scott went into a shallow dive and leveled out as he began skimming through the tops of the clouds, slipping in and out of the sunshine. When he popped out of each cloud his head was on a swivel, and his eyes were straining as he looked for another tiny dark speck in the sky, a speck that could in seconds mushroom into a Japanese fighter.

The clouds were breaking up now, becoming separated, and he could see the ground far below. The gas gauge was creeping closer to the big "E" on the lower left side of the fuel gauge. It was eight minutes past nine a.m. when he sighted a Japanese aircraft straight ahead, coming toward him on a collision course. It was a twin-engine bomber, probably about to make a sneak attack on one of the fighter bases that Scott commanded.

Scott flicked on his gun switch, pushed the propeller to low pitch and the throttle to full military power. The mighty Allison changed from a smooth kittenish purr into a deep and throaty roar. The P-40 was singing its battle song.

But even as Scott's finger squeezed the trigger, he was given a fighter pilot's moment of grace: he realized the bomber had an escort. Three Japanese fighters were flying top cover, weaving back and forth a few thousand feet above him. And he remembered Chennault's inviolate rule: It is suicide for a single P-40 to attack a bomber escorted by fighters.

But chance and destiny had converged, and Chennault's rule did not matter. Destiny had to be fulfilled. Scotty continued his head-on pass, guns blazing, and as the two aircraft merged at almost five hundred miles an hour, he shoved the stick forward, dove under the bomber, then racked his P-40 around in a high-G turn, firing at the bomber in a full deflection shot, very much aware that the fighters were diving on him.

His P-40 quivered with shock as Japanese bullets thudded into the fuselage. Scott's blood was high, his sinews were stiffened, and his heart was full. This moment was the culmination of all his boyhood dreams and prayers. The Big Sky Boss had put him in this place at this time, and there could be only one outcome.

A fighter roared by the front of his P-40, and Scott got off a snap shot. As he pulled up, the Zero that had been firing at him went for separation and Scott squeezed the trigger, knowing with the intuitive knowledge of a long-time bird hunter that many of the two hundred rounds he had fired had slammed into the Zero. He reversed his turn to make another pass at the bomber, holding the trigger down as bullets hammered into the engines and wing roots of the bomber. The bomber came apart before his eyes, and he watched the smoking remains spiraling toward the earth.

Because two of the fighters were attacking him, and because he was running on fumes, he did not see the crash of the fighter he had shot up. He pushed over into a dive and used the weight and power of the P-40 to escape the pursuing Japanese fighters. Scott's fuel gauge was bouncing off the big "E."

Scott raced to a nearby emergency field, and when he arrived did not bother to determine the active runway: he was running on fumes, and he had no choice but to make a straight-in approach.

As his airplane rolled out, the Allison gurgled to a stop. Scott dismounted and counted the bullet holes in his P-40; there were seventeen and all were near the tail. Scott laughed and shook his head in derision. The Japanese pilots obviously had never been bird hunters. They did not know how to lead a target.

The sound of a jeep coming at high speed caused him to turn around. The driver told Scott that his bomber kill had been confirmed by local villagers and that the wreckage was not far away. Did Scott want to visit the site?

Scott was poking through the wreckage, examining the bodies of the dead crewmen and hoping that one of them might be wearing a highly prized samurai sword, when another jeep arrived. The driver said that Chinese observers had reported the wreckage of a burning fighter aircraft a few miles away.

Scott abandoned his search for a sword. His boyish enthusiasm knew no bounds. At long last he had been blooded.

He had seen the elephant.

Scott had taken on a bomber and three Zeros and he had shot two of the aircraft out of the air.

He was a thirty-four-year-old colonel, a man too old and with too much rank to be a fighter pilot, and in his first air-to-air engagement—when he was outnumbered four to one—he emerged victorious.

The Big Sky Boss was on the job.

Scott knew that those years of practice—wing shooting, the snap shots at birds, the many full-deflection shots he had made with a shotgun, the intuitive feel of leading an aerial target, the hours spent in the woods honing predatory instincts—all had paid off in a few quick minutes. Shooting at sharks in Panama Bay had not been wasting bullets.

That night Scott wrote a long letter to his mother explaining in detail his grand adventure.

Scott's superiors in New Delhi wrote him a note again reprimanding him for flying so much. The general said it was unbecoming of a colonel to be flying so many missions.


Now the full miserable might of the monsoon season was upon eastern China. The rain was heavy, steady, and prolonged, turning every piece of exposed ground into a slippery and glue-like mud. And the missions flown by the Twenty-third were across mountains, across long and desolate and virtually unmapped sections of China. Rivers and railroads and towns were the landmarks for pilots who might fly hours using a compass heading and a watch, often losing sight of the ground a few seconds after takeoff and not seeing it again until they made a letdown and broke out near their target. If they had not been blown off course by winds, and if their timing was spot-on, they might break out of the clouds only a few hundred feet above the ground and in a valley away from mountains or near a river that would lead them to their target. In addition to the usual rigors of combat flying, the navigation and the distances and the hours of sitting behind a thundering engine induced a fatigue that settled in the marrow of the bones and never seemed to go away. On July 26, Scott wrote in his combat diary that after weaving between mountains on a flight to Kunming, flying in heavy rain with limited visibility, "I respect this country more for its ruggedness each day."

Scott continued to fly solo sweeps through enemy-controlled skies. Chennault urged Scott to consider the dangers of such flight. That he did not make it an order is revealing. Scott was bringing even greater glory to Chennault's command. Plus, going against the odds was what these Southerners did.

Scott's lone-wolf tendencies had produced an unexpected backlash on the day of one of his victories.

When a P-40's ammunition containers were filled with .50-caliber ammunition, it was customary for the armorers to put a small piece of tape over the mouth of each gun. The tape served several purposes. It gave notice that the guns were fully loaded. It protected the barrels from ingestion of dust or mud as the aircraft taxied for takeoff. And to some degree it prevented the accumulation of moisture inside the barrels, moisture that would freeze at high altitude and render the guns inoperable.

One day Scott shot down a Japanese fighter and stopped at an auxiliary field to refuel. As was customary, while the gasoline was being pumped the armorers replenished the ammo and put tape over the gun ports.

Scott landed back at his home field and claimed his victory. Other pilots saw the tape over the gun ports and shook their heads in disbelief. And soon there was talk among pilots that Scott had returned from a mission claiming a victory when he had not even fired his guns.

On the cover of the August 10 issue of *Life* was the deeply lined face of General Claire Lee Chennault. The cover story, written by Jack Belden, told how Chennault was fighting to hold China, and that the victories of the Twenty-third had done more to hold back the Japanese "than a hundred of Roosevelt's speeches."

Belden wrote how Chennault had accomplished near miracles with "only his own genius . . . the most brilliant air combat unit the world has ever seen . . . and the best air-raid warning system in existence."

Belden said Chennault had pulled to his side "two of the most colorful, adventurous and skillful pilots in the world." These were two fellow Southerners: Caleb Haynes was in charge of bomber operations, and Robert Scott commanded all pursuit operations.

Scott was described as "probably the most romantic American in China today." The article said, "Reckless, flashing, romantic, he is likely to become the D'Artagnan of the air in the Far East. He gives a damn for neither man nor beast, weather nor Japs, and is a regular hell on wings."

Belden said Scott might have become one of the youngest generals in the Army "had he not thrown over his prospects for a chance to get at the Japs."

Scott was the only pursuit pilot at Haynes's Ferry Command airfield in India. Scott, wrote Belden, had flown the AVG and even though he was a colonel he flew as a wingman because he knew the Flying Tigers could teach him much.

Belden's conclusion was that Chennault, Haynes, and Scott formed "the smartest, don't-give-a-damned-est trio Asia has ever seen."

Scott's combat diary is filled with anguish about the lack of letters from Catharine. On August 20, he wrote her that some of his friends received packages of as many as twenty-five letters, and that he had received letters "from everyone—friends—relatives—enemies—but none from you."

But Kitty Rix was confused about Scott's address, and the letters she wrote went astray. It was August—almost four months after he landed in Karachi—before he received his first letter from Catharine.

He was flooding her with gifts. Rubies. Rugs. Finely crafted furniture. She wore the jewelry and she proudly installed the rugs and the furniture. But when Scott's mother came to visit, she referred to them as "Rob's rug" or "Rob's jewelry" and Ola's tongue was a lash as she told Catharine she was not good enough to be the wife of such an extraordinary man.

It was during the months he was in China that Scott's relationship with Catharine began to unravel.

Scott wrote letters by the dozen, mostly to his mother, but often to Kitty Rix. In one letter he wrote, "Smoke all you want if you don't exceed 10 a day—eat and even gain 18 pounds—I'll never make you mad again—unless you smoke too much—or are late—or work on your nails all night." He said everyone was receiving more letters than him.

Scott was so famous that movie stars back in Hollywood were writing him and a maharaja in India was sending him gifts. Letters were arriving from people all around the world.

He told Kitty Rix that he had been terribly disappointed to be assigned to the ABC Ferry Command but that it had turned out to be the biggest break he ever got; that only days after Haynes and he took over, he had one of the most important jobs in the Air Forces. The ABC Ferry Command was the lifeline to China, and he brought in every round of ammo, every bomb, and every gallon of gasoline. Every bit of food or medicine going to China, he carried in unarmed transports through Japanese-controlled airspace.

When officers he knew were rotated back to the States, he sent them to Kitty Rix with diamond and emerald rings that he had acquired in India. He sent her embroidery from China that he said had taken a year to sew.

Scott flew to Kunming, Kweilin, Linchow, Nanchang, Myitkyina, Dinjan, and he often roared into battle quoting Kipling at the top of his lungs, radio switch pressed down.

On August 11, he shot down another enemy aircraft.

On August 17, he accompanied bombers to Lashio, and as they dropped their bombs he dove to extreme low level to strafe the streets of the town as bombs burst on either side of his aircraft.

Foolhardy Scott might have been. But he had dash, flair, and panache, and he always had a good quote for the correspondents who clustered around him. Scott brought glory to the Twenty-third. He also brought a lot of attention to Chennault and his lack of airplanes, parts, and pilots.

Scott's brother pilots shook their heads as they talked of seeing Old Exterminator scorching along at rooftop level, its six fifties blazing as bombs burst on either side. Colonel Scott might be an old man, but he pressed the fight.

To use a Southern expression, he had a set of balls that were too big to fit into a number-two washtub.

On September 2, he shot down another Japanese aircraft, and yet another on September 25. Now he was an ace, a member of the most exalted club in fighter aviation.

Scott had become a legend in the CBI. He was the man in the cockpit, the man who was not only killing Japanese, but was willing to talk in great detail of his victories. His Southern expressions and turns of phrase made for great quotes. Scott was the man Americans wanted to read about.

And read they did. Americans connected Scott with the Flying Tigers, and newspapers across the country replayed his exploits. So did the big national magazines. In *Life,* Teddy White wrote, "Greatest of all the pursuit men was their commander, Colonel Robert Scott."

No wire-service story about Scott was too long for the *Macon Telegraph* to use. The town's very own Rob Scott, that boy who had failed his last year at Lanier, that wild boy always shooting his bow and arrow and who dressed up like an Indian and swam the Ocmulgee River, was—if you can believe it—the most famous fighter pilot in the war.

The news of another aerial victory by Scott caused the church bells to peal in Macon, the taxis to blow their horns, and factory whistles to screech. People congregated on the streets to talk of Colonel Rob and say, "Guess you heard Rob got himself another Jap." And someone would nod and say, "He's gonna win that war all by himself if he ain't careful."

And there was no doubt in the minds of Maconites that every "probable" the newspaper talked about was in reality a Japanese aircraft that had been shot down. The government called them "probables" only because Scott was a Southerner and they were holding him back.

Give our Rob credit for his victories, for goodness' sake.

# 21

# LEAVING CHINA

CHENNAULT'S GENIUS FOR TACTICS AND SCOTT'S GENIUS FOR COLORFUL leadership turned the Twenty-third into a fast-moving, nimble, and unpredictable combat organization that had an impact far out of proportion to its size. It would be more than four decades before the qualities manifested by these two men would become codified by a retired Air Force colonel named John Boyd, who talked of "OODA Loops" and "getting inside the enemy's decision cycle."

An example of the agility displayed by the Twenty-third came in September, when Chennault issued orders for Scott to launch an attack against Japanese shipping at Pajang. Within an hour, Scott took off with four aircraft, picked up four more at Changi, and then landed, refueled, and loaded bombs for a mission that would launch at daylight the next day. He and his men arose at 4 a.m., had a preflight briefing, took off at 6 a.m., and began dropping bombs at 7:45 a.m. They sank seven of the ten vessels in the harbor.

Scott's group landed and refueled, attacked a troop train, landed and strapped on more bombs, and in an unexpected and slashing attack, again bombed the harbor north of Nanchang.

Scott's skill at low-level bombing was rarely equaled. When his men asked him how he became so good at such an esoteric art, he said that tossing crenshaw melons out of the cockpit taught him most of what he knew. They did not know whether or not to believe him.

After Chennault and Scott linked arms in China, they took the initiative from Japan. And the Japanese were never again able to regain that initiative. The two Southerners were legatees of men who had been fighting all their lives, men who knew how to use the old rules of war and to invent new rules. Masters of surprise, speed, and violence—the three ingredients of any successful attack—Chennault and Scott showed the Japanese they no longer ruled Chinese skies.

Chennault craved respect, but he knew he would never have the respect of Arnold and Bissell. Scott craved the approval of his mother, but because he could never please her, he could never please himself, and he was always looking over his shoulder out of fear that the people in the Training Command would call him home.

Chennault and Scott often escaped administrative chores by going bird hunting. And the monsoon never sent enough rain to stop their hunting trips. In September, Scott and Chennault went on a four-day dove-hunting trip and, as they often did, shot dozens of birds for their Chinese cooks to prepare for the mess.

Both Chennault and Scott liked an occasional drink of scotch. But it was rare for either to drink to excess. The scotch was a lubricant so the stories could come easier. The scotch was a propellant for griping about Bissell and the grinding administrative orders being sent down by the Tenth Air Force. The scotch was a fuel for head-shaking complaints about Stilwell and his nonsense about infantry soldiers.

While scotch eased the rigors of constant combat, both Chennault and Scott were serious men engaged in serious work. They knew they were fortunate enough to have a war, which, after all, is the ultimate purpose of warriors, and they were not going to squander their opportunity.

At night, after dinner, Scott and Chennault would talk for a while about tactics and missions, or hunting and fishing, about back home. Afterward they went to their rooms. Chennault planned strategy and tactics and how to get around Bissell and Hap Arnold. Scott wrote letters to his mother, long detailed letters about his adventures. His letters to Catharine were brief and far less frequent.

The *Macon News* of September 19 described Scott as "the most famous flyer in the Far East," but said people back home remembered him as a "Georgia Tom Sawyer."

On September 28, the Twenty-third strafed a Japanese convoy on the Burma Road and destroyed tanks, forced cars over cliffs, and left burning trucks filled with dead troops. According to an Air Forces monograph "History of the China Air Task Force," "This devastating attack was led by Colonel Scott who set an example personally accounting for over a dozen of the vehicles."

Scott wrote Kitty Rix that in five months he had received only six letters from her. He had received mail from strangers around the world, from movie stars, from family and friends, but not from her. He said that pilots in training schools across America were flooding him with letters wanting to fly with him. But Catharine did not even respond to his cablegrams asking if she had received money he wired to her. He groused that her only job in the war was to write to him and that if she did not write more often, he would stop writing. He said that his mama sent him more mail than his wife.

She complained that the checks she wrote to pay bills were bouncing, and that she didn't know how much money was in the bank because the account was in his name.

She said her mother came to have dinner with her, but then complained of how much she hated to eat in such a small house; that Catharine's house was not at all like the Green family home in Fort Valley.

And when her allotment check did not come in, she asked Scott's parents if they would go to the post office and check on it again. Mrs. Scott chastised her, saying, "You can't do anything. You couldn't make a living if your life depended on it." Mrs. Scott then delivered to her daughter-in-law the most caustic insult that can be delivered to a young wife in the South: "You weren't brought up right."

Ola said, "Rob must have lived in hell while he's been married to you."

Kitty told Scotty, "Mrs. Scott is highly jealous of me, and I am desperately afraid of her." She said that Mrs. Scott had ordered her, "Don't tell him anything—he's enough worries of his own."

"But she better leave me alone, Scotty—I simply can't stand her heartless words or manners towards us any longer. Maybe you have been through hell with me—maybe I haven't been an asset to you, but rather a hindrance—I don't know—maybe she's right.

"She is the only person on earth that has caused me real heartache and anguish since you've been gone."

But Scott was concerned about other things. When Kitty Rix mentioned that she had gotten her hair done before going out, Scott wrote a letter and said, "Catharine, what in hell are you doing?" He said he was anxious and wondered "about the secret of the rendezvous" and he wrote several pages before asking her "Where did you go" that night.

He accused her of "running around," but quickly apologized. Scott sent her a prepaid telegram of twenty-five words, but when she responded only with "All my love" he complained that he had paid for twenty-five words and that he wanted twenty-five words.

Kitty Rix wrote back and said she was "sick of trying to explain about my letters." As to the prepaid telegram, once she had included his address and her return address, there were only three words remaining.

Scott sent a letter addressed to two-year-old Robin Lee that said, "As I guess your Mama is smoking or writing to some other man or gadding about I suppose I'll just have to write to you."

It is clear from the letters between Scott and Kitty Rix that their two different personalities were pushing them apart. Scott was detailed, organized, and focused on his work. Kitty Rix smoked heavily, drank, spent a lot of time on her nails and hair, and was somewhat undisciplined. She couldn't quite cope with the stresses of being a young wife and mother left alone in her husband's hometown, where she was at the mercy of his demanding and domineering mother.

One day Chennault told Scott that Wendell Willkie was returning home from a visit to Russia and would stop over to take a look at air operations in China. Roosevelt had defeated Willkie in the presidential race of 1940; afterward, he persuaded Willkie to serve as an ambassador-at-large and personal emissary.

In his diary that night Scott wrote, "I'd like to ask W.W. why in the hell this 100% air show in China has to be held up and retarded by an old infantry general. I guess the higher ups are still fighting wars of yesterday, are still jealous of the Air Corps—but now that petty jealousy is working against the success of our country."

On this visit to China, Willkie is known to have consummated his affair with Madame Chiang. She said later that they planned for Willkie to run again for president; that he would rule the West, and she would rule the East, and together they would rule most of the world.

Chennault asked Willkie to carry a personal letter to FDR. In the letter, Chennault outlined his ideas for an air war against Japan. The letter caused a scandal in military circles, both because Chennault had gone around the chain of command and because his ideas ignored the infantry. Hap Arnold and George C. Marshall dismissed Chennault's ideas as impractical.

Few parts of America honor their war heroes with such ardor as does the South.

In the early fall of 1942, the city of Macon decided to hold a Robert Scott Day. And they wanted to do it immediately, because, given his penchant for going into combat alone, it was just a matter of time before he got shot down. Better to hold a Robert Scott Day now in order to honor the man while he was still alive. The city leaders consulted *Grier's Almanac*, which promised fair weather in early October, and picked October 3 as the date. Cherry Street was decorated with flags in preparation.

Two companies of soldiers and an Army band participated in the parade. More than twenty thousand people packed downtown Macon to hear stories of Rob's bravery.

The same month saw one of the most famous missions of the Twenty-third, a mission remembered for its great success, and a mission that Scott would later write about on multiple occasions, and in each instance with considerable variation in events. The mission was one of the largest Chennault had ever mounted: twelve bombers and seven fighters, a minuscule force compared with the hundreds of bombers and fighters the Eighth Air Force was beginning to launch out of England in missions over Europe.

Not only is the mission illustrative of the paucity of the limited resources available in the CBI, it is illustrative of how Chennault and Scott were able to use those aircraft as what the military calls "force multipliers"—that is, obtaining results far out of proportion to the resources used to obtain them. *Life* magazine's Teddy White was aboard one of the bombers on the Hong Kong raid. White wrote that flying above the bombers in a protective screen were P-40s "commanded by dark and daring Colonel Robert Scott."

That day the Twenty-third shot down an estimated eighteen enemy aircraft over Victoria Harbor. Scott was credited with shooting down two fighters. And when the attack was over, and he was ripping along at low altitude, he sighted the famous Peninsula Hotel, a building that intelligence reported was the headquarters for senior Japanese generals. Scott peeled off and loosed his guns at the top floor of the hotel, shattering glass and ripping the building apart.

On October 31, Scott wrote a "Dear Mama and Daddy" letter saying that he had been receiving letters from old girlfriends at West Point, and letters from "my movie actress friends in Hollywood" asking about his exploits.

The weather turned bitterly cold in November. Scott was flying almost every day, often taking off before dawn, sometimes getting in two combat missions a day—in all, more than seven hours of combat flying. He could not get enough flying, could not get enough missions against the Japanese, could not drop enough bombs or shoot enough bullets. He sucked in the dangers of aerial combat the way a man lost in the desert sucks in water. There was never enough.

On November 27, Scott downed two more enemy aircraft near Canton.

Tokyo Rose branded Scott a war criminal, and announced that the Japanese government had put a price on his head. Chennault congratulated Scott for joining a rather exclusive club. Such an award had been on Chennault's head for years.

In one five-day period, the Twenty-third hit Hanoi, Canton, Hangchow, Lingling, and Youyang. Chennault's strategy was to keep the Japanese off balance, never knowing where or when his aircraft would attack next. And Chennault and Scott grew ever wilier in planning those attacks. Chennault had his pilots appear to drink too much and talk too much in bars favored by the Twenty-third. He knew their talk of a "big mission on Kweilin" would soon be passed along to the Japanese.

Scott led the mission and formed his fighters up as if they were going to Kweilin. Radio reports were relayed to them of how the Japanese were massing to meet the attack. But over Kweilin the bombers and fighters turned for Hong Kong, where, despite marginal weather, the bombers made their attacks. When one Japanese fighter attacked the lead American bomber, Scott banked sharply, and fired at a fighter. When he landed back at Kweilin, he claimed two victories and two probables. Scott's probables were growing in number.

When Scott dismounted from his P-40 that day, Chennault was waiting, his eyebrows raised in an unspoken question.

Scott looked at the man who was his hero, his mentor, his brother Southerner, and his voice was choked with emotion when he said, "General, we got 'em all."

In early December the Army Air Forces created the Air Transport Command (ATC). While the new command had a worldwide mission, its primary purpose, as had been the purpose of its predecessor, the ABC Ferry Command, was to fly supplies across the Hump to Chennault and Chiang. Now bigger aircraft and more pilots were arriving, and the ATC was about to become the most professional cargo-hauling outfit in the world.

And now, in recognition of the dangers they faced on every flight, the AAF was awarding combat pay to its crews.

Scott and Haynes had developed the routes and the techniques for these Hump pilots, who would become some of the most legendary pilots of the war.

On December 12, Scott ferried a bomber in need of repairs to Karachi. There, while awaiting the delivery of a new P-40 that was being ferried in from Africa, he took a few days off for rest and recuperation (R&R). He had been in combat eight months.

It was on this trip that Scott began to have intimations of just how famous he had become and what lay in store for him back in America.

He spent his first night with the maharaja of Cooch Behar, a young man in his twenties who had graduated from a British university. The young maharaja prepared what Scott called a "royal dinner," after which the maharani gave Scott a gold scarf for his wife.

In India he found that the British not only knew of him, they considered him a famous man. The Brits weren't quite sure how many aircraft Scott had shot down. But it did not really matter. He was a double ace who had wreaked havoc in the skies over a dozen enemy-held cities, a man with a price on his head, and was the combat commander of the famed Flying Tigers.

Given that the Brits had no great combat heroes in the CBI, it was natural that they would be drawn to the American ace.

Scott was invited to many social events, especially the dances so loved by the British, and the sight of so many lovely and well-dressed women made him ache for home and Catharine and Robin Lee. And in his diary he wrote, "Oh, Lord, the more I see other women, the more I talk to them, the more I think of my own wife." He said the very thought of Catharine and Robin Lee "makes me want to do things to get this war over with," and then ended with the plaintive words, "Catharine and Robin Lee—take me back to them soon."

Tired of Karachi and tired of being in one place, pushed by that unscratchable itch to keep moving, Scott flew on to Bombay and Delhi. He saw the Taj Mahal and buzzed the maharaja's palace in Cooch Behar.

He picked up the new P-40 and when he was ready for departure, a gaggle of officers argued over who would carry his luggage. An amazed Scott wrote, "I had a lieutenant colonel fight to carry my bag to the ship."

On the return trip through Karachi, he was waylaid by General Bissell, who "cussed me out for I was lost in the wilds of India during the last eight days."

Scott's flight log of the vacation showed that he still had his love of geography. He went to considerable length to include names of rivers and towns. Scott had seen much of the CBI and been honored at elaborate balls, but his observations remained those of a small-town Southerner. Of the Ganges, a river holy to those of the Hindu faith, he wrote, "Looks dirty as hell to me."

He wrote of flying over Poona City, Gaya, Dinjan, and Cooch Behar. Up the Brahmaputra to Dinjan. In one day Scott flew twelve hundred miles in the P-40 and that night he still felt in his bones the noise of its Allison engine. Scott crossed the Salween and the Mekong and, pushed by a strong tailwind, in one hour traveled 335 miles, which he said was a record speed for a P-40.

Upon his return to Kunming, Scott and Chennault went bird hunting. They were in a life raft in the middle of a lake, Scott lying on his back facing Chennault, Chennault lying on his back facing Scott.

Bird hunters know they can't go hunting with just anyone. When two men hunt together for the first time, they watch how the other person carries his weapon, observe each other's woodcraft, and listen to each other's thoughts about the hunt. Sometimes after five minutes, one hunter knows he will never again go hunting with the other person.

That Chennault and Scott could lie head-to-feet in a life raft and shoot at ducks and geese flying overhead shows not only the hunting skills of each man, but how much they trusted one another.

On this hunt the birds were plentiful, and Scott and Chennault were blasting away, causing a pinwheel effect with the life raft, and as they spun about in a lake in a distant corner of China, they laughed so uproariously they had to stop shooting.

But they got enough birds so that the mess ate well that night.


Upon their return, Chennault flew away to consult with the Gissimo about a new offensive. The meeting must have gone well, or perhaps Chiang simply wanted to show his affection for Chennault and Scott. He presented Chennault with a bottle of Haig & Haig, an expensive scotch. Chennault gave the scotch to Scott and suggested he keep it as a souvenir. After all, not everyone can point to a bottle of Haig & Haig and say, "Generalissimo Chiang Kai-shek gave that to me."

The Japanese continued to conduct bombing raids on American holidays. The raids were always expected and they were always met in force. On Christmas Day, 1942, Scott received the Distinguished Flying Cross, and that afternoon at three twenty-five the Japanese bombed Yunnan. Chennault called Scott and, possessed of the tactical ability to know the mind of his enemy, said that the Japanese would be back at the same time the next day and that Scott should hit them hard.

On the twenty-sixth, Scott took off to set the trap. Nineteen bombers attacked at two forty-eight that afternoon, Scott saw the glint of the sun off a windshield and came out of the sun, firing his .50-caliber guns. The bomber caught fire and exploded.

Scott said that he and his men shot down thirteen of the nineteen bombers that attacked but only eight were confirmed. "I know I got one, and probably two others," he said.

Scott now claimed thirteen aerial victories and nine probables. And sometimes he claimed the probables as victories.

Now Scott was one of the leading American aces in the war. He had flown 388 combat missions since arriving in the CBI.

On December 26, Scott received a letter from Joe E. Brown, mailed a week earlier, saying that his son Don had been killed in an airplane crash back in October. Christmas Day would have been Don's birthday. Brown told Scott, "If you get a Japanese plane on Christmas Day, dedicate it to him."

Christmas Day in the States was December 26 in China. Scott wired Brown that he had shot down two Japanese aircraft that day and dedicated both victories to Don.

J. Reilly O'Sullivan, an Associated Press war correspondent in China, wrote an open letter to Joe E. Brown that was published on the front page of newspapers across America.

The story began, "Your request has been amply met. Col. Scott got at least two for Don on the birthday your son didn't live to see." The story told how Scott's "heavy machine-gun slugs ripped into" the first bomber and then told how Scott and his men shot down ten Japanese aircraft and broke up an attack on an American airfield.

"Don would have liked that, the colonel is sure, and maybe it will give an uptwist to that wide mouth of yours," O'Sullivan wrote.

A few days later, newspapers across America ran a photo of Brown reading Scott's cable. Tears streamed down Brown's face.

People across America fell in love all over again with the brave colonel who shot down Japanese aircraft and dedicated them to a former student who was the son of a beloved comedian.

After that Christmas, Joe E. Brown added something to his shows. After his performance was over and the curtain had closed, he would take a folding chair and sit in front of the crowd and tell how his friend, the famous Colonel Robert Scott, had led the Flying Tigers to a magnificent aerial victory on Christmas Day. And that Colonel Scott, who had taught his boy how to fly, had dedicated those victories to his son.

On December 29, Scott flew his P-40 to a remote area on a hunting trip. He shot eighteen geese, and threw them in the baggage compartment of the aircraft. As he flew back, Scott wondered what would happen if he was shot down and goose feathers flew everywhere. That night the men of the Twenty-third feasted.

The scuttlebutt was that Scotty would soon be going back to America to make a tour for war bonds, and then to the Training Command to teach young pilots what he had learned in combat.

On January 2, Lieutenant Colonel Bruce Holloway moved into the headquarters building as executive officer of the Twenty-third. At last, Arnold and Bissell were adding long-overdue and much-needed staff for Chennault.

On January 5, Chennault radioed Scott and asked him to fly to Kunming.

"Scotty," Chennault said. "Orders have come in transferring you back to the States. You are to train fighter pilots."

That evening after dinner, Scott opened the bottle of Haig & Haig, saying there was no one he would rather drink it with than General Chennault. It was a night for slow drinking, soft talking, and sweet memories.

At some point in the evening, Chennault said, "Scotty, we've fought and suffered together. We've seen some good men die and we have hurt the Jap." Chennault paused. "I guess ties made over here in war will last a long time."

Scott said later that what Chennault had told him that night was the greatest compliment he ever received. "Scotty, I can't run this place without you. You've learned a lot and you've done a great job. I'd figured someday to see you lead our fighters over Tokyo. But if you are going back to teach how it's done, it's a good move. Send us back lots of men who know how to fly formation, shoot, and navigate."

Chennault had a good sense of what was going to happen to Scott upon his return, and he said, "Tell them the truth about China." He paused. "Then come back out here," he said.

Both men were in tears. Two men whose spirits were annealed by war. Two men who had fought the Jap together and won when no one else was winning. Two men bound in a brotherhood impossible for civilians to understand.

Chennault was losing his flamboyant combat leader, who had brought so much glory to the Twenty-third. He was losing a trusted friend. He was losing a hunting buddy, his confidant, his brother. He was losing the man who had earned the respect of the Gissimo and Madame Chiang, the man who had watched his back in the battles with Bissell and Arnold, and especially with that ornery damned ground-pounding Stilwell.

On January 4, General George C. Marshall sent Scott his personal congratulations "for outstanding performance in combat."

Scotty was swamped with administrative work for several days, showing Holloway how to keep the wheels turning for the squadrons of the Twenty-third. He went to every man under his command, officer and enlisted, shook their hands and said good-bye.

He wanted to make one more combat sweep through enemy territory before he went home. He wanted to take a P-40 into enemy skies just one more time, and hope and pray that the Jap would rise against him.

The Lone Wolf of the Chindwin needed a victory lap. The One-Man Air Force needed to dominate the skies yet again. He had the victory flags painted under his canopy to show the "thirteen yellow bastards I shot down in aerial combat." Plus, he had nine probables that he believed should have been credited as victories. It was a most impressive combat record. But it was not enough.

This time Chennault prevailed. He told Scott that he had seen seven men with orders to go home who wanted to make just one more mission. They had all been shot down.

"I would rather have pleased Claire L. Chennault than to have been a four-star general," Scott wrote. So he did not go.

That night, his last night in theater, Scotty, group flight surgeon Tom Gentry, and Chennault again opened the bottle of Haig & Haig. This time they threw away the cork and they drank to the death of all Japanese. Chennault, who rivaled Scott in his paranoia, said to Scott, "These people who hate me are taking you away.

"We kept the record clean," Chennault said with pride. In his understated way, relaxed with close friends, he said, "And in some places we added to it."

The three men finished off the bottle of scotch and Chennault threw his glass into the fireplace. Scott and Gentry did the same.

Scott's final breakfast in China was with a group of his fighter pilots. He told them, "I'm not going to say good-bye because I'm supposed to be tough." With tears in his eyes and a catch in his voice, he waved, said "So long," and was off to his waiting aircraft. As the aircraft taxied out for takeoff, Scott saw the pilots and enlisted men of the Twenty-third gathered on the tarmac, all waving at him, and his heart was full. He believed that nothing would ever again affect him in this manner.

But a few minutes after takeoff he looked out the window and saw a formation of P-40s, led by Bruce Holloway and the senior pilots of the Twenty-third, among them several of the original Flying Tigers. They escorted him over the hills of Yunnan all the way to the Mekong, and along the way they did slow rolls over the transport in which he was riding, and they dived past at high speed and then roared up in an Immelmann, the red shark mouths and white teeth gleaming in the early-morning sun. The greatest pilots in the war were paying homage to their leader.

On the morning of January 9, 1943, Scott looked over the land he had fought to defend. And as his transport crossed into Burma, the formation of P-40s, one by one, roared past his window, wheeled in the sun, and returned to the fight.

# 22

## HOME IS THE HERO

CHENNAULT WAS RIGHT WHEN HE TOLD SCOTT THAT UPON HIS RETURN to America he would be a famous man. But then, the Old Man was always right.

Scott was an early ace to come home from the war. On his chest he wore ribbons representing the Silver Star and the Air Medal, the first an award for bravery in combat, the second for extraordinary flying. Both ribbons were adorned with an oak-leaf cluster, signifying that each medal had been awarded twice. Scott's hat had a fifty-mission crush, and it was tilted to the side at a cocky angle that defied regulations. On his left shoulder was that most mysterious, most evocative, and most beautiful of all unit patches: the CBI patch. It was shaped like a shield, which has been the fundamental design for many American military patches, and the bottom half was covered with the vertical red and white stripes of the U.S. flag. Side by side at the top were the twelve-point Chinese sun and a star representing India.

A hound-dog grin covered half of Scott's face, his blue eyes sparkled, and he was ready to talk to anyone, any place, any time, about his thirteen victories and nine probables, the genius of Claire Chennault, and the obstructionism of General Joseph "Walking Joe" Stilwell, who, by the way, was the man who lost Burma to the Japanese.

With great passion, he set about following Chennault's instructions to tell people about China and to use his fame to get more airplanes and more men sent to Chennault.

The AAF not only wanted to know all that he knew, the AAF wanted to put him on display across America. At that moment in time, Scott was the greatest of American heroes, and a walking advertisement for air power.

In Washington, Scott talked to Hap Arnold and his senior staff. Afterward, Arnold ordered Scott debriefed. The resulting thirty-one-page text was classified "Secret" and circulated among the AAF's high command. It contained the inside scoop on China from a senior officer who had been there and who knew all the players, American, Chinese, and British.

The debriefing clearly showed the amazing role of the AAF in the CBI, a theater where Stilwell and the Army had been humbled. Scott's debriefing was invaluable ammunition for Arnold to use in the coming postwar battle for independence as a separate and autonomous department of the military.

Scott was prepared, and his numbers were hard, definitive, and impressive. In three months, using unarmed Gooney Birds, the ABC Ferry Command had dropped two million pounds of rice to the Chinese army and brought eight thousand wounded British soldiers and refugees from Myitkyina and Lashio to safe haven in China. He told of Chennault's air warning system, of how some of the Flying Tigers were men he had taught to fly in California, but that in China they were the teachers, and he flew as their wingman. He told how the Twenty-third had been organized and activated in combat, and how on the first day of operations it had shot down nineteen Japanese aircraft.

In the briefing, Scott continued to demonstrate his paranoia about the Training Command, saying he had "devised a scheme" to go to war and "devised a scheme" to be assigned to fighters. He knew that Arnold had little regard for Chennault, but his loyalty to the Old Man was greater than his desire to please Arnold. Chennault's ideas about aerial tactics are woven throughout his debriefing. At the end of the thirty-one pages, when the interviewer asked for any final thoughts, Scott said that Chennault should be given full authority to run the air war in the CBI, that Chennault should become the senior military man in China, and that the military should recognize that Chennault knew the Chinese better than anyone else.

After the debriefing, Scott was given leave to go home, where Mama and Daddy and Kitty Rix and Robin Lee and the good people of Macon, Georgia, were waiting. In fact, so many people in Macon were waiting that Scott said he had to sneak into town so he could meet Kitty Rix without being disturbed.

Two-year-old Robert Lee Scott, Jr. (Museum of Aviation—Robins Air Force Base)

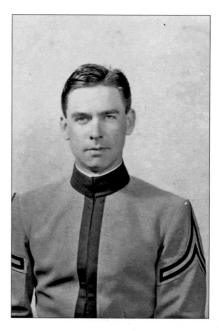

Scott at West Point. (Museum of Aviation—Robins Air Force Base)

### ROBERT LEE SCOTT, JR.
#### Macon, Georgia
#### Army

IT is with a great deal of fear and trembling that we approach the enormous task of writing a resume of this man's hectic existence. If there is any one who can put his finger on something Scott has not done we beg of him to come forward and tell us so that we can make note of it here. He has been in turn aviator, lawyer, doctor, marine, sailor, chauffeur, rancher, stock-broker, and so many other things that the stories of his experiences alone would occupy many volumes. But one very important thing that we must not fail to include here is his ability to recite reams upon reams of poetry and to sing yards of funny songs and never exhaust his supply. In one way or another his ability in this line has brightened many of our hikes and trips and although we must admit that we have by this time learned many of his favorites by heart; yet we still like them all and like Scotty for making the Lord take down the darkness.

A page from the *Howitzer,* the West Point yearbook, during Scott's senior year. The biographical sketch shows why Scott was known as "bugler" during his West Point years. (U.S. Military Academy)

Scott on Soyer motorcycle. After graduating from West Point, Scott rode across much of Europe on this motorcycle. (Museum of Aviation—Robins Air Force Base)

Kitty Rix in Panama holding an orchid grown by Scott. (Museum of Aviation—Robins Air Force Base)

Scott standing in front of a Boing P-12 while stationed at Albrook Field, Panama, in the mid-1930s. (Museum of Aviation—Robins Air Force Base)

Robin, Kitty Rix, and Scotty in 1941 when stationed in California. (Museum of Aviation—Robins Air Force Base)

General Claire Cennault and Scotty study a photograph in China. (Museum of Aviation—Robins Air Force Base)

The wreckage of a twin-engine Japanese bomber, a KI-48 "Lily." This was Scotty's fifth aerial victory, and shooting it down made him an ace. (Museum of Aviation—Robins Air Force Base)

Colonel Scott pointing to his victory flags painted on "Old Exterminator." When this photo was taken in late 1942, Scotty was one of the most famous pilots of the time. (Museum of Aviation—Robins Air Force Base)

Roland Scott standing in front of his B-26 in England. Shortly after this photograph was taken, Roland led the famous and disastrous low-level attack on Ijmuiden. (Museum of Aviation—Robins Air Force Base)

Scotty and Kitty Rix with their movie counterparts, Andrea King and Dennis Morgan, on the set of *God Is My Co-Pilot*. (Museum of Aviation—Robins Air Force Base)

A street in Macon during the movie premiere. (Museum of Aviation—Robins Air Force Base)

Scotty and Kitty Rix at the premiere. (Museum of Aviation—Robins Air Force Base)

General Dwight David Eisenhower speaks to a young pilot at Furstenfeldbruck Air Force Base in Germany in 1952. Wing Commander Scott looks on with approval. (Museum of Aviation—Robins Air Force Base)

Elephant taken by Scott on safari in Africa. (Museum of Aviation—Robins Air Force Base)

Scott and famous comedian Joe E. Brown at Williams Air Force Base in 1957. Scott was reprimanded by his superiors for awarding Brown the fictitious rank of six stars. (Museum of Aviation—Robins Air Force Base)

Scott in retirement. (Museum of Aviation—Robins Air Force Base)

Riding a camel somewhere along the Great Wall of China. (Museum of Aviation—Robins Air Force Base)

Scott in 1980 standing on the promontory known as The Old Dragon Head, where the Great Wall of China ends at the sea. Some thirty-five years earlier, he had flown along the Great Wall in a P-51. (Museum of Aviation—Robins Air Force Base)

When the Museum of Aviation finally acquired a P-40, Scott welcomed it with a kiss. (Museum of Aviation—Robins Air Force Base)

Scott flying one of his first fighter aircraft, the fabric-covered open cockpit Curtiss P-1 Hawk. (Museum of Aviation—Robins Air Force Base)

The Super Saber---F-100C---
Just before I got the message from
being fired so much and retired...
1957..
Luke Air Force Base...

The last aircraft Scott flew on active duty was the supersonic F-100 Super Sabre. (Museum of Aviation—Robins Air Force Base)

As Scott left the banquet, he turned and waved good-bye to the crowd. It was his last good-bye. He died two weeks later. (Anica Hollar)

The *Macon Telegraph* of February 8, 1943, had a story about Scott returning to Macon. The headline read:

## COLONEL BOB
## BACK AT HOME
## FOR 2 WEEKS

Scott's privacy was brief. A national hero had come home, and restraint was not the order of the day. A second Robert Scott Day was held, and all of Macon and much of middle Georgia turned out to see in the flesh this Macon boy who was now a national figure. People in Macon could not remember another native son who had been so famous. But they could remember Rob—they learned from the papers that now he was called "Scotty"—and what a free-spirited boy he had been.

The first Sunday he was home, he and Kitty Rix and Robin Lee, along with his parents, went to the Tattnall Square Baptist Church and sat in the family pew where Scott had sat as far back as he could remember. He was in uniform. The silver eagles gleamed on his shoulders, and the combat ribbons shouted on his chest. He wore more combat decorations than anyone in Macon had ever seen.

Around him was the palpable aura of fame. He was *from* Macon but no longer *of* Macon. He might duck his head and grin and pull his aw-shucks routine, and he might remember the names of everyone in the congregation, but no longer was he one of them. He had led the most famous fighter outfit of the war against an enemy of his country, and he had been victorious in battle: a double ace.

He knew General Claire Chennault and General Stilwell and Chiang and Madame Chiang and all those stuffy British generals. He even knew General H. H. "Hap" Arnold and all the bigwigs up in Washington, DC.

No, he was not of Macon.

That morning, Kitty Rix sat on one side of Scotty and his mama on the other. The two women in Scott's life had grown so resentful of each other they could barely speak.

The preacher looked out from the pulpit and the aura around Scott was so great it was as if a light from above were shining upon him. Everyone in the congregation was sneaking glances at Colonel Scott and barely paying any attention to the preacher. Whatever the preacher had to say that morning would not be heard and certainly would not be remembered.

So after a few hymns were sung and a few prayers delivered, the preacher looked over his congregation and said, "Robert, won't you come up here and take my place today? Won't you tell us something about your safe return from mortal combat? We have all been reading about you, and we want to hear from you."

Scott did not need a second invitation. Both Chennault and Arnold had ordered him to spread the word.

Scott stepped out of the pew, tugged at the bottom of his tunic to make sure he was squared away, and marched down the aisle, tall, lean, and with a bit of fighter-pilot swagger. He had lost weight in China and his new tailored uniform made him look like a walking recruiting poster. He shook hands with the preacher, stepped into the pulpit, and delivered the gospel according to Robert Lee Scott Jr. It was a gospel born in the dozens of letters he had written home to Mama, a gospel born in what he had written in his combat diary. It was a gospel born in the simple fact that he was a bugler, and it was his nature to talk.

Scott said he had grown up in this church, and he knew those in the congregation expected him to say he had prayed his way through combat, and that it was those prayers which brought him through great danger. If that was the case, he was going to disappoint them. He admitted that he did not pray at all while in combat; he was far too busy. But he was comforted nevertheless because he knew that his mama and the members of this church were praying for him, and it was those prayers that had brought him home.

As he talked, he stared at his mother and tears filled his eyes.

He said that one of his mama's favorite quotes from the Bible was "Seek and ye shall find," and all his life he had sought. He had a goal and that goal was to become a fighter pilot and to go to war and kill the enemies of his country.

That he had realized his dream was due entirely to his mother.

Then Scott began telling stories. He told the congregation what it was like to fly in combat against the Japanese, of the Hong Kong raid, of several of his victories including the first bomber he had destroyed on the ground.

But even at the moment of his great fame, pushing to the forefront of his thinking was the idea that he had "lied" to get into combat: he said he had told Colonel Cooper he had a thousand hours in the B-17 when in reality he was not qualified to fly the aircraft.

And Macon being Macon, and the South being the South, the women nodded in slight bewilderment as the men smiled in appreciation and looked at each other and grinned. That ole Rob Scott had pulled a fast one. He got in one of them B-17s for the first time, and he flew it off to Karachi, India. Crossed the Atlantic Ocean, by God he did, and he had never flown that big old airplane before. They nodded their heads, and their admiration of Scott soared with his rhetoric. Hot damn! Hold my beer and watch *this*. Yessireebob, no sumbitch from New York City could have done what Rob Scott from Macon, Georgia, had done.

In the South, when the truth is in conflict with the legend, people go with the legend. And the legend of Robert Scott was in full flower.

Scott needed to feel guilty about something, and already he was feeling guilty about being back home when Chennault needed him in China. He felt guilty that people were calling him a Flying Tiger when he had never been a Flying Tiger. He felt guilty that he was being assigned to the Training Command. "They" had finally caught him.

The good Baptist in the Tattnall Square Baptist Church worshipped an Old Testament God, a God who did not forgive or forget transgressions, and who demanded payment in full and running over for every mistake made. The Baptist God knew when a sparrow fell, knew when a man wandered from the straight and narrow. Robert Lee Scott Jr. was standing in the pulpit of a Baptist church and confessing that he had told a lie to go to war. He oozed contrition, and it was clear from his demeanor that if the heavens had parted and a bolt of lightning had struck him dead, he would have understood. But the people of Macon, Georgia, forgave him. They were proud of him, and his story would become their story.

Scott could have stayed in the pulpit all day. He had stories he had not even thought of yet. But unlike Baptist preachers, he had a sense of timing, and he knew when to sit down. He knew to exit while the crowd still wanted more.

All this was stressful in the extreme for Kitty Rix. Rob was home at last—home with her and Robin Lee. But Ola was constantly at the house, hovering, her glacial stare indicating her disapproval with just about everything she saw. She did not like the way Kitty Rix had arranged the rugs Rob had sent home. She did not like the placement of the new furniture. And she thought that the heart-stopping beauty of the jewelry that Rob had sent home was just too much for Catharine. She did not deserve such finery.

When Catharine mentioned all of this to Scotty, he ignored the biblical admonition that in marriage a man must leave his mother and cleave unto his wife. Scott told Kitty Rix to learn to get along with his mother.

# 23

# ON THE ROAD AGAIN

SCOTT HAD BEEN BACK IN THE STATES ABOUT TEN DAYS WHEN HE began receiving messages from Chennault.

"What happened?" Chennault asked. "Have they softened you up with a cushy job and made you forget China? Things are the same out here. There is no shortage of Japs."

Scott was working on a paper to present to Arnold, a paper containing everything he had learned about aerial combat in China. His plan was to give the paper to the general, say "That's all I know," and then hope that the Big Sky Boss would work the levers that would send him back to China, back to Chennault, and back to flying combat against the Japanese.

It was a dream born of hope rather than reality. The AAF wanted to show off its biggest hero, and going back to China was not part of the plan. America was the plan. *All* of America, from sea to shining sea. America needed someone to boost the sales of war bonds. America needed someone to help end the embarrassing and shameful absenteeism of defense workers. America needed someone to boost the spirit of the country. And the AAF had just the man. He was tailor-made for the job, straight out of Hollywood casting, a certified war hero and a natural-born bugler.

Arnold spoke to Scott along these lines: "I am sending you around the country to talk to defense workers. Inspire them. You will be making a lot of speeches. Stay out of political matters. You will be attending lots of parties where you are expected to make a good impression for the Army Air Forces. If I hear that you have had more than one drink at a party, I will transfer you to a place you do not want to go."

He gave Scott a brand-new tricked-out P-40, in drab war colors but bright and shiny in new paint, replete with the shark mouth, the lolling salacious tongue, the malevolent eyes, with the Twenty-third Fighter Group's insignia painted on the rear fuselage and—best of all—the thirteen Japanese flags painted under the left canopy rail. Old Exterminator was in the air again.

There was no more commanding, sexy, jaw-dropping aircraft in America. This was the aircraft of legend, the aircraft whose deadly .50-caliber guns had shot down at least thirteen enemy aircraft, maybe twenty-two. And just in case there was someone who had been a hermit in recent months, "Colonel Scott" was painted on the fuselage under the canopy rail. It was an aircraft to stir the heart of every man, and it was flown by a pilot who stirred the heart of every woman.

Scott had been away from home more than nine months. Now he was going on the road again. After all those weekend round-trips from San Antonio to Rome, Georgia, after all those letters saying he would never leave home again, he was leaving. And he was again leaving Kitty Rix in Macon with a demanding three-year-old girl and an even more demanding mother-in-law.

America by now was reaching toward its full and mighty industrial strength. Warplanes were rolling off assembly lines by the thousands. The idea that the bombers would always get through still reigned supreme in the AAF, and top priority was given to rolling bombers off the assembly lines in ever-increasing numbers for the fighting fronts in England, North Africa, the Pacific, even China.

Because of the Flying Tigers and the Twenty-third Fighter Group, in the spring of 1943 the P-40 still remained the embodiment of America's wrath against Japan. And now Scott had been ordered to take his P-40 and go see America. Tour AAF bases and show young pilots a bit about gunnery and bombing. Know that a big crowd will be waiting at every stop, and that your job is to put on a show. Let them hear the war song of that mighty Allison engine. By God, let them know a fighter pilot is in town. And while you are at it, talk to the media about the war in China and the critical role of the AAF in that war.

Talk to workers at defense plants about how important their jobs are if we are to win the war. Inspire the workers on the home front. Motivate them or shame them to cut the absenteeism rate and get back to work on the assembly lines.

Few military pilots have ever had such an open-ended and relatively unsupervised mandate. Scott would revel in the assignment.

Hap Arnold knew that Scott could be very good indeed for the AAF, but he did not like the lanky, smiling, mush-mouthed Georgia colonel. Scott was entirely too close to that renegade Chennault. And Chennault was in cahoots with Chiang and his Dragon Lady of a wife—what a pair—who had the ear of Roosevelt. The unholy trio of Chennault, Chiang, and Madame Chiang disliked Stilwell, and they were doing all they could to undermine his leadership. And already Arnold was tired of Scott pestering him about returning to China.

Arnold was a complex man. He would later have the distinction of being the only man ever to reach five-star rank in both the Army and the Air Force. He was a ruthless, hard-driving leader who made brutal decisions easily. He trampled on feelings and ambitions as if he were a runaway bull elephant. Arnold wanted his way, and he went to great lengths to get it. But he also was a visionary who would be one of the men most responsible for creating the new and independent United States Air Force after the war. Sometimes it seemed as if every move Arnold made was intended to further that goal.

To Arnold, Scott was nothing more than a pilot. And generals have little respect for men who are only pilots. They know how very little pilots contribute to strategy and logistics, and the role that politics plays in both. They see pilots as one-dimensional. But Scott was famous. The American people idolized him, and he could bring much glory to the AAF. To Arnold, Scott was a pawn in a national chess game.

Scott's innate sense of showmanship matured during the next few weeks. At an Army base where troops and even hundreds of civilians might be waiting, Scott would come roaring out of the sun in a three-hundred-mile-per-hour dive, that gleaming shark mouth causing a frisson of trepidation, then level off at maybe two hundred feet and then pull up into a victory roll followed by a zoom up to a thousand feet or so to bleed off airspeed, then circle around and land. Aerobatics were forbidden over Army Air Forces fields, but this was Colonel Scott, and whatever he wanted to do was just fine. Good for recruitment. Good for military and civilian morale. Made the AAF look good. Real good.

Scott favored long white scarves, and as he landed he would slide the canopy back and flick his scarf out into the slipstream, so that when he arrived in front of the reviewing stand his scarf would be fluttering along the fuselage, and when he stepped onto the wing it would hang in luminous counterpoint to his uniform. Dash. Élan. Panache. Playing to the bleachers.

Adulatory young fighter pilots would gather around, and there would be lots of talking with their hands—fighter pilots are rendered mute if they are forbidden to use their hands in conversation. There might be a short speech, and then Scott would climb back into his airplane to demonstrate his ability with the six .50-caliber guns. There is no doubt that Scott was one of the best shooters in the AAF. He had proved it on the Burma Road, the Salween Gorge, the barges on the Chindwin, and with thirteen Japanese fighter aircraft.

Finally, Scott would perform a few aerobatics, refuel, and move on to the next town, maybe to a defense plant. One Friday morning Scott talked to a crowd of hundreds at the Curtiss-Wright Corporation in Buffalo, the plant where his beloved P-40 had been manufactured, and that afternoon to thousands more at the nearby Packard plant where they made twelve-hundred-horsepower turbocharged engines for PT boats. The next day he talked to workers at the Bell Aircraft Corporation factory, and by the end of the day he was weary. But he was guest of honor that evening at a party hosted by the top executives of the Curtiss-Wright Corporation, and in attendance would be the executives of several other defense contractors, all of whom were anxious to meet the famous pilot in a social setting, call him "Scotty" as if they were old friends, and leave knowing that their stories of being with the famous colonel would later make them the star of many a social gathering.

So Scott went and nursed a drink all evening telling yet more stories about China and Chennault, the Flying Tigers, and the battles that he and Chennault had fought together.

Late in the evening he felt a gentle touch on his arm and a soft-spoken man introduced himself as Austin Pardue, dean of St. Paul's Cathedral, a large and prominent Episcopal church in Buffalo.

"I've heard all of your talks here," Dean Pardue said, "and I wonder if you might speak at the cathedral tomorrow morning. Would you take my place in the pulpit?"

Before Scott could answer, several nearby women chimed in and agreed that this would be a wonderful idea. Many of the defense-plant executives and their wives belonged to St. Paul's.

Scott remembered that Arnold had told him he was the face of the AAF, and this was a most influential audience, so of course he agreed.

The next morning, as he walked down the aisle of St. Paul's, he remembered what Chennault had told him about using his fame to help out the Twenty-third; to do what he could to get more airplanes and equipment and gas and bullets and bombs back out to China.

That morning Scott began bugling in a voice he did not recognize as his own. He said he was a boy from middle Georgia, and all he had ever wanted to do was fly, and how he wangled an appointment to West Point, flew the mail, and told a big lie to get into combat. He spoke of the dangers in flying the Hump in unarmed Goons, and how he had used the P-40 that Chennault had given him to bomb barges and became the Lone Wolf of the Chindwin, of how he had painted his prop spinner different colors between missions to become the One-Man Air Force with a price on his head, and how he strafed the penthouse of the Peninsula Hotel and saw Japanese generals running down fire escapes. He told them of how very little Chennault's valiant men had to fight with, and what a great job they were doing and how they needed the help of every American to win the war against Japan. And of course he told of shooting down twenty-two Japanese aircraft but "they" would only give him credit for thirteen.

Scott picked up Dean Pardue's Bible from the lectern, waved it overhead, and said, "All this sitting here and asking God to help us win this war, every word in this Bible is not enough. The tools of war must be produced for soldiers such as me to use, fighter planes and PT boat engines such as come from here in Buffalo."

He said Chennault had worked miracles in China but never had more than fifty operational aircraft at any one time. If Japan was to be defeated, then Chennault needed more airplanes, more parts and supplies, more bombs and ammunition, and more men.

When Scotty was in full bugle mode, there were few orators—preachers or otherwise—who could touch him, and that morning he *owned* St. Paul's Cathedral.

And when it was over, when dozens of people had shaken Scott's hand and told him what a great sermon he had delivered, Dean Pardue took Scott by the arm, stared at him almost in adulation, and said, "I was looking at the congregation as you talked, and they were fascinated by what you had to say. It was so inspirational to everyone. I wish I could hold their attention in such a fashion."

Scott demurred, but Dean Pardue held on to Scott's arm. "Your story should be a book," he said. "A book. I want you to go with me to New York tomorrow. I want you to meet my friend Charles Scribner and tell him the stories you told today from the pulpit."

Scott says he shook his head and explained that he had a job in the AAF—he was due in Arizona at the end of the week, and he wanted to spend the next few days with his family in Macon before he took over the new job.

But given what we know of Scott's bugling abilities, his small-town Southern defensiveness, and his desire to please his mama, it is possible that the idea for the book was already burning inside Scott. Perhaps he had already given it much thought.

In any event, Scott jumped at the opportunity for an audience with a publisher. He and the dean took an overnight train to New York City, and the next morning caught a taxi to the Scribner Building on Fifth Avenue, where they met Charles Scribner. A Princeton man like his father and grandfather before him, Charles Scribner headed the most distinguished publishing house in America, the house of Maxwell Perkins, the house of Hemingway, Wolfe, Fitzgerald, and Rawlings. In short, a house containing some of the most celebrated writers in America.

Scribner and Pardue took a seat. But Scott found it difficult to talk sitting down. He paced back and forth across the office, and he used his fighter-pilot hands to illustrate the maneuvers of Old Exterminator, and to retell the stories he had been telling for the past few days. Scott's intensity thickened his accent until his voice was mushy and slow. Scribner's ears were not used to the Southern accent, and often he had to ask Scott to repeat himself.

Scribner had a pronounced stammer, perhaps the result of being corrected so much when he was a boy, and the interruptions were sometimes prolonged.

One man talked easily and at length while the other had difficulty with the simplest sentence.

But several hours after Scott began talking, he paused to take a breath. The courtly and urbane Scribner exhaled and said, in effect, I think you have a book, Colonel Scott. But what will be its title?

Scott says he leaned toward Scribner and said, "I've thought about that a lot, Mr. Scribner, and I think the title should be *God Is My Co-Pilot.*"

Scribner was speechless. The sheer boldness of the title, the ambition, the scope, even the arrogance of the title, what some would consider blasphemous, hit Scribner with a visceral impact. But he was a conservative man and practical, and he shook his head and said, "I don't know. People will think it is a religious book."

Scott's eyes widened and he moved closer to Scribner. He held out his hands and said, "Oh, no, Mr. Scribner. There is a spirit abroad in the land. What are the songs you hear today? 'Coming In on a Wing and a Prayer,' 'Praise the Lord and Pass the Ammunition.' People will understand."

Scribner was not convinced. Moving on, he asked, "How long will it take you to write it?"

Scott grinned his wide lopsided grin, shrugged, and his eyes sparkled when he said, "Mr. Scribner, I have a new assignment in Arizona. So I have to do it in three days."

Scribner was gobsmacked. He was an urbane man who thought he knew and understood the unusual ways of writers. But this lanky, grinning Southerner, this barely intelligible man from Georgia who somehow had made it through West Point to become a full colonel in the AAF and a nationally known war hero, had stunned him. Write a book in three days? The very idea was ludicrous. No one had ever written a book in three days. Scribner walked to the window, looked outside, collected himself, and after a few minutes said, "Colonel, I've been in this business many years . . . and if you think you can write a book in three days, well . . ."

"Oh, I won't write it. I'll talk it."

Scribner was again rendered speechless. He turned from the window and stared at Scott.

"I've heard about these new Dictaphones," Scott said. "If you will get me a hotel room and a Dictaphone, I will give you a book in three days." He paused and repeated, "I'll talk it."

A New York editor knows how to call a bluff. It would be worth the cost of a hotel room to see what, if anything, Scott could deliver. Scribner told his secretary to reserve a room at the Waldorf-Astoria for Colonel Scott. Make it for three nights. And send over a Dictaphone and a box of cylinders. (The Dictaphone of that time used wax cylinders for recording.)

Pardue accompanied Scott to the hotel and then took his leave, no doubt feeling proud of his accomplishment. Scott, of course, was tightly wound, with stories racing through his mind, seeing in vague form the contents of the book and how he would tell the story. He had barely settled in his room when there was a knock on the door and a hotel employee brought in a Dictaphone and a box of cylinders.

The Dictaphone was relatively simple to operate. Having made history, Scott was now ready to write it.

In a few moments Scott had loosened his tie and taken off his shoes, and was sitting in the middle of the bed with his legs crossed. He picked up the microphone, raised his eyes toward the ceiling, thought for a second, and began to speak:

"Even the angels in heaven must have shrugged their wings after the few seconds of my first flight."

## 24

# THE BOOK . . .
# AND THE MOVIE

By late afternoon, Charles Scribner could no longer contain his curiosity. He walked from Fifth Avenue across to Park Avenue and up to the Waldorf-Astoria, got on the elevator, and rode to Scott's floor. At Scott's room, he knocked on the door, and after a brief pause was admitted by a smiling, courteous, slightly manic Scott.

Before Scribner could ask how much work Scott had done, Scott said he didn't know what to do with all the wax cylinders he had filled with words, so he had put them into a pillowcase. Scott handed the bulging pillowcase to a nonplussed Scribner, who said that he would have a secretary transcribe them, and that he would get back to Scott.

"Mr. Scribner, I'll have a lot more for you tomorrow," Scott said as he closed the door.

Scott loved to tell this story, and he would do so many times over the years. Behind the story was a Southerner's pride at turning upside down the world of a famous New York City publisher.

Scott says it was not yet noon the next day when there was a knock on his door and Scribner entered, nodding in approval. The publisher told Scott to keep on doing what he was doing, that even though his secretary was having some difficulty in understanding everything Scott said, a good story was emerging from the wax cylinders.

Scott was freshly shaven and well turned out. But his tired eyes showed he had been up for much of the night. He handed Scribner another lumpy pillowcase, said that the book was going just fine, thank you, and that he would soon need more wax cylinders.

Scribner stared at the pillowcase, nodded, and said he would have them delivered.

And that is how it went until late Thursday, when Scott dropped off the last pillowcase at Scribner's office, took a train to Buffalo, jumped into his P-40, and flew to Luke Field, near Phoenix, where he was to assume command of a training wing.

Upon arrival he found that there had been a mix-up in his orders, and that another colonel had taken over what Scott thought was to have been his command. Scott said he thought that once again he had "escaped from the Training Command." He did not call Washington for a clarification of his orders or to ask where he should report. He had things on his mind. So he climbed back into his P-40 and continued flying west, on to his prewar command at Cal-Aero Academy, in California.

The *Los Angeles Times* of April 2, 1943, ran a story and photo with a headline saying "China Air Hero Here to Train New Flyers." In truth, Scott made a speech at the Curtiss-Wright Technical Institute, retelling the stories he had spent the past three days talking about, and then he was off to Hollywood.

Scott is vague regarding what happened next and who was involved. As he told the story, a friend at Cal-Aero introduced him to Jack Warner of Warner Bros. Pictures. But it was almost certainly Joe E. Brown who made the introductions.

Whoever the intermediary was, Scott was soon in the office of one of the most famous movie producers in America. There he told his story. He told Warner of his book with Scribner's, and a few hours later he and Warner had agreed on a movie contract.

Scott had no idea if there were military prohibitions against officers writing books. A member of Warner's staff called Washington, was connected to Hap Arnold, and said he had a Colonel Robert Scott in his office and that Warner Brothers had just bought the movie rights for his book.

He listened a moment then handed the phone to Scott.

"Yes, sir, General Arnold," Scott said.

"What in the hell are you doing in Hollywood?" Arnold said. "I thought I sent you to Arizona. And what is this about movie rights and a book?"

After Scott explained, Arnold told Scott to make sure the book and movie reflected well on the AAF, and to return to Arizona, where new orders would be waiting.

The manuscript for *God Is My Co-Pilot* had not yet been finished. The secretary transcribing the wax cylinders simply could not understand Scott's Southern accent, the military terminology, and the Chinese place names. She was winging it, and parts of the manuscript would later appear to be in some strange new phonetic version of the English language.

On April 8, 1943, Warner Brothers and Scott signed the movie contract. Scott received $100,000 for the sale of the movie rights, the money to be paid in annual $20,000 installments. He also agreed to serve as technical advisor to the movie.

Jack Moffitt, a Warner executive, wrote an interoffice memo to Hal Wallis, another executive, saying he found a boy-like quality about Scott that irritated military superiors. Moffitt said Scott always did more than he was ordered to do, always had to put a little fillip atop whatever job he was doing.

Right in the middle of the early hubbub about the book and the excitement about the movie, there came a bombshell that made both publisher and producer know they were riding a good horse. And it showed the people of America the greatness of the Flying Tigers and their leader.

Teddy White's story of the Hong Kong raid by the Twenty-third Fighter Group appeared in the April 12 issue of *Life*. Why the story took so long to appear in a weekly magazine is not known. Perhaps it was the growing paper shortage that caused the delay. Or wartime security issues.

In any event, the story was a blazing paean to Scott and his pilots. White said that on the raid, Scott and his pilots shot down twenty-seven Japanese aircraft without losing a single American aircraft.

White said that nowhere else in the war was America or its allies using the "ancient and rickety" P-40, but that Colonel Scott thought the aircraft was splendid, and if a way could be found to make them watertight, "we'll use them as submarines."

White described Scott as the greatest of fighter pilots. "He has a thick Southern accent that gets smoky with suppressed excitement when he is angry. . . . He is the lone-wolf type of pilot—likes to get out on his own and shoot up the field or break away from formation and head after that Zero in the corner which seems to be slipping away. His men are crazy about him."

White observed that the top command of the China Air Task Force "is almost entirely Southern. The Southern mentality I find is essentially a combat mentality and a glorious one."

During the spring of 1943, Scott was involved in so many overlapping events that it is difficult to keep track of him. He had just returned from China, was making speeches all over the country, had a new duty assignment at the School of Applied Tactics, near Orlando, Florida, was working with Scribner's on the book and Warner on the movie, and was well into writing his next book, a novel.

Chennault still wanted to know when Scott was returning to China.

Scott was caught between the Scylla of Hollywood and the Charybdis of Chennault. And Scott being Scott, it was inevitable that he would overreact to the pressure—that he would step over the line. And he did.

On Saturday, May 1, 1943, Scott made a speech in Orlando to a women's club. Numerous newspaper reporters were present.

At the time, John L. Lewis, the beetle-browed and contentious labor leader, had told his workers to go on strike, and the resulting drop in war production was significant. Lewis was very much in the news, and many in America questioned the patriotism of the fiery labor leader. But Lewis was adamantine in protecting what he saw as the interests of his union members.

After Scott's speech, one of the good ladies in the audience asked Scott what he thought of Lewis. Scott, remembering Arnold's admonition to stay away from political matters, demurred. But the lady insisted.

Scott was unable to turn down an invitation to talk, but made it clear he was speaking as a private citizen and not as a colonel in the Army. He looked straight at the good lady and said he thought it would be a good thing if the .50-caliber guns of his aircraft, "which you ladies have commended me for using so well," were turned on Mr. Lewis. Shooting Lewis, Scott said, would be a "definite step towards ultimate victory" in the war.

The next sound heard was the sound of reporters kicking over their chairs as they ran from the room to call in the story. And the next day the front page of the *Orlando Sentinel-Star* carried a two-column picture of Scott and a story saying he would be glad to shoot Lewis. The story was picked up all across the country.

In May, Churchill and Roosevelt and legions of their aides met in Washington for the Trident Conference to talk about the future of the war. As Churchill settled in and looked about the room, he recognized Stilwell, but then his eyes came to rest on an AAF brigadier general who had a face like leather left too long in the sun, burning dark eyes surrounded by crow's-feet, and an air of seething impatience.

"Who is that man?" Churchill asked an aide.

The aide looked, leaned close to Churchill, and whispered, "Chennault of China."

Churchill harrumphed and muttered, "I'm glad he is on our side."

The Brits have long had a practice of awarding their leading military heroes a title that references the name of their greatest military victory. The most famous, of course, is Lawrence of Arabia. But there was Roberts of Kandahar, Kitchener of Khartoum, Montgomery of Alamein, and, of course, Mountbatten of Burma.

Such honorifics were never bestowed upon Americans. General Douglas MacArthur would never, except in his own mind, become MacArthur of the Philippines. There would be neither Eisenhower of Normandy nor a Patton of France.

But there was a Chennault of China.

Stilwell presented his ideas about how the war in China should be conducted. Chennault presented his ideas. This time Chennault got everything he wanted, everything he had asked for in the earlier letter to Roosevelt that had been squelched by Marshall and Arnold.

The president and the prime minister were quite taken with Chennault, and Roosevelt let it be known that he would welcome more back-channel letters.

A few months later Chennault was promoted to major general and given command of the newly created Fourteenth Air Force. Chennault would be autonomous; he no longer worked for Bissell, and no longer would Stilwell have a voice in his air operations. In fact, Stilwell was ordered to give Chennault all possible cooperation.

But Stilwell got one concession. Bissell was also promoted to major general, and he was promoted one day ahead of Chennault. Bissell was still senior.


A few weeks after the Orlando incident, Scott was in Hollywood to meet with General Arnold and Jack Warner. Arnold wanted to make sure the movie reflected favorably on the AAF. The meeting was in a hotel bar, and Arnold assiduously avoided Scott during the proceedings. But after it was over and most everyone had departed, Scott saw Arnold sitting alone at the bar and joined him. For a long moment, Arnold said nothing. And then, his eyes staring back over the bar, he asked Scott if he had really said he would like to shoot John L. Lewis.

Scott said that he had voiced the quote attributed to him, but that he was speaking as a private citizen and not as an Army officer.

Arnold turned to face Scott and exploded in anger. As long as you wear that uniform, you have no private opinions, Arnold said. For several minutes he blistered Scott about his duties as a senior officer, and then he stalked off with no good-bye.

On May 14, while Scott was being revered as a war hero and was congratulating himself on a book and movie deal, his younger brother, Roland, was about to experience a pilot's worst nightmare.

A year earlier Roland had gone to McDill Field, in Tampa, Florida, the same place where Scott trained in the B-17, for training in flying the B-26 Marauder, a twin-engine medium bomber with a reputation for killing its crews. "One a day in Tampa Bay" was the word. "Widowmaker" was another. The plane had such short wings that it was called the "flying prostitute" because it had no visible means of support. But for those young men who mastered the beast, it was like flying a fighter: powerful, agile, and unforgiving.

Roland went to England in March 1942 for further training. On May 14, 1943, Roland and his crew put on their new custom-tailored dress uniforms, snugged up their ties, and adjusted their caps. This would be the first Marauder mission over Europe, and Roland was leading the raid. His crew would be the first B-26 crew over Europe, and Roland wanted them to be the best dressed.

At the pre-mission briefing, Roland looked around the room and saw a number of signs saying, "Flak Is Not A Lethal Weapon. It Is A Deterrent."

Roland took off, leading a flight of twelve B-26s to attack a power plant at IJmuiden, near Amsterdam. Both Roland and his copilot were from Georgia, and their aircraft had an idiosyncrasy that made it almost impossible to synchronize the two propellers. The aircraft made occasional "jerking" motions in flight. As a result, Roland had had "Gawja Jerk" painted on the nose of his aircraft.

The raid on IJmuiden was the first extreme-low-altitude attack made by B-26s, and the idea was to come in fast, hit hard, and get out quickly. The Marauders were below one hundred feet when they came in off the sea. But the Germans knew they were coming, and they had placed weapons in church steeples and tall buildings. From the time the B-26s crossed the beach, they were under heavy and sustained fire. Two aircraft were shot up so badly they broke off the attack, salvoed their bombs over the North Sea, and limped back to England.

A second after Roland released his bombs, the aircraft took a twenty-millimeter round in the cockpit. Both Roland and his copilot sustained serious injuries. Roland took 263 pieces of shrapnel in his face and neck. He lost his right eye.

The flight sergeant had been trained for such emergencies—to level the wings and pick up a heading that would take the aircraft back to England. The flight sergeant was wrestling the aircraft when he noticed a movement on the floor. Roland was sweeping his hand back and forth.

"Sir, I thought you were dead," the sergeant shouted. "What are you looking for?"

"My eye."

Back at home base in England, Roland, his face half shot away, refused all medical attention and ordered medical personnel to take him to the briefing room. There he tore down every sign from the wall, collapsed, and was taken to the hospital.

Roland was hospitalized for months in England undergoing reconstructive surgery, and then for additional months at a military hospital in Augusta, Georgia.

While there he was fitted for a glass eye. Later he had a second one made that was a replica of the Confederate battle flag, a third showing the U.S. flag, and a fourth representing a fish.

For the rest of his life he would wear the glass eye with the Confederate flag on May 14, the anniversary of the day he was wounded. Every July 4 he would wear the glass eye with the U.S. flag.

Looking Roland Scott in the eye could be a disconcerting experience.

When word came to the Scott family that Roland was in Augusta, Ola casually mentioned "Roland is back," but she did not go to visit him.

Roland had flown one mission, was shot down, and the mission was a failure. Her Rob had flown 388 missions, had never been shot down, and was one of the most famous pilots of the war.

Roland would bear the effects of his wounds for the rest of his life. But he rarely talked about his wartime experience. If asked about the B-26 raid on IJmuiden, about all he ever had to say was "It was an honor to have been there."

The newly formed AAF School of Applied Tactics (AAFSAT) was located near Orlando, Florida, in the town of Winter Park. It was to become a place where the Air Forces developed new aerial tactics, tested new weapons, and improved existing equipment. It was a toy store for Scott. That is, when he was in town.

Scott and Kitty Rix—using part of the money from the movie—made a down payment on a ten-acre estate in Winter Park replete with a large manor house, guest bungalows, and about a thousand orange trees. The estate was called "the Anchorage," and it was befitting for an author who had written a book and sold the movie rights.

But Scott had not yet paid off all the bills incurred from setting up Kitty Rix in the house in Macon a year earlier. And now he was spending movie money on a run-down estate. But Kitty Rix was ecstatic. At last, she and Scotty and Robin Lee had a home of their own, and away from Scott's mama. Scotty had a good job, and he would be at home. They could settle down, raise Robin Lee, and have at least two or three quiet years before Scotty was transferred again. This was Kitty Rix's dream realized. They could live like a normal civilian family.

Or so she thought.

Scott received the typed manuscript for *God Is My Co-Pilot* and the suggested edits were far too lengthy and numerous for him to scribble in the margins with a pencil. Plus, because the stenographer had so much trouble understanding Scott's Southern accent, much of the book was gibberish.

For more than two weeks, Scott worked late every night retyping the manuscript.

Charles Scribner continued to have doubts about the title. In one letter to the publisher, Scott spent more than a page attempting to justify the title. He said he had been thinking about it for three years, and that the movie people thought it was just fine.

Scott received no advance for his book. The book was almost ready for publication before Scott received the contract. Scribner offered Scott a loan of $250 against future royalties but said that if Scott needed the money, he could raise the offer to $1,000.

Scribner congratulated Scott for completing the book "in one tenth the time that even a journalist would normally take."

On April 21, 1943, Scribner began sending pieces of the manuscript to Warner Brothers. Wrote Scribner, "Everyone I have spoken to groans at the title *God Is My Co-Pilot*, but if you and the colonel are set on it we shall have to follow suit."

Scott did not know whether he or Scribner's controlled the subsidiary rights to the book, but that did not stop him from attempting to peddle them to every newspaper and magazine reporter he talked with. And they were numerous. Several newspapers wrote to Scribner's asking to print parts of the book, but they were turned down because *Life* and *Reader's Digest* were already considering the book.

On April 26, Charles Scribner wrote Scott, "The story is really fine, far ahead of anything I dared hope for."

Scott attempted to speed up production of both the book and the movie by telling Scribner's and Warner Brothers that he would be returning to China. He did not tell either that Arnold had rejected every such overture. But as a result, Scribner wrote Scott on May 10 and said, "We're following your wishes and pushing the production as hard as we can."

The book that Scott wrote during three days in March would be published in July.

# 25

# GOOD REVIEWS . . . AND BAD

THE YEAR 1943 WAS THE MOST REMARKABLE YEAR IN THE 150-YEAR history of U.S. publishing.

So said *Time* at the end of the year.

Americans would buy some three hundred million books that year, up about 25 percent over 1942.

"It's unbelievable. It's frightening," said Bennett Cerf, then president of Random House.

He said 1943 was the year that book buying pushed beyond the insular intellectual world and became part of the life of the literate population of America.

The surprise number-one publishing success that year was *One World*, Wendell Willkie's saga of his trip around the world. Not all the details of his stop in China were included.

Number two, also a surprise, was *Under Cover*, an account of journalist John Roy Carlson's four-year experience living among crooks and fascists. The book sold 550,000 copies.

So many Bibles were sold in 1943 that Manhattan bookstores had to ration them.

Then there were the war books. And at the top of the list, where it would remain for several years, was *God Is My Co-Pilot*.

While reviewers rightly categorized it as a war book, it was far more. It was the book America craved, the book America needed. Tales of glory. The saga of one man who came out of nowhere and, against all odds, achieved his dream of being a fighter pilot.

To put the book in perspective, it was published a year before D-day. Marines were leaving trails of blood—their own as well as that of Japanese soldiers—across unknown little islands in the Pacific. But most Americans had never heard of those islands, and there were so many of them and they were so hard to find on the maps.

The Allies had invaded North Africa the previous November, but Africa was so far away and so bewildering that it was difficult to understand the significance of that campaign.

The invasion of Sicily began in mid-July, about the time Scott's book was published, and while it gave Americans a better mental picture of the war, Sicily was still a preamble to the invasion of Europe. Americans knew a European invasion was coming, but no one knew when. It was all so vague.

But America could read Scott's book, and it was as if they were in the cockpit with him as he strafed the Burma Road or dropped bombs on barges in the Salween River or shot up the penthouse in the Peninsula Hotel. They could visualize the enemy aircraft in his gun sight, and they could feel the cold hand of the Training Command reaching out to pull Scott back to America and thwart his destiny.

The book made it appear that Scott was winning the war in China by himself. He was at the center of the story and, to civilians, the story was a magnetic one. But Scott's military colleagues knew enough about the CBI to realize that much of the story was exaggerated. Within the AAF, the book soon became a burden to Scott.

Young men could nod with approval of the big lie he told about flying the B-17. American boys had a history of lying about their ages in order to fight for their country. What ole Scotty did was the same thing. He just wanted to go off and kill Japs. He left his wife and baby daughter to go off to China. That's what men do.

We wanted to know America was winning, that we were defeating the sneaky and treacherous Japanese who had bombed Pearl Harbor without first bothering to declare war. In answer to that need, here came Colonel Robert Lee Scott Jr. of Macon, Georgia, made all the more glamorous because he was such an unlikely hero.

And just as Scott was a symbol of America's need to triumph, he was a symbol of every American's desire to overcome the circumstances of his birth, to triumph over adversity, achieve great things, and make his parents proud.

The AAF had thought Scott was too old to be a fighter pilot, too old to go to war. But he had gone to war and become a fighter pilot and shown he could shoot better, bomb better, and fly better than the hotshot young pilots. To use a phrase beloved by editors, the book worked on two levels: as a war book, and as the story of an unlikely man achieving great things.

On both levels the book was an unqualified success.

The man of action had become a man of words, equally famous in both worlds.

Charles Scribner hoped to publish *God Is My Co-Pilot* before Doolittle Raider Ted Lawson's book *Thirty Seconds over Tokyo* was released, on July 12. But Scott's book was slow to make it through the wartime censors—a number of place names had to be omitted—and July 26 was the publication date. Once again, Jimmy Doolittle had beaten Scott to the target.

Scribner continued to think the title was "unfortunate."

The book cost $2.50. It was dedicated to Hap Arnold, "who, more than any other person, is responsible for the Air Force coming of age."

Arnold never acknowledged the dedication, a silence that devastated Scott. He was so tone-deaf that he never realized that Arnold was probably miffed that Chennault had written the introduction.

Chennault wrote that when Scott was under his command, Scott had scheduled himself for all possible missions but "specialized in the most dangerous, such as long-range flights to strafe from minimum altitudes Jap airdromes, motor vehicles, and shipping deep in enemy territory."

He said Scott's story of "persistence, determination, and courage from early boyhood . . . should be an inspiration to every American boy."

John Chamberlain of the *New York Times* said that, while Scott had no flair for titles, he had a "downright genius for writing about his own Gargantuan living." Chamberlain said Scott's work was "a great American biography as well as a great war book."

The *New Yorker* sniffed at the "faintly megalomaniac title" but agreed the book was a "humdinger," and that Scott's writing was "just about as *sui generis* as Davy Crockett's and in the same tradition."

The *American Mercury* said, "Easily the most fascinating book by an American military man to come out of World War II."

Wolfgang Langewiesche, the most famous aviation writer of the day, had the best insight into the nature of the book. He said it was "really an old-fashioned success story—the kind that used to mean to people all over the world the story of life in America." In parallel to this was an additional insight into what made the book so popular with boys: "Scott's respect for regulations and red tape is not excessive."

But as any writer knows, it is the critical reviews that are best-remembered. More than fifty years after publication, Scott would often quote a review: "Here is presented, under the misleading title, *God Is My Co-Pilot*, what I must call not only a new style in literature, but a new form. The author doesn't attempt to write in any known language, but a sort of colloquialism I can only classify as Georgiaese. . . . In my opinion, if all the dangling participles and split infinitives—drawled as they are—were placed end to end, they would reach to China."

Scott did not remember the publication, only the words.

Scott appeared on a radio show to promote the book. With him were Ernest Hemingway and Marjorie Kinnan Rawlings. Scott began by apologizing for even being there. He said he was not in the same league as his fellow Scribner's writers. Hemingway interrupted and said it took him years to write a book and Scott had written one in three days. Stop apologizing for writing a best-seller, Hemingway told him.

A week after publication, the book went into a third printing. In August, the book was the main selection for the Book of the Month Club. By October, fifty-five thousand copies were in print. By December it would be eighty-five thousand, and Scribner told Scott, "You can expect a telegram from me some day early next year when we print the one hundred-thousandth copy." For two years the book was on the best-seller list. Ripley's *Believe It or Not*, a popular syndicated newspaper feature for decades, featured it as the book written in three days.

By today's lights, the book is dated wartime propaganda. It has technical flaws and factual errors. The book is episodic, has little sense of proportion, and has no sense of Scott's marriage or child. He refers once to "my wife," and once to "Catharine," but talks at length of his mother and her impact on his life. Scott mentions friends, fellow pilots, and crewmen often, but only by their last names. He would devote a full chapter to a single flight in China but almost nothing to his family.

The dialogue is stilted, wooden, tone-deaf, and clearly re-created. In his comments about the war, Scott shows that, while he operated well at the tactical level, he was neither a strategist nor a historian. Or an honest reporter.

The book is marked throughout by Scott's paranoia. He was always looking over his shoulder because "they" wanted to ground him or make him be an instructor or keep him out of combat.

One of the most curious omissions of the book is the story of how he came by the title. It would be years before he explained that when Old Exterminator was shot up by a Japanese fighter pilot over Victoria Harbor, some of the bullets hit the armor behind Scott's seat and slammed rivets into his back. He would later claim that the injury required surgery performed without anesthesia in a mountain cave where he had seen in dancing flames the words "God Is My Co-Pilot."

In the book, he never mentions being wounded on the flight. And if he was wounded, why did he not receive a Purple Heart? No one as medal-hungry as Scott would have let such a medal slip by.

But the book works. While not a great, or even a good, writer, Scott was a great storyteller. He later would write—by his count—sixteen books. But *God Is My Co-Pilot*, which would become known simply as "the Book," is the truest, almost certainly because he talked it in three days, and because the legend of Robert Scott was still forming. Scott was just beginning to grapple with his fame. And given that the book was spoken, he could not go back and read what he had said. Then there was the rush to publish. As a result, readers received Scott's first, and therefore most important, memories. Most of Scott's later books are elaborate, fanciful, and even fabulist extensions of the stories told in *God Is My Co-Pilot*.

The value of the book is threefold. First, for untold thousands of boys in the middle and late 1940s and beyond, this was the first book they ever read that had no pictures. The book caused a generation of boys to draw shark-mouthed P-40s in their school notebooks and on scraps of paper. And more than sixty years later, the shark-mouthed P-40 remains a favorite among airplane modelers.

Second, the book motivated thousands of boys to go into aviation. And even as late as 2015, the book was often found in the libraries of retired fighter pilots. Well-thumbed. The book remains in print to this day.

Third, the book is a paean to the Flying Tigers. Granted, they had a certain measure of fame before Scott's book. But whether or not that fame would have lived on is open to question. That it did live on is due in large part to Scott's book and to the movie based on his book. Scott made the Flying Tigers immortal.

A final, more general comment about authors in general. Those who write books are granted an intellectual status that may not be deserved. Granted, one must have a modicum of intelligence to conceive and execute the prolonged experience of writing a book. But qualities other than intelligence are more important. Perseverance, for instance.

Scott was not greatly burdened by his West Point education. His writing career can be attributed more to Southern defensiveness, determination, and a desire to stay ahead of the IRS than to a great intellect.

In November 1943, Scott beseeched the publisher to send him $15,000 against royalties so he could "cover payments on my home when they become due in December as well as solving the 1943 and 1944 income tax." Scribner agreed.

Scott said he would soon have the new manuscript in the mail. Again, he dictated a book. But this time he had the manuscript edited by a historian before he sent it to New York.

As an early Christmas present, Scott shipped several cases of oranges from his grove in Winter Park to the people at Scribner's.

# 26

# MOVIE STAR

Scott was becoming a problem child for Arnold. No one in the AAF was so good at bringing attention to U.S. military aviation. The media loved Scott. Reporters flocked to him, and they could not get enough of his stories.

Arnold thought Scott should devote more attention to his duties and less to the publishing and movie business.

But he knew, as did anyone who came in touch with Scott, that in January Hodder & Stoughton, a British publisher, had bought the rights to the Book. They knew that Scribner's had printed ninety thousand copies and soon would print more. They also knew that Scott had almost completed his next book, *Damned to Glory,* and would soon send it to New York.

With the book out and the movie coming along, more publicity would accrue to the AAF. It did not matter that most people in America did not know the difference between the AVG and the Twenty-third Fighter Group. It did not matter that Scott had never been in the AVG. All that mattered was that Scott's book had caused America to fall in love with the Flying Tigers and the AAF.

Arnold did not like Scott, but he needed him. Arnold was as tough-minded as a general is supposed to be, and he would keep his eyes on the higher goal. He would indulge Scott. But invariably there would be what psychologists call "leakage." Arnold's anger toward Scott would emerge, and Scott would be devastated.

On February 7, 1944, an official at Warner Brothers sent a telegram to the Pentagon asking that Scott be assigned to them while the script was being written, and then that he be allowed to serve as technical advisor to the movie, the shooting of which would start upon completion of the script.

Arnold agreed. Scott was now assigned indefinitely to Warner Brothers. The studio put Scott up in the Sunset Tower, where, according to Scott, his fellow tenants included Frank Sinatra and Jack Benny.

Kitty Rix didn't care who his fellow tenants might be. She and Robin Lee had been left behind in Florida, all the way across the country.

What Kitty Rix did not yet know was that Jack Warner owned a house in Malibu, and that he had given Scott keys to it. Scott spent many weekends at the beach house, almost always in the company of a beautiful movie star.

It is possible that the genesis of Robin's later estrangement from her father had its roots in the empty big house in the orange grove.

On March 20, 1944, Warner Brothers' Jack Moffitt sent an interoffice note to Hal Wallis, saying that the script was "excellent," and that it had a "freshness that differentiates it from previous air stories." That letter may have crossed in the mail with a March 26 letter Scott wrote on Sunset Tower stationery to Scribner's in which he complained about how difficult it was to find copies of the Book in California. It was the first of many such letters he would write from many places and, according to Scott's correspondence with Scribner's, marks the beginning of his becoming a very difficult and demanding author. By now paper shortages had hit America hard, and Scott would become impatient in the extreme with the lack of books.

When Scott's mother heard that Humphrey Bogart had been offered the role of playing Scott in the movie, she was outraged. She did not like Bogie, and she wanted someone else to play the role of her son. Scott relayed her concerns to Warner Brothers.

Scott's mother need not have been concerned. Bogie refused to take the role, and he was suspended without pay for forty-two days as a result. Dennis Morgan was cast as Scott instead.

At some point in the shooting, Scott says, he flew to Washington to ask Arnold to send him back to China. As Scott began talking, Arnold stood up behind his desk, walked to the window, and looked at the view. He listened, and when Scott finished, Arnold never turned around. He continued looking at the view as he told Scott the movie was important to the AAF, and that it would help in the postwar unification battle. Scott was to go back to California, and he was to do what he was told.

The flying scenes in the movie were splendid, no doubt because the combat scenes involving the P-40s were flown by Ed Rector and Tex Hill, two of the original Flying Tigers. That two Flying Tigers flew in the movie is important. First, it added greatly to the credibility of the combat scenes. Second, in later years when it was said that the Flying Tigers disliked Scott, this incident would be used to rebut that argument.

During the filming of an aerial sequence on August 22, 1944, a B-25 and an AT-6 trainer—the latter painted to resemble a Japanese Zero—collided. Four men were killed. Even as *God Is My Co-Pilot* was under production, Scott's second book, *Damned to Glory,* was set for publication in October. In the meantime, Scott had written twenty thousand words of his third book, *Runway to the Sun.* By his count Scott would eventually write sixteen books. But that number is inflated, since Scott counted translations and condensations as separate books. And one of his books was self-published.

Readers should not feel deprived if they have not read all of Scott's books, or when they find that all but one is out of print. If you have read *God Is My Co-Pilot,* you have read Scott.

The script writing, filming, and editing were conducted almost as rapidly as the book. The movie was set for release in early 1945.

Like the book, the movie has numerous technical flaws and factual errors. The movie, for instance, has Scott being shot down.

Like the book, the movie is of a heroic man winning the war by himself, a pilot who flies with brave Americans and achieves victory over great odds.

Scott took a copy of the movie to Washington and showed it to Arnold and his staff. Scott reported that Arnold believed the movie would be good for the military. But, as later comments from Hollywood would indicate, several of the viewers, including Arnold, thought it was a stinker.

On October 19, 1944, Stilwell received notice that he would soon be sent home. Barbara Tuchman and others all have good and compelling theories as to the reasons for the recall. But Stilwell had tried a power play, and the effort failed. Chiang, at Chennault's urging, delivered an ultimatum to Roosevelt: I cannot work with Stilwell. Any other officer you send will be acceptable.

Stilwell was a brilliant officer, but he had acerbic opinions about America's allies in the CBI, and he could not keep those opinions to himself. He was the wrong man for the job that he had been given.

Chennault had won. Both he and Scott were pleased.

Hap Arnold was not. Maybe his bombers did not always get through, but he was a five-star AAF general, and he did. A day of payback was coming.


Catharine and Robin Lee had come to Hollywood for a few weeks that same month. But about the time that Stilwell received notice that he was being sent home, Scott told Catharine and Robin that it was time for them to return to Florida, to the big house in the orange grove. He sent them home by train, and he said he would fly home later.


On February 11, 1945, Scott wrote Wallace Meyer, his editor at Scribner's, that he was at Winter Park awaiting the premiere of the movie in Macon. He said that he had been notified that there would be a possum hunt and a Junior League dance before the premiere, and that a camellia had been named after him.

Scott said that he had pulled up 135 diseased orange trees and replaced them with "perfect specimens" of "Temple, Parson Brown, Lui Gen Gong, and Valencia."


On February 21, 1945, the world premiere of *God Is My Co-Pilot* was held in Macon. City fathers wanted to have a third Robert Scott Day, but they were trumped by Governor Ellis Arnall, who issued a proclamation that decreed February 21 as Robert Lee Scott—God Is My Co-Pilot Day, not only in Macon, but all across Georgia.

To the good people of Macon, and to all the people of Georgia, the idea of a movie premiere about a local man was an event of near-biblical proportions. The idea that Hollywood was coming to Macon was almost impossible to grasp.

But seventy-five thousand people came to Macon to see a parade featuring Scott and the stars of the movie, Dennis Morgan and Andrea King.

Even by today's standards, and even in a town much larger than Macon, it is difficult to imagine a parade drawing so many people.

The parade took two hours to pass.

This was Scott's second parade down Cherry Street in the town where he grew up, and where he recognized many in the crowd. He was up front in the parade, and he rode in what the newspaper called a "bullock cart" symbolizing conditions in China. He was flanked by the uniformed members of Boy Scout Troop 23.

People cheered when Scott rode by. But he was from Macon, and it was the movie stars that the people of Macon came to see. And their enthusiasm had only increased when the movie stars approached the Grand Opera House for the premiere.

The *Macon Telegraph* reported, "Matinee idol worship became uncontrollable and almost reached hysterical proportions."

Women charged Dennis Morgan armed with large scissors; one cut a button and "a large swath" from the front of his coat.

Women broke past the police guard in front of the Dempsey Hotel and attempted to enter rooms where the stars were staying.

The parade, the Robert Scott Day, the premiere, having movie stars in the Dempsey Hotel, all brought out what in middle Georgia is called the "country-come-to-town" syndrome. It was rubes in church clothes acting like what they were. This was Macon in full gaga mode for Hollywood glamour. This was something to remember, like Ely's crash back in 1911. If Maconites would steal pieces of clothing from a dead pilot, they could certainly snip off items of clothing from live movie stars. This was mass hysteria. And it all centered on Rob Scott, who grew up over on East Napier Avenue. You remember Rob? He was the one who flunked his last year at Lanier. Since then he has really come up in the world.

The day after the premiere of the eighty-nine-minute movie, a Warner Brothers representative who signed his telegrams "Mort" sent word back to a man named Charlie Enfield at the studio in Hollywood saying, "Just had what probably the finest civic demonstration ever given a world premiere." His summary: "Simply magnificent."

———

To celebrate, Scott took Catharine to New York for a shopping trip at Saks. That venerable store was so impressed by the visit that a giant photograph of Scott was placed in the window.

The tabloid *Film Daily* reviewed the movie under a headline that said, "THRILLS AND EXCITEMENT APLENTY IN STIRRING TALE OF HERO'S AIR EXPLOITS." It summarized the movie as "Rousing entertainment packed with thrills and red-blooded antics."

*Motion Picture Daily* said that during the first weeks in the box office the movie led movie sales across the country, bringing in "an outstanding $183,500" in nine key cities, where the par was $153,700. Extended engagements were common.

The *Hollywood Reporter* of May 22 said that *God Is My Co-Pilot* was "one of the best of all the air pictures."

The *Time* issue of April 2 wrote of "swift and explosive air combat" that was "about as exciting as such material can hope to be." And *Variety* of February 22 wrote of "a surging feeling of drama." But the *New Yorker* continued to dislike the title, and in the March 24 issue the magazine's reviewer damned the movie with faint praise.

Fame is a bitch; a savage and heartless Circe who demands far more than she gives. Fame can destroy a man. If he is not careful, one day he will wake up and find that the streets of glory have become alleys of despair.

Scott was in his mid-thirties when Fame sucked him into the maelstrom. At heart he was an uncomplicated young man from middle Georgia who wanted nothing more than to be a fighter pilot. Flying was all he cared about.

But now he was famous beyond his wildest dreams.

Adulation came from all quarters save one: Scott's brother officers in the AAF. They could read between the lines. They knew some of the people who had served with Scott, who had flown with him, and many of these veterans considered him a bullshit artist of epic dimensions. The most charitable would shrug and say something about how "Scotty sure knows how to tell a good story," or "Scotty likes to pump things up a bit." Those less charitable, and perhaps those with a bit of jealousy, dismissed him as just another Southern blowhard, a windbag who took credit for winning the war. "Hell, he was never a Flying Tiger. He was regular Army who took over when the military federalized the Tigers."

And there was that story about the masking tape over the gun ports.


Chennault's letters now chided Scott about his "cushy job," and said that Scott's skill and experience were needed back in China with the young pilots.

If there was one man on earth Scott wanted to please, it was Claire Chennault. Again he flew to Washington to ask Arnold to send him back to China, but Arnold was too busy to see him. Scott holed up in a hotel near the Pentagon and began calling. Arnold would not take his calls. On the third day he told Arnold's secretary that he was going to call every hour until his call was put through. The idea of a colonel calling the commanding general of the AAF to demand an assignment is contrary to the fundamental hierarchy of the military. But Scott was a decorated combat hero, the author of a best-selling book, and the subject of a movie. He *knew* Hap Arnold. They had watched his movie together.

Scott was put in his place when he heard Arnold's secretary announce that Colonel Scott was calling again, and in the background Arnold's gruff voice: "Colonel Scott? Do you mean God's personal pilot?"


Scott's months in Hollywood during the shooting of the movie came at a pivotal time in his life. He had been married for more than a decade and he had the desire of the long-married man to fall in love one more time. He was lionized by the most beautiful and best-known movie stars of the time. He knew Hedy Lamarr and Frances Langford and Ann Sheridan and Bette Davis and Rosalind Russell and Arlene Dahl and Rhonda Fleming and a beautiful model-actress named Phyllis Kirk, and many others. Some of them he knew rather well.

His fame was different from their fame, and they were drawn to Scott. And he to them.

Today there is a strong magnetism between Washington politicians and Hollywood stars. But in 1944 Hollywood was fascinated by the military and military heroes. It was a moment in time, and both Scott and those

Hollywood leading ladies, perhaps impelled in part by the war, took full advantage of it.

All the way across the country, back at the prison in the orange grove, Kitty Rix roamed the big rooms and drank big drinks. She never acquired the polish, urbanity, and ease that had grown on Scott. She was still the princess of Peach County, the daughter of the mayor, the drama major, the girl who still did her nails after she went to bed.

The book and the movie generated a certain amount of animosity toward Scott that would hound him beyond his retirement. They also generated more money than Scott knew how to handle. Though the amount was modest by today's standards, it was enough—when combined with Scott's lack of experience and his desire to spend everything he made—to create problems with the Internal Revenue Service. He owed the IRS some $25,000.

He would remain in trouble with the IRS for most of the rest of his life.

By now Arnold had had enough of Scott and ordered him back to China, not so much to satisfy Scott's heartfelt desire as to get rid of him. Arnold wanted Scott out of the country as much as Scott wanted to be out of the country.

Scott thought it was a good thing when he returned to China. But Kitty Rix did not. She was about five months pregnant and saw no reason for Scotty to be dashing off to China again.

And she saw no reason to return to Macon as she had done when Scott first went to China. This time she and Robin would remain in Florida, far away from Scott's mother.

# 27

## CHIAROSCURO

APRIL 1945 WAS A PIVOTAL MONTH IN WORLD WAR II. HITLER COMmitted suicide. Germany surrendered. Roosevelt died and Truman became president. The U.S. Marines invaded Okinawa. *God Is My Co-Pilot* opened in theaters across America, and Colonel Robert Lee Scott Jr. returned to China.

He was an altogether different man from the Robert Scott who had first come to China, three years earlier. Scott had come to the war as a refuge from the Training Command, and he returned as one of the most famous officers in the theater. He had a flair and a dash possessed by no other man in the CBI. His book had made the rounds in China, and he was moving heaven and earth to get copies of the movie there so that everyone could see how he had already won the war.

Scotty brought a Confederate battle flag with him, showed it to all, and said he brought it for General Chennault to sign.

It is a measure of Scott's fame that when he returned to China, Hap Arnold had transferred him to the General Staff. Scott was no longer a combat pilot, but a staff officer. His collar insignia no longer was a tiny propeller superimposed on gold wings, but the Great Seal of the United States upon which was imposed a silver star.

And he carried orders that specifically said he would not fly missions behind enemy lines.

Were he to be shot down, the propaganda value to the Japanese would be incalculable.

---

If Scott had changed, so had the CBI. So had the war.

The dream, the promise, the chance for glory that Scott had found when he landed in Karachi back in April 1942 were gone when he returned.

The end of the war was approaching, and the end of a war can be as confusing and jangled as the beginning.

The Fourteenth Air Force, commanded by Major General Claire Lee Chennault, was not the scraggly expeditionary force it had been back in the summer of 1943. Now the Fourteenth had twenty thousand men and more than a thousand aircraft. New fighters, including the P-51 Mustang, at last were coming into the theater. Big bombers lined the edges of many airfields. Transports flying the Hump were landing every two minutes on Chinese fields, bringing gas, bullets and bombs, all necessary bureaucratic supplies, and even luxury items for the Gissimo and Madame.

Chennault's aircraft dominated the skies of China and, with the full backing of the Gissimo and the Princess, he pressed Hap Arnold to let the Fourteenth Air Force take its bombers to Tokyo. Arnold said no.

By now the end of the war in Europe was in sight. The great Stilwell had been sent home in disgrace, and the CBI was viewed as the place where careers went to die.

Bissell had been transferred to the U.S. and later to England, where there were allegations about his involvement in a coffee-smuggling business. Bissell retired and, several years later, when called to testify before a congressional committee, further tarnished his legacy by suppressing a report that Soviet forces were behind the mass killing of Polish officers at the Katyn Forest massacre.

Chiang and the Dragon Lady had grown more imperious and more demanding, Chennault had the bit in his teeth, and all three were impossible to deal with. The Chiangs wanted more money for themselves and more men to fight the Communists . . . and, oh, yes, the Japanese as well. In a few more years the Communists would emerge triumphant, and Chiang would flee to Formosa (now Taiwan) trailing behind him odious allegations of mass corruption, indulgence, and incompetence.

He was the wrong man for the job.

As for the Brits, Dickie Mountbatten's wife, the not-so-fair Edwina, was having affairs with numerous men, including an Indian politician named Jawaharlal Nehru. Dickie, Edwina, and Jawaharlal would draw the lines of partition that created Pakistan and later Bangladesh. Like most lines drawn by colonial masters, especially the British, the lines were disastrous.

But for now Dickie was Mountbatten of Burma and demonstrating that he was the wrong man for the job.

The CBI had begun with such glory, hope, and promise. Now it had devolved into a snake pit of clashing personalities, conflicting desires, and colliding disunity.

America was winning everywhere. May 8 was Victory in Europe Day—VE-day. The Marines and the Army had marched across the Pacific, and now there was talk of invading the Japanese homeland. Everyone sensed that Japan's days were numbered.

Chennault's days were numbered, too. He was in trouble with Arnold, but thought he would be allowed to stay the course in China. He had been there before the beginning.

Chennault had heard the rumors that Scott had changed—that Scott had come to believe he was as important as people told him he was. The rumors were true. Scott had spent most of the past two years in the bubble of celebrity surrounding his return as a war hero, his book, and the movie. Not only had he slept with many of the most famous and most beautiful actresses of the day, he had boasted about it.

It was decades later before Scott wrote of his return to China. But because Scott was living the legend rather than the facts, we must proceed carefully, very carefully, in recounting the facts in the spring and summer of 1945. Scott's official personnel records appear to have been altered, and thus the events of the time are hazy. Moreover, Scott began to merge events in the movie with events in his own life and to believe it was the movie that was true.

On May 25, Scott wrote a letter to a Warner studio executive asking why Chennault had not received a copy of the movie as promised.

On June 6, the studio executive responded by saying that Chennault soon would have a copy, that "the picture is a great box office hit" and "is being held over everywhere," and that even though people in Washington had said that the movie was a turkey, they had been proven wrong because the movie "is going very big everywhere."

———

When Scott returned to China, events in his life were happening quickly and overlapping with events in Chennault's life.

Scott's story of his return to China centers around high-velocity aircraft rockets (HVARs). But there is no way to reconcile his story about the rockets and the Air Force history of those rockets in China. Scott says he was responsible for sending 200,000 rockets to the CBI. The Air Force says it had seventy-five. Scott says that in a single day his men blew up forty-nine locomotives and that his program was so successful that Japanese trains moved only at night. Air Force history says that only 25 percent of the rockets hit their targets, and that the program was ineffective.

The rockets arrived in the CBI late in the war, and it was August 1 before the first HVAR mission was flown. Scott led the mission and, according to the history of the Fourteenth Air Force, he demolished a flak tower and took out part of a small bridge. The last HVAR mission was flown on August 6. Thus, the HVAR missile program of which Scott makes mythic dimensions in reality was a brief and irrelevant sideshow.

But no matter. Scott tells one story of those days that is worth repeating. The story may not be true, but Scott made it true and later would often retell the story.

He says that one day he was flying far north in China and returning from a mission that had taken him almost to Shanghai. It was one of those days when a pilot can see forever. He has several versions of the story but the thrust of it is that on the return flight he followed the Great Wall west to the mountains north of the Yellow River. He flew a low, high-speed dance, wingtip to wingtip, and swung back and forth across the wall, looking for Nankow Pass, the place he had first seen as a Boy Scout in the doctor's office, the panoramic photograph he had carried for years. He could see his shadow on the ground and positioned his aircraft between the wall and the sun so that his shadow tracked along the wall at more than three hundred miles an hour. He keyed his microphone and said, "Thank you, Lord for guiding me here. But please, oh, please, may I return someday and walk down there where my shadow walks?"

He was almost at sea level as he approached what he recognized as the promontory of the Old Dragon's Head, the end of the Great Wall.

"Some supernatural force had drawn me there like a magnet," Scott later wrote.

Several weeks earlier, on July 6, 1945, Chennault received orders bringing him home. The same orders said that all offensive air operations would cease until the new commanding officer arrived.

Arnold had prevailed. Chennault had committed what for a military man is the most egregious of mistakes. He had used unorthodox tactics and he had been extraordinarily successful. His men had destroyed more than two thousand Japanese aircraft, sunk more than two and a quarter million tons of enemy shipping, killed more than fifty thousand Japanese, and held a million Japanese troops at bay. The aerial-combat tactics that he had devised were the template for American fighter pilots in the Pacific.

Chennault had enjoyed a second act in his life such as few men are privileged to know.

Because Chennault had been so close to Chiang and Madame Chiang, and because of the Chiang's extraordinary influence in Washington, Arnold had left Chennault in China long after he wanted to bring him home. Chennault had been a major factor in General Marshall's recall of Stilwell. He was a part of the reason Bissell had been reassigned to England. But now the Japanese were on the run. Now the war was winding down. Arnold knew that Chennault would request retirement when he returned. And Arnold knew that he would approve that request.

This was the second time the Air Force had pushed Chennault into an unwanted retirement. And the scars from the first time were not enough to cover the pain of the second.

Scott had nominated Chennault for the Medal of Honor, and many of the men who had served under Chennault endorsed the effort. But Stilwell's shadow was long. As Chennault's superior for several years in the CBI, he still had a voice in the approval process. And he turned it down, surely with no small degree of satisfaction.

Chennault had been in China for eight years, and he had written history large. If Arnold refused to accept Chennault's accomplishments, the Chinese were more than willing to embrace them.

Rarely has China put on a display for an American as it did for Chennault. General Xue Yue, known as the Tiger of Changsha, was still fighting both the Communists and the Japanese, but he marched for two days to reach Chennault. The general gave Chennault his Sam Browne belt, and there were tears in his eyes as Chennault flew away.

Chennault left China on August 8, three days after the first atomic bomb was dropped on Hiroshima. And as he departed from Kunming, the base long associated with the Flying Tigers, thousands of firecrackers exploded. The Chinese believe that firecrackers frighten away devils and they wanted Chennault's path free of devils.

Chennault was approaching Cairo on August 9 when the pilot informed him the second atomic bomb had been dropped on Nagasaki.

The date is not known, nor are the details, but sometime while Scott was in China, Kitty Rix had a late-term miscarriage. She was carrying twins, a boy and a girl.

Her grief was great, both over losing the twins and because she had to go through the ordeal alone.

On August 12, 1945, Scott wrote a letter to "Mama & Daddy" from the Hotel Mount Everest in Darjeeling, where he had been grounded by monsoon rains while ferrying a P-51 to China. He said he would be coming home soon and was glad because he was tired of war. He ended by telling his parents he was quite near Everest and Kanchenjunga but if it were not for the rains he would try to climb them both.

This is typical Scott bravado. Climbers plan such trips months in advance, are part of a group, lug equipment, hire guides, and then there is the trek, which can take weeks. But if it were not raining he would climb them both.

Scott still had to impress Mama.

On September 2, the Japanese formally surrendered at a ceremony held in Tokyo Bay aboard the battleship USS *Missouri*. Most of the American generals and admirals who had fought the Japanese were given the honor of being present, as were their Allied counterparts. Chennault should have been there. He had fought the Japanese longer than anyone else. But Arnold deprived Chennault of his heart's desire. When the Japanese surrendered, Chennault was back in the swamps of Waterproof, Louisiana.

Scott later wrote that he led a flight of P-51 Mustangs as part of a vast victory armada that flew over the battleship USS *Missouri* during the surrender ceremony. He said that he cracked open the canopy of his fighter and pushed the Confederate battle flag out to fly in the slipstream as an honor to Chennault.

On September 27, Scott wrote a "Dear Charlie" letter to Charles Scribner. Scribner was a "Mr. Scribner" sort, maybe Charles to close friends, but he was most assuredly not a "Charlie" and the salutation must have surprised him.

Scott's letter came on the stationery of the Beverly Hills Hotel, and he said he was in Hollywood to talk about a movie based on *Runway to the Sun*. Wrote Scott, "I had to travel all over California to find six copies of" the Book, and he complained that some bookstores had not even heard of it. Scott griped, "The book was never advertised—in most cases not even announced." And he complained that his new book was being promoted as a book for juveniles rather than as another book by the author of *God Is My Co-Pilot*.

Scribner's reply, as always to Scott and, one cannot help but believe, to all of his writers, was patient and courtly. Scribner said the new book had always been considered a juvenile book, and that to position it as an adult book would open it to the criticism that it was a rehash of the first part of *God Is My Co-Pilot*.

Scribner goes on for more than a page, patiently and courteously.

On October 5, Scott wrote another "Dear Charlie" letter and picked up the conversation by saying, "Now don't you go and get mad with me and agree with Mr. Perkins that ALL would be writers are bastards."

He asked Scribner to forget the September 27 letter from Beverly Hills, admitting with an unusual degree of self-analysis, "When I am out there maybe I don't think right."

Then Scott took off for South Dakota to shoot pheasants, and then for Wyoming to shoot elk.

In late 1945, Charles Scribner's Sons published Scott's second book, *Runway to the Sun*, the book he had been working on since shortly after sending off the manuscript for *God Is My Co-Pilot*. Again, Scott dictated the text, and it was an updated and supercharged version of the Book. For example, in this book the queen of Romania and her daughter visited West Point while Scott was a student. He danced with the princess, and had her ask her mother to request the commandant to grant amnesty to all cadets who were facing hours of punishment. It was a great story, but it was fiction.

Also in this book, Scott recounted how, when he was a teenager on the crew of a tramp steamer, he had tied a rope around his waist and persuaded the crew to lower him over the side so he could swim in the middle of the ocean while, only a few feet away, there was a twenty-ton propeller "trying to pull me through it and cut me into small pieces."

# 28

## TWILIGHT

Scott did not realize that when the war ended, so did his usefulness to Hap Arnold.

Now Arnold would have his pound of flesh. The retribution would be painful, prolonged, and humiliating. Although Arnold would retire in another six months, his successors, and some of Scott's contemporaries, would work to marginalize the One-Man Air Force.

When Scott came home in September, his military career was essentially over. The war in which he had served so bravely was finished. His destiny was realized. Now there would be a reduction of forces and the pale between-the-wars jobs. It would be another eleven years before Scott retired, and the first five of those years would be spent in a series of short-term and relatively inconsequential jobs.

Scott was still living in his glory days in the immediate postwar period, but now his stories had to get bigger and better and even further from the truth. He could not help himself, and he would continue to embellish his life story even when he knew that many people did not believe him.

In 1948, Scott was assigned to Williams Air Force Base. Located about thirty miles southeast of Phoenix, Arizona, it was only a four-hour drive or a short flying hop from there to visit his friends in Hollywood.

Scott wanted Catharine and Robin Lee to stay in the big Winter Park mansion while he was in Arizona. He said he would fly home on weekends.

Catharine would have no part in such a plan. She presided over the sale of the house, and then she and Robin Lee moved to Williams, where the Scott family lived in a converted hospital ward.

Catharine was tired of being left behind. Living in a cramped former hospital ward with one's husband and daughter was better than living alone in Florida. Catharine wanted Robin Lee to grow up in something approaching a traditional home. And she may have thought that if the Scott family lived together, then Scotty would not succumb to the pull of Hollywood.

On April 6, 1948, Scott wrote a bitter letter to his publisher saying that it was impossible to find his book even though there was a "popular demand" for it, that he did not understand why the book was not available and why Scribner was not pushing it when in fact "it would have sold better than books that you continue to keep publishing."

Scott was so upset about what he perceived as a lackadaisical attitude at Scribner's that—without notifying the publisher of his intentions—he began negotiating with Doubleday about reprinting *God Is My Co-Pilot*. It was the beginning of his breakup not only with a publisher that had done so much for him, but with Charles Scribner, who, if his letters to Scott are any indication, had both respect and affection for Scott. And it goes back to three things. First, Scott was like many writers, in that his expectations for his book were unreasonable. Second, the national publicity Scott had received in China, the great success of his book, and the popularity of the movie based on the book had all turned his head. Third, the relationship between Scott and several movie actresses had caused Scott to lose his moorings, to become adrift in a world with no reference points. Now that Scott was stationed in Phoenix, about to become qualified to fly jets, and commander of the first jet-fighter school in the new and independent Air Force, he was an even more glamorous figure to Hollywood stars, and he would resume some old relationships, begin some new ones, and drift even farther from the shore.

Scott was forty years old when he came to Williams. But his need to impress people was such that he was making speeches from the time he arrived. Many of the speeches were in venues quite distant from Phoenix, and they were made at government expense. Scott's idea of his place in history was such that he ordered his public information office to provide the Wing historian with copies of each speech he delivered.

In March 1949, Scott delivered six speeches, three of them local and one each in Texas, Ohio, and New York.

That same month Scott wrote a "Dear Charlie" letter to Scribner, telling the publisher of the speeches he was making, plus the fact that almost six hundred aviation cadets were coming through Williams every five weeks. He wanted Scribner's to send twenty-five copies of the Book "right now" and begin sending at least a hundred copies every month to the base for sale in the BX.

Scott said he had spoken to more than 700,000 Boy Scouts in the past year, and he figured that had books been available at his speeches, he could have sold fifty thousand copies.

Scribner replied that when Churchill asked to have copies of his book at events, no more than ten books were ever sold after a speech. He told Scott what every publisher knows, and what no writer wants to accept: There is little connection between speechmaking and bookselling.


In July 1949, Scott wrote Scribner saying "The income tax people are still worrying me" and asked for a detailed breakdown of his sales.

Scribner replied with a table entitled "Amount reported to Government" on all of Scott's books: $26,153.44 in 1943; $17,236.36 in 1944; $15,444.27 in 1945; $7,560.12 in 1946; and $489.55 in 1947.

It was impossible for Scott to stay ahead of the IRS.

And it was impossible for Scott to stay away from Hollywood.

The August 4, 1949, issue of *Variety* reported that Scott was in Hollywood "dickering with several studios" over what the paper called a "new jet pilot story."

Wherever Scott traveled he visited bookstores to see if his books were in stock and how they were displayed. On one of these trips to Hollywood he sauntered into a used-book store and saw a used copy of *God Is My Co-Pilot* he had signed to Phyllis Kirk, a famous model and sometimes movie star who was close to Scott. The sale price of the book was fifty cents.

It is hard to know which was more painful to Scott: that a woman with whom he had a long public affair had discarded a book that he had autographed for her, or that its price was only fifty cents.

———

Having been qualified to fly jets, Scott could fly a jet fighter on his weekend trips to Hollywood. At the airport he was often met by movie stars such as William Holden, who drove a sleek and muscular Ferrari roadster.

Sometimes Scott drove to Hollywood for the weekend. Like most fighter pilots, he drove at high speed, and he was angered that he had to stop at the agricultural inspection station at the border town of Blythe each time he entered California. Scott was a decorated colonel in uniform, and he thought a lowly agricultural inspector should simply wave him through. But Scott had to wait in line and then get out, open the trunk of his Cadillac, and prove he was not smuggling some exotic fruit or plant into the great state of California.

And when he left California, it was the same story all over again: stop, wait in line, open the trunk, submit to the inspection, and then drive on.

As Scott tells the story, one Monday he returned to Williams after a particularly lengthy and frustrating stop at the California state line. He sat at his desk stewing. Then he ordered one of his men to check out a truck from the motor pool, go to a nearby farm, and buy a load of watermelons. Scott would pay for them.

He had the watermelons loaded into the bomb bay of a twin-engine Douglas B-26 Invader, a light bomber, and took off.

Nearing the California state line, he eased the nose over and pushed the throttles up to full military power until he was scorching across the desert at cactus-top altitude. As he approached the agricultural station, he opened the bomb bay and released a long, tumbling thread of watermelons, causing them to cascade to the earth and explode in a spray of red juice, black seeds, and green rind.

By the time the officials at the station heard the B-26, Scott had already passed overhead and, still at very low altitude, exited the area, climbed to altitude, and returned to Williams.

During the next year he was anxious each time he approached the agricultural inspection station. But he never complained about having to open his trunk. One day the agricultural inspector waved a hand over his shoulder and pointed. Scott looked and as far as the eye could see was a long string of lush green watermelon plants, growing in a straight line for almost a mile.

Scott waited, not knowing what to expect.

The inspector told the story of what happened. When he was finished,

Scott—with no small amount of apprehension—asked if anyone had gotten the tail number of the aircraft.

"Hell, Colonel," the laughing inspector said, "it was going so fast we are not even sure it was one of ours."

When Scott left Williams he was shown his fitness report. And when Scott was in his nineties, he could still recite the contents: "This officer has developed such a penchant for public speaking that he is consistently far from his primary duties. Such sidelines, doubtless personally generated to a great degree, indicate he is unsuited for higher responsibility at this time."

It was a devastating report for a senior colonel, enough to have guaranteed that Scott would not be promoted to general.

Years later Major General Leroy Svendsen Jr. recorded an oral history, part of which recounted his time as a junior officer at Williams under Scott's command.

Svendsen said he and his brother officers looked upon Scott as "a very famous personage" due to the Book, but that they had "mixed emotions" about Scott because there were so many stories about him that conflicted with the Great Man image, one of which was the story about landing with masking tape over his gun ports but claiming an aerial victory.

During Scott's time at Williams an incident took place that reveals much about the state of Scott's marriage.

Scott, Kitty Rix, and Robin drove to California to visit his brother, Roland. Scott's parents stayed with Roland while Rob and Kitty Rix stayed in a motel. Ola and Kitty Rix could not stay in the same house.

Catharine had been drinking and when she saw Ola she loudly pronounced, "I need a drink."

Ola gave Catharine a look that would have frozen over an active volcano, and said, "You've had enough."

Ola was right. Catharine had had enough. She was no longer the subservient daughter-in-law wanting to please. She had spent years at home without her husband. She was raising Robin almost by herself. And when her husband was home, he chastised her for smoking and drinking, rebukes made all the more painful because by now she knew of the many affairs he was having in Hollywood. She knew about Jack Warner's beach house. And she knew that after seventeen years of marriage, Ola was still criticizing her. Catharine mixed a big drink, held it up, and stared defiantly at Ola.

Yes, Ola was right. Catharine Rix Green of Fort Valley had had enough.

Ola made a tart reply. But before Catharine could respond, Scott put his hand on Catharine's shoulder, squeezed, and said, "Catharine. That is my *mother.*"

Catharine had another drink.

Scott's men held a going-away party for him his last night at Williams. That afternoon, Scott had checked out an aircraft and flown to Los Angeles, where he borrowed an ape suit from the Warner Brothers Studio—a big bulky suit that was probably used in the Tarzan movies of the 1950s.

Scott put on the suit before he got into the cockpit. When he landed at Williams and taxied up to the prime parking space in front of the tower, he climbed down as an ape. He wore the suit to the party that night and told everyone he was "the ape who became a full colonel."

Only a psychologist can affix some sort of meaning to this.

In 1950 Scott was ordered to the U.S. Air Force base at Fürstenfeldbruck, Germany, to take command of a fighter bomber wing.

He left Catharine behind to close up the house at Williams and have the furniture packed and shipped. Then she and Robin Lee would go across the country by train to the East Coast, where they would board a passenger ship bound for Germany. Scott would visit his parents and then meet Catharine and Robin Lee at the dock before the ship departed.

Near Columbus, Georgia, Scott collided with a truck carrying a concrete mixture, and the crash broke his hip. From his hospital bed at Fort Benning, the large Army base near Columbus, Scott wrote his mother that after the crash he was sorely tempted to pull the truck driver down from the cab and give him a good thrashing.

Mama was impressed with Rob's spunk.

At Fürstenfeldbruck, Scott provided proof of the adage that flying is like sex: No man gives it up until he must.

Scott was still a time hog. While most wing commanders like to get in a little stick time now and then, the job is essentially administrative. But Scott sometimes flew an hour before he went to his office. He flew during his lunch hour. He flew in the late afternoons. He flew on the weekends. He flew all over Europe and over much of Africa.

There was a war going on in Korea, an air war where F-86 Sabre pilots were going up against MiG-15s. Unlike many other distinguished pilots of World War II, Scott was not invited to this war, but that did not mean he could not fly a fighter and fly it often.

The Republic F-84 Thunderjet, or as the pilots called it, "the Hog," was a fighter-bomber with an infamous reputation for "flameouts" and crashes. The plane was a lieutenant-killer that intimidated many pilots. But not Scott. He gave the pilots under his command a new confidence in the aircraft.

Not only did Scott want to fly the F-84, he wanted people to know who was driving. His F-84 had the squadron identification stripes painted in blue on the vertical stabilizer. The tip tanks were blue and gold, and the nose was painted red, not a shark mouth but close. On the fuselage and on the tip tanks was the insignia of the Twenty-third Fighter Group.

Scott's glistening helmet was blue and white and gold and also emblazoned with the Twenty-third insignia.

To maintain the aircraft, Scott had not one but two crew chiefs. When Scott landed at bases throughout Europe, one look at the aircraft shouted that the famous Colonel Robert Scott, former commanding officer of the Twenty-third—now universally known as the Flying Tigers—was in the cockpit.

"Distinctive" was a kind word for the appearance of the aircraft.

Scott flew so much and was gone so often that Kitty Rix confronted him and asked, as she had in Panama, why he flew so much, what was so great about flying. But rather than explaining that he needed to hone his skills, he put her in the backseat of a Lockheed T-33 and took her for a ride.

Not only was taking a family member up in a fighter illegal, there was a certain amount of risk. Catharine had no training in how to use the ejection seat or parachute. Scott simply strapped her into the seat, fitted her with an oxygen mask, told her to breathe normally, and took off.

It is axiomatic among pilots that when taking up a nonpilot for a first ride, the flight should be straight and level with gentle turns and no aerobatics. But Scott, in his words, "wrung out the aircraft." He did loops and rolls and Immelmanns, followed by a split-S, steep climbs, and high-G maneuvers. It was a flight designed to turn a nonpilot against aviation. It was a mean-spirited, even cruel thing to do.

Years later there remained pride in his voice when he told of this experience and ended with, "She never asked me again what I liked about flying."

While stationed in Germany, Scott made six trips to Africa on hunting safaris, became certified as a hunter, was voted into the East African Professional Hunters Association and served on committees that picked the Big Game Hunter of the Year. He was a member of the Shikar-Safari Club, a group of big game trophy hunters all devoted to gun manufacturer Roy Weatherby and his big-bore hunting rifles. He had a half-dozen custom-made rifles, the stocks inlaid with mother-of-pearl or silver.

One cannot help but wonder how a commanding officer of an air base that was only six minutes away from Russian-controlled territory could take off so much time during the Cold War. Members of the military are given thirty days of leave each year. To fly to Africa, collect the members of the hunting party, go into the bush and return, spend nights at the hotel, and then return to Germany is easily a two-week trip. Two such trips a year would take all of Scott's leave. He had no time left to vacation in Europe with Kitty Rix and Robin. But he did have a coat made for Kitty Rix from the skin of a leopard he had killed, and perhaps she found it comforting during the cold winters of Germany.

After one of his safaris, Scott wrote about the event for the Fürstenfeldbruck base newspaper. The piece was far longer than is usually found in a base newspaper, that is, unless it was written by the wing commander. The text became the foundation for *Between the Elephant's Eyes*, a book Scott wrote about big-game hunting published by Dodd, Mead & Company (associated with Doubleday).

The dedication to the book is one of the few times Scott gave Kitty Rix more than an obligatory nod in any of his books. But even then the dedication is more about Scott than it is about his wife. The dedication is to "my wife Kitty Rix who stayed home while I flew three million miles in fighter planes and walked a great many more after lions, leopards, buffalo and elephant."

In 1951, the year after Scott arrived at Fursty, General Dwight Eisenhower became supreme commander of NATO. Ike was an avid fly fisherman, and he frequently flew into Fursty to go fishing in the nearby Traun River, a famous trout-fishing river but one that historically was made available only to the German aristocracy.

Scott was Ike's host during these trips, and he was able to put the supreme commander on such productive stretches of the river that newsmen asked Scott if he had sergeants hiding in the water and hanging trout on Ike's hook. On one of these fishing trips, a relaxed and expansive Eisenhower asked, "Bob, what has retarded you on the promotion ladder?"

Ike knew that Scott, once the youngest colonel in the Air Corps, was now one of the U.S. Air Force's most senior colonels. Why had the famous war hero and author not made flag rank?

Scott gave Ike a straight answer. He said he flew too much, made too many speeches, had written a best-seller book, and was too outspoken.

Ike nodded, and Scott thought that was the end of it.

As Scott's tour was ending, he received word that he would be attending the National War College in Washington. This was an unusual assignment for such a senior colonel. Usually students at the NWC are fast-rising lieutenant colonels who are marked by their superiors as worthy of higher command. Attending the school is a requisite for being promoted to general officer.

Scott objected to the assignment. He wanted to stay in Germany. He wanted a flying job.

As Scott tells the story, his boss, who was studying Scott's personnel file, looked up and asked, "Do you know who recommended you for the War College?"

"No, sir."

His boss turned the file around and pushed it across the desk to Scott.

The man who had recommended Scott was General Dwight Eisenhower, now running for president of the United States.

Scott was bound for the War College, like it or not.

When Scott left Germany, he brought with him what he said was the record for flying time in jets. He had accumulated more than a thousand hours of jet time, which he said translated to more than a half-million miles.

# 29

# THE MORE THINGS
# CHANGE . . .

SCOTT ENTERED THE NATIONAL WAR COLLEGE IN THE SUMMER OF 1953. The NWC is the most prestigious of the various colleges operated by the U.S. military. Students are from all branches of the military, along with State Department and CIA middle management. All NWC students wear civilian clothes. The permanent faculty is comprised of generals and admirals; its visiting professors are retired senators and senior government leaders.

Scott was the senior officer in his class and thus automatically became class president. He used his position to inveigh against the Pentagon, talk about flying, and tell of China and Chennault and his dealings with the generalissimo and Madame Chiang Kai-shek. He said that at Fursty he had lived in Carinhall, a house Hitler built for Hermann Göring, head of the Luftwaffe in World War II. But students at the NWC know their military history, and they knew that Carinhall was located northeast of Berlin, more than three hundred miles north of Fürstenfeldbruck. Further, to prevent his home from falling into the hands of the advancing Red Army, in the spring of 1945 Göring had ordered that Carinhall be demolished with explosives.

Scott's classmates grew weary of his never-ending flying stories. At one point, when Scott boasted that he could fly a T-33 Shooting Star, a two-seat training jet often used as a courier aircraft, from Washington to the West Coast and return in a single day, an admiral assigned to the War College called Scott out. It can't be done, he said.

Scott told the admiral to put on a flight suit and be at Andrews Air Force Base in suburban Washington for a 5 a.m. takeoff.

From Washington to Los Angeles is roughly 2,300 miles. The T-33 cruised at 450 mph and had a range of about 1,000 miles. Allowing for two refueling stops on the westbound leg, a refueling in California, and two more refueling stops on the return leg, a round-trip required at least twelve hours.

It was a weary admiral who crawled from the cockpit after his round-trip flight. And it was a boastful Scott who regaled students with the story.

Scott made few friends at the NWC.

He graduated in the summer of 1954 and was ordered to the Pentagon.

In that same year, *Between the Elephant's Eyes,* Scott's book about big-game hunting, hit the bookstores. *Reader's Digest* bought the condensed version for what Scott called "a pretty fat sum."

Now Doubleday was publishing *God Is My Co-Pilot* through an arrangement with Garden City Publishing Company. But Scott continued to hector Scribner's about not being able to find copies of the book. Charles Scribner had died, and all of Scott's correspondence went to Wallace Meyer. Scott wanted to rewrite and update the Book. Meyer said no.

On January 3, 1956, Wallace Meyer wrote an office memorandum saying that Scribner's was returning all rights to *God Is My Co-Pilot* to Scott, and that the contract was terminated. Meyer had no choice, because Scott, without consulting Scribner's, had negotiated a new contract with Doubleday, where he thought he would have a more enthusiastic and supportive publisher.

At the time, other than his inability to handle money and his ongoing problems with the IRS, the decision to leave Scribner's, then the most prestigious of publishing houses, ranked up near the top of Scott's bad business decisions. But even worse business decisions and consequences were ahead.

At the Pentagon, Secretary of the Air Force Harold Talbott read the Book, saw the movie, and met the man. Because of Scott's affable and smiling ways, Talbott believed that Scott would make the ideal front man for the Air Force and—over strong objections of Air Force generals—promoted Scott to brigadier general and made him the chief public affairs officer for the Air Force.

Given the poor performance evaluation Scott had received when he left Williams, and given the almost universal animosity toward Scott from the

Air Force senior leadership, this was a promotion that could have come no other way. Had Talbott not imposed his authority as secretary of the Air Force, Scott would have soon been retired as the most senior colonel in the Air Force.

The influence of Eisenhower and then Talbott adds much credence to the belief in Scott's family that he led a charmed life. But it was not to last.

In August 1955, Talbott was replaced by Donald Quarles, who might have kept Scott in the job were it not for a speech that Scott made at a commanders conference in Puerto Rico on January 23, 1956.

The theme for the conference was "A Decade of Security through Global Air Power," a not-so-subtle self-congratulatory title.

In the early 1950s, the Cold War was in full flower and the cause of great rivalry among various branches of the service. The rivalry was about competing roles, different strategic views, and prestige. But it was mostly about money. Since gaining its independence in 1947, the Air Force had received the biggest share of the defense budget, and it would continue to do so for years. To maintain that status quo, the Air Force needed to make nice with everyone, to be politic, collegial, and professional.

Scott did not see it that way.

His speech at the conference shows the sly good old boy at work. He did not directly attack the other services but instead made a devastating attack by using their own words against them. For instance, he commended General Stilwell for wanting to fight his way out of Burma with his teeth and a bayonet.

That was only the beginning.

At the time, most people were not sure what a Communist looked like. But the word "communist" was a powerful epithet. Scott lined up with General Curtis LeMay and the Strategic Air Command against the Communist menace. The Army and Navy, Scott said, did not understand the threat of communism, and even if they did, they were not capable of responding to that threat. Only the Air Force and air power could do that. So let the Army and Navy sit back and watch the mushroom clouds bloom while SAC took care of business.

Secretary Quarles was in the audience and became so angry as he listened that he interrupted Scott several times. Quarles wanted harmony, and here was his senior public-relations man launching a bitter attack on both the Army and Navy.

Scott compounded his intemperate speech by giving a copy of the text to *Time*. The magazine expanded Scott's speech to a June 4 cover story titled "Fight in the Pentagon," and the article talked of Scott's "slam-bang, let-out-all-stops press campaign" to prove that the Air Force was superior to the Army and Navy.

It was as if Scott had deliberately painted a target on his back and invited the Air Force to take a shot at him.

Quarles had had quite enough of General Robert Scott.

Scott knew that he was about to be reassigned. He had hoped for a second star and command of the Fourteenth Air Force, Chennault's old command. But Quarles was listening to his generals, and the generals wanted Scott out of the Air Force.

(After the war, Chennault had returned to China. He called upon a number of former AVG pilots, men who would go to the ends of the earth for him, and—with help from both the Chinese and American governments—formed Civilian Air Transport. The new airline bought U.S. military cargo planes at giveaway prices and began airlifting supplies to Chiang's bases in northern China. In 1949, when the Communists pushed Chiang off the mainland to the island of Taiwan, CAT went along. It soon morphed into Air America, a paramilitary arm of the CIA, and it expanded its operations throughout Southeast Asia.)

A general officer, especially one with Scott's combat record and fame, had to be handled gently. Judging by what happened, someone who knew Scott well simply decided to give Scott the rope and let him hang himself.

In August 1956, Quarles assigned Scott to Luke Air Force Base as commander of a training wing. Not only was he back in the Training Command, he was a general doing the same job he had done years earlier as a colonel.

"They" had finally caught up with him. He had been humiliated by the Air Force high command. He knew his days were numbered.

On August 25, 1956, a story in the *Phoenix Gazette* reported that "one of the Air Force's most colorful personalities" was coming to take command of nearby Luke AFB.

Phoenix newspaper reporters asked Scott if he had been fired from his job in the Pentagon. He said yes, but all in all it was a good outcome because now he was back in the cockpit.

The presence of the reporters illustrates an often overlooked point about Scott. He was in the newspapers and on radio and TV far more than most other officers. Much of the coverage was self-generated. But Scott was also a magnet for reporters. Whatever he did or said was news. He could walk outside his office, look up at the sky, and pronounce it a good day for flying and the local paper would trumpet that General Scott loved the weather in Phoenix.

Scott's superiors ordered him to cut back on his speechmaking, to stay in his office and do his job. Afterward when Scott received a request to make a speech, he would turn down the request. But he told the people who had invited him that if they asked their congressman or an influential business-man to call the Air Force chief of staff, something might be arranged.

When a congressman or businessman called Washington and said they wanted General Scott to make a speech, the request was granted. But Scott's superiors in Washington knew what Scott was doing, and their resentment grew even stronger.

Scott was writing a biography of Chennault, this time on a typewriter, at night and on weekends.

Scott was at Luke a relatively short time, but he was there long enough to show that his judgment had not improved with age.

Joe E. Brown came to Luke and did a free show for the personnel on base. Afterward, Scotty gave Brown an officer's hat with six stars and pro-vided a car on the front of which was a tag bearing six stars. He posed for gag shots with Brown and the car with six stars. The photos made the papers across the country.

Scott's superiors thought he had crossed the line in awarding a come-dian the fictitious rank of six-star general.

In addition, several female movie stars came out from Hollywood, and Scott entertained them in the officers' club and took them for a ride in a T-33. He did not wring out the airplane as he had done with Kitty Rix aboard.

The model-actress Phyllis Kirk often called Scott at home. Naturally this angered Kitty Rix.

Scott occasionally took Kirk to see a play in New York City. They made a striking couple: two tall, slender, recognizable people.

"I think that made Catharine mad," Scott said later, regarding his trips with Kirk.

Perhaps it did, because once when Scott took off his wedding band and watch before taking a shower, Catharine picked up his ring and threw it away. She said she did it because she believed Scotty no longer loved her.

Afterward, Scott wore his West Point ring on the finger where he had long worn his wedding band.

Almost exactly a year after arriving at Luke, Scott was relieved of duty and forced into retirement.

Scott tells two stories of what happened.

One version approaches the truth. Scott said that various movie stars came to visit, and he entertained them at the officers' club. There he enjoyed the double takes of the men under his command who entered the club and saw him laughing and joking and leaning in close for conversation with such famous faces. He says that jealous officers accused him of billing his entertainment expenses to the government and that Pentagon officials audited the officers' club accounts but found no evidence of malfeasance.

There may have been some jealousy involved. But the men in Scott's command also knew he was married and had a daughter. Both were at home while he was in the club. It is quite possible that such flagrant neglect offended some brother officers, who turned him in. By now, Scott had become in the eyes of many brother officers a blowhard. Talk, talk, talk. That's all he did. And he was at the center of every story he told.

Scott often talked of his devoted wife and beautiful daughter, and how much he loved them both. But his actions, which are always more revealing than words, were different. He rarely saw his family.

Roland Scott Jr., Scott's nephew, said that Kitty Rix and Robin "knew he had numerous affairs." And when Scott went to Hollywood on weekends, they figured he was back at Jack Warner's beach house.

By now Kitty Rix was a full-blown alcoholic and smoking several packs of cigarettes daily. She no longer cared what Scotty thought. Her anger at Scott was such that she and Robin moved into a small apartment.

Robin was by then a teenager and in a few more years she would be going away to college. Kitty Rix saw herself as a future empty-nester, and she didn't like the prospect. After four months in the apartment, she and Robin Lee moved back into the condo. Despite all the problems, she still wanted her marriage to work. She believed the secret was for Scotty to stay at home more, be more of a father and husband. But Scott was the Running Man. If only he could figure out where he was going.

Scott says he was making too many speeches against communism, too many speeches talking of the Soviet Union's superiority in weapons and in space. He says that one day he went to his office and found two generals from the Pentagon waiting to see him. They told Scott he had made another "unauthorized" speech against the Soviet Union.

In his oral history, General Svendsen, who had served under Scott back at Williams, said of Scott that "eventually he got in trouble and was kind of summarily asked to retire."

The truth is that Scott was filing flight plans for cross-country flights, and that while he was supposed to be halfway across the country on official travel, he was shacked up in a Phoenix hotel with one of the best-known movie stars of the day, a leading lady who also happened to be married.

Scott was given a choice: He could face a general court-martial on charges of falsifying official documents, and conduct unbecoming an officer—offenses punishable with heavy fines, imprisonment, and a dishonorable discharge—or he could retire forthwith.

Scott retired on October 31, 1957. He was forty-eight, had been in uniform twenty-six years, four months, and twenty-five days, which, for the sake of convenience, he later would round off to forty years. He had fifteen thousand hours of flying time, more than any man in the Air Force, but in later years he would round it off to thirty thousand even thirty-five thousand. He was a double ace in the CBI, but to the end of his life he would say that he had shot down twenty-two enemy aircraft but "they" had taken numerous victories away from him. He had flown 388 combat missions and taught more than one thousand men how to fly. His first flight had been in a fabric-covered biplane and his last in a supersonic F-100.

When Scott retired, there was no parade, no flyby, no moving ceremony with speeches by senior officials, and no bouquet of flowers for Kitty Rix.

The absence of these honors shows how the Air Force felt about one of its most decorated and celebrated heroes.

It was an embarrassing and ignoble end to a glorious career.

# 30

# STILL IN THE RACE

THERE IS LITTLE TO SAY ABOUT A MILITARY MAN AFTER HE RETIRES. HE takes up residence, often at the town nearest his last duty station, he shops at the PX—not so much for the good prices, but more in the hope that some-one will recognize him—and hangs out with fellow military retirees. He bores his civilian neighbors who were not in the military.

But Scott was not the ordinary man, and he still had two great things in his life to accomplish. Just as the between-the-war assignments of a career military man are important to his life story, so are the events between Scott's two major post-retirement accomplishments.

He bought a tenth-floor condominium in Phoenix. What he called the "residential payment" was $78,000 with a monthly fee of $2,300. He never let Kitty Rix know the price.

Scott said he wanted Kitty Rix to have a comfortable home after all those years of living alone. And it was comfortable, with a view that seemed to stretch forever. But perhaps Scott bought it more because it fit his image of where a famous writer ought to live. Or he may have bought it because the only way to pay for it was by making speeches—going back on the road, and again leaving Kitty Rix and Robin at home. For Kitty Rix, the condo was a prison in the sky.

Upon retirement, Scott signed a contract with a speakers' bureau and found he was one of the most popular speakers in America. It seemed people all over the country wanted to hear from him. And they paid him up to $5,000 per speech.

He would stand before a crowd, adopt a hangdog expression, and proceed to say that when he went to war he had never been in a B-17 and that "I lied to get into combat." Many in the audience would smile and nod in appreciation. *That fellow Scott is okay. He did what he had to do to go off to war and fight the Japs. Couldn't even fly that big bomber. But he got that thing off the ground, flew it halfway around the world, and became a hero. Yes, sir. He sure did.*

The watermelon story—the truth of which cannot be documented—was guaranteed to have the audience roaring. As was the story about being lost near Pittsburgh, landing his mail plane, and seeing the road sign for Mars. The follow-up line, "I didn't know I was *that* far off course," always got a laugh.

In one ninety-day period, Scott made eighty speeches.

He was now on the road more than ever. And he traveled in style. He bought a new Cadillac. To those affected by the Depression, owning the big soft-riding Cadillac was the ultimate symbol of success. For the rest of his life, Scott bought a new Cadillac almost every year.

He bought expensive new suits. Men who wear a uniform for much of their lives are rarely comfortable in mufti. Oftentimes it shows in the choice of fabric, style, even the fitting. Such men look frumpy and they can thus be identified either as ex-military or merely someone who doesn't know how to dress. But not Scott. He wore expensive dark suits that fitted his lean frame. With his hair turning to silver, he presented an elegant appearance.

When he was at home, he slept in a separate bedroom at the far end of the big condo from Kitty Rix. He said it was because "She snored. She smoked."

And it was a terrible time for Kitty Rix, as she was about to be home alone. Robin Lee was leaving to attend college at Stanford University, where she would find the man she wanted to marry. Bruce Fraser was the manager of a Kmart store, and Scott made no secret of the fact that he thought his daughter could do better. He tried to talk Robin out of the marriage, but why should she take advice from a father who often spoke of his love for her in public, yet who in private had virtually abandoned her and her mother? Robin knew about her father's affairs, and she defied him in a way that ended up hurting him the most: She eloped. Her father was deprived of the joy of attending the wedding of his only child.

In between making speeches, Scott was rushing to finish a biography of Chennault. It was a labor of love, respect, and veneration, and Scott wanted

Chennault to read the book. He needed Chennault to see on paper how Scott felt about him.

But the Old Man was ill and failing fast.

It is a measure of the situational morality of the Air Force that its leaders, who a little more than a decade earlier had disdained Chennault and ordered him home from China, now recognized him as a great leader, a great thinker, and one of the greatest tacticians in the history of aerial warfare.

The Air Force recognized that in this instance the Brits had got it right: Chennault of China.

A new and insecure branch of the military needs the inspiration of every great leader that it can claim for its own. And thus the Air Force awarded Chennault another star shortly before he died, at sixty-four, on July 27, 1958.

At last, the Old Man was senior to Clayton Bissell.

Chennault was buried with full honors in Arlington National Cemetery. Scott was one of the pallbearers.

The *New York Times*'s obituary of Chennault was on page 1.


Scott's biography, *Flying Tiger: Chennault of China*, was published a year after Chennault died. It might have been published much earlier, but when the publisher that commissioned the book, Henry Holt & Company, received the manuscript, an editor deemed it "unpublishable." Scott was outraged and refused to return the advance. The publisher later obtained a $10,000 judgment against Scott. Eventually, Doubleday & Company published the book. It was dedicated to Chennault and Merian Cooper as "Americans who recognized the cancer of Communism long ago."

It was a passionate and eloquent book, filled with insights about Chennault of China, and far and away the best-written of Scott's books. But it was a hagiography, and that failing attenuated its impact.


After retiring from politics, former Georgia governor Ellis Arnall became chairman of the board of a large life-insurance company based in Atlanta. He remembered Scott, and he believed that a man who talked so much and so well would make a good insurance salesman. Arnall offered Scott a job selling life insurance, giving him the title of regional vice president. For the sign on the door of his small office in Phoenix, Scott dropped the "Regional" part of the title.

The job called for Scott to travel to a half-dozen Southwestern states. As a result, if Scott was not on the road making speeches, he was on the road selling insurance. He was driving fifty thousand miles a year, and while on a road trip he often stopped, alighted from his Cadillac, and ran several hundred yards by the side of the road before returning—a journey within a journey.

While Scotty was always on the move, Kitty Rix was rattling around in the big condo in Phoenix, looking out the large glass windows through which she could see for miles. She could also see that her life had turned out quite different from what she expected. The man who had spent so many hours driving toward her, now was spending even more hours driving away from her.

She was, in every way imaginable, a long way from Fort Valley, Georgia.

When Scott was in town he would drive to Luke AFB, where, among the young pilots, he was a venerated figure. After his speeches, he would sit and spend hours talking to them.

These young lieutenants did not care about the stories of masking tape over the gun ports. All they knew, and wanted to know, was that this man had written the book that made them want to fly airplanes. And many of them had tears in their eyes when they told him of how his book had influenced their lives.

It was the same when he spoke to classes at the Air Force Academy. Many of the young cadets said it was Scott's book that made them choose to go to the academy.

Scott's speeches and his talks with young pilots were a collection of stories with a few recurring themes: his "big lie" and his many failings. One of his failings was, as he said, "I was not a complete partner with my wife." He would rather be in a cockpit alone at thirty thousand feet than be with wife and daughter at ground level. His atonement was to buy gifts—the condo: "I bought it for you"—and to make promises: "I'll be at home from now on."

All Kitty Rix wanted was a family like the one she had grown up in back in Fort Valley, a family such as she might have had if she had married one of the fraternity boys.

And on every trip that Scott took, Kitty Rix followed him to the elevator, where she cried, and bemoaned the fact that Scotty was retired but was still gone all the time.

Scott was naive in many respects. And when businessmen who wanted to take advantage of his name talked him into business ventures, the results were predictable.

A July 6, 1964, article in *Arizona Days and Ways* magazine titled "From Hero to Zero" told how Scott had appeared in bankruptcy court asking for dismissal of $37,000 in debts, leaving him $31,000 to pay on another debt. He told the bankruptcy referee, "You might say, sir, that I didn't know how to enter the civilian market after thirty-three years in the military." Scott told how "unscrupulous men" had taken advantage of him and his reputation and how they had put him on boards and enticed him into deals that would benefit them.

The reporter who wrote the story took pleasure in noting that while Scott was inside the courthouse declaring bankruptcy and getting out of debt, his new Cadillac, with its distinctive "23 FG" tag, was parked at the curb.

The year 1967 was another year of bad business deals for Scott. That year he was sued in Maricopa County in a civil action titled Arizona v. Scott Productions, Inc. It seems that some stock was sold in Scott's name to finance a TV series. The producer was a Texan who, as they say out that way, was all hat and no cattle.

Scott painted himself as the naive war hero who was taken advantage of by an unscrupulous Texan. He was probably right.

That same year, Scott self-published a book called *God Is Still My Co-Pilot*. He sent out a mailer to a thousand people seeking to raise the $31,500 he was told it would take to publish the book. Enough money came from 882 people to go ahead with the project. The book cost $40 and was designed to resurrect the glory of Scott's first and most famous book.

The foreword was written by Senator Strom Thurmond of South Carolina, Scott's cousin. Thurmond was an unreconstructed Southerner famous for his segregationist views and for having a wife one-third his age.

Scott said criticism of Chiang and Chennault was "diabolical communist propaganda."

References to Kitty Rix and Robin are brief, even perfunctory. Kitty Rix is "the Georgia girl," "the girl," or "the wife." But long passages are devoted to Scott's mother, "to whom I practiced writing, in a thousand letters from all over the world, which, in time became the notes for all of my books; and to her, most especially, for the inspiration and guidance she always provided."

How the institutional Air Force looked upon Scott was revealed in an article written by General Bruce Holloway and published in the November 1967 issue of *Air Force* magazine. In China, Holloway had been Scott's executive officer and had replaced Scott as commander of the Twenty-third Fighter Group upon Scott's return to the States. When Holloway wrote the piece he was vice chief of staff of the U.S. Air Force.

Holloway's article spoke of all the accomplishments of the AVG, but it never mentioned Scott.

Strictly speaking, the article was correct. Scott had not served in the AVG. But he took the article as a slap in the face. Scott could not take on a four-star general, but his brother, Roland, could and did. Roland wrote the editor about Scott's role in China. The editor replied that General Holloway's article was accurate and the fact that Scott had flown guest missions with the AVG and been the first commander of the Twenty-third Fighter Group—an entirely different organization—was "hardly germane to the point at hand."

Not only had Scott been forced to retire, he had been banished from the Air Force hall of heroes.

Scott's nephew Roland remembers his famous uncle of those days. Roland was living in California, and from time to time Scott would visit. Roland would open the door and see his uncle running up the driveway, hands raised high in the air, a big smile on his face and a loud "How are you?"

What Roland remembers most about his uncle is his unfailing ebullience, good humor, and consideration of others.

But Scott's smiles and exuberance were balanced by periodic onslaughts of depression. Those dark moods were becoming darker, and they became worse after his mother died, on January 3, 1966.

She was not buried in Macon, where her children had grown up and where her husband still lived. Instead, she was taken back to Aiken and buried in the family plot at Millbrook Baptist Church. To the right of her grave stretched generations of Burckhalters. The cemetery is a small one, and is engulfed by what has grown to be one of the largest churches in Aiken.

Scott took charge of all the burial arrangements while, as always, his younger brother and sister stayed in the background.

The slab over Ola's grave is distinguished by its size—it is larger than any other slab within sight—and by the effusive and disjointed sentiment carved upon it.

OLA BURCKHALTER
OCTOBER 3, 1885–JANUARY 3, 1966

WIFE OF ROBERT LEE SCOTT
DAUGHTER OF LILLIE WISE AND
LLEWELLYN J. BURCKHALTER
OUR MOTHER
ELIZABETH SCOTT HAGAN
ROLAND B. SCOTT LT/COL USAF
ROBERT L. SCOTT B/GEN USAF

TO OUR DAD SHE WAS A DEVOTED WIFE FOR 58 YEARS
TO HER COMMUNITY SHE GAVE A HELPING HAND WITH
DIGNITY AND GRACE
TO US, HER CHILDREN, SHE TAUGHT AMERICANISM BY
EXAMPLE . . . WHEN HER SONS FLEW AERIAL COMBAT OVER
EUROPE AND CHINA, SHE REFUSED TO BE AFRAID, BUT
INSTEAD WENT TO WAR HERSELF, SERVING AT AGE SIXTY
ASSEMBLING FUSES IN A NAVAL ORDNANCE PLANT . . .
FRIENDLY, GENTLE, LOVING AND COMPLETELY SELFLESS,
SHE EPITOMIZED MOTHERHOOD . . .
UNSELFISH LOVE FOR HER FAMILY AND HER SERVICE
TO OTHERS EXEMPLIFIED THE BEST IN CHRISTIAN FAITH . . .
TO HER THE ONLY RULE IN LIFE WAS THE GOLDEN RULE . . .
IN ALL HER WORLD SHE NEVER MET A STRANGER

THE KISS OF THE SUN FOR PARDON
THE SONG OF THE BIRDS FOR MIRTH,
ONE IS NEARER GOD'S HEART IN A GARDEN
THAN ANYWHERE ELSE ON EARTH . . .

To combat his depression, Scott began writing another book, with the working title *The Maverick General*, and it was a replay of many of the stories Scott had previously told so often.

It was in this new memoir that Scott first wrote of how he had decided on the title for his first book. He may have talked about it in the past, but this was the first time that the story appeared in print.

It was stories like this that caused Scott's exasperated brother to explode with "Goddammit, Rob" and ask Scott why he told such stories when it was so clear they were not true. Scott would shrug, smile, and admit, "I know. I know. But I can't help it." When Roland was asked why his uncle waited forty years to tell of this experience, he said, "It probably took him that long to come up with it."

By 1970, Kitty Rix had become quite frail. For the past fifteen years she had been spending more and more time with doctors. Now she had been diagnosed with liver cancer, and she was growing weaker and weaker.

There are many reasons for Robin Lee to have been estranged from her father. The last year of her mother's life ranks near the top of the list. Despite the fact that Kitty Rix was becoming more and more ill, Scott did not cease his travels. Instead, for most of the last year of Kitty Rix's life, Scott was on the road.

One morning as he was leaving for yet another trip, Kitty Rix followed him to the elevator. There she gave him a sealed envelope and told him not to open it until he was in his hotel that night.

Addressed to "Scotty Dearest," the letter talked of Scott's need to travel and then said, "I only wish you were half as bent on being here with us. Have you ever dared to say to yourself, how will I live this life, I am happy because those around me are happy.

"Scotty, is your life always going to be tomorrow and tomorrow, with here and there bitter memories of yesterday. Is there no NOW to your existence?"

Kitty Rix asked Scott if his life were like an express train and he a passenger, forever going, whizzing, hurrying and impatient at every stop.

"Why so hot, little man? You shall pass this way but once. The hearts that beat for you; those who love you, you shall never find again. The days now here briefly shall be gone. Why not stop just once; sit down, take life in your two hands and taste it? Why not <u>live</u> and be forever just passing the time?"

In 1971 Kitty Rix rode with Scott from Phoenix to Hollywood for a party at the Beverly Hilton Hotel. She should not have gone, but this was a Hollywood Party, and Scotty insisted on being there, so she steeled herself, and dressed, and they drove to Hollywood.

At the party she collapsed. Scott swaddled her in blankets, helped her into the backseat of the Cadillac, and began the four-hundred-mile drive back to Phoenix. Much of the time he drove with his right arm over the seat so he could hold hands with Kitty Rix.

Back in Phoenix, Kitty Rix was rushed into intensive care. She had metastatic liver cancer so advanced that nothing could be done except to take her home, give her pain medication, and wait for the end.

Kitty Rix was in a semi-coma for six weeks. On the morning of January 25, 1972, Scott was struggling to raise her into position to take her medicine when she opened her eyes. Scott could see the fatigue and resignation in her eyes. She smiled and said, "Scotty, you are trying to play God." She died a few minutes later.

The obituary in the *Phoenix Gazette* was more about Scotty than about Catharine. It said that he had commanded the Flying Tigers in China and that he had shot down twenty-two enemy aircraft.

The apex of Catharine Rix Green's life had been her high-school years in Fort Valley and her two years at Shorter College in Rome.

Then she married and discovered the true dimensions of loneliness, the insidious effects of alcohol and tobacco, and the equally enervating price of being the wife of a famous man who chose to have more affairs than she could number. Other than the joy of raising a daughter, Kitty Rix's adult life was one of misery and sadness. The darkness did not end with her death. After her cremation, Scott had Catharine's remains placed in an urn and put in storage.

After Kitty Rix died, Scott wrote, "Oh fairest of the fair—my dove— why did you fly away? Leaving me earth-bound, cursed by my loss, forever. Like the eternal sea of loneliness I ride, my heart pounds out endless waves of guilt. You are lost to me forever."

So it goes for several hundred words of purple prose, of the self-pity that, in middle Georgia, is read as the anguish of a broken heart.

# 31

# RESURRECTION

AFTER KITTY RIX DIED, SCOTT FOUND THE BIG CONDO TO BE A HAUNTED place. He was alone and in his early sixties, and as large as his personality might be, it was not big enough to fill the condo. Scott sold it and bought a small house on Buccaneer Drive in Sun City, Arizona. There he was close enough to Luke Air Force Base to hear fighters in the landing pattern.

Scott was surrounded by people his age and older, and he was miserable. "Depressionville" was his name for Sun City. "People come here to die," he said.

The spells of depression grew more severe. It was to combat depression that he began a program of rigorous exercise. His obsessive side kicked in and soon he was running three to six miles every day. While the running helped to alleviate his depression, it did nothing for his impatience with Sun City residents—those people old and stooped and endlessly curious, who, when they saw him running, croaked, "Why are you running?"

The August 17, 1975, issue of *Texas* magazine contained a piece about Scott that described him as "tough and outspoken" and "brash and contemptuous of red tape" and a hero to millions. The article said that his most famous book was still in print after more than thirty years, and that he remained one of the nation's most sought-after speakers. Scott liked to end his speeches with the line: "I sold air power by example."

And the stories were getting better over the years. In these stories he defied generals, broke regulations, and had a grand old time because "All I ever wanted to do was fly, fly, fly."

Scott had a bad year in 1977.

Bruce Holloway had retired and he was asked to record an oral history covering the high points of his career. Usually these interviews are setups, an opportunity for the general to replay his career as he sees it and without rigorous questioning by the historian.

Holloway's oral history is unusually full of vinegar and bile and mean-spiritedness. He had few good things to say about anyone. And while he took gratuitous swipes at Chennault, Bissell, and Stilwell, he emptied his bile duct on Scott.

In the beginning, Holloway tried to balance his remarks. "I didn't think much of him" and "He was awfully good to me." Then "I was for a long time a booster and would defend him against anybody" followed by an assertion that Scott had "sided with gangsters" in a business venture.

Holloway said Scott "is the hero image of anybody I have ever known" but "there is very little truth in any of it."

He said that *God Is My Co-Pilot* "alienated a bunch of friends" because Scott took the experiences of others and made them his own.

But most damning of all was Holloway's accusation "Nobody ever saw him shoot down an airplane, ever." He said that Scott was "one hundred percent dishonest" in counting his aerial victories.

Holloway's words were meant to be a lasting record. These oral histories are available at the Air Force Historic Research Agency at Maxwell Air Force Base in Alabama for anyone who wants to read them.

At one time, Holloway had been Scott's loyal and trusted subordinate. Scott picked him to take over the Twenty-third Fighter Group when he returned to America in January 1944.

Part of the equation may be that Holloway had been retired for five years when he was interviewed, and living in Florida, where the sun quickly bleaches the arrogance out of generals. More and more people did not know how powerful he had once been and they did not pay him the deference he expected and he could see himself slowly deflating. And, despite what Holloway saw as the truth about Scott, the world at large viewed

Scott as a colorful war hero and the author of a popular book that had influenced so many young men. Holloway was jealous of Scott.

On May 10, 1978, one month after he turned seventy, Scott underwent surgery in a small hospital in Aiken, South Carolina. He had annual physicals there because Aiken was the town where Scott's longtime Air Force doctor had retired.

The doctor had found a shadow atop Scott's right kidney and feared it might be malignant.

That morning, the doctor told Scott to count backward from ten. Instead, Scott counted backward from twenty-three.

Scott said the mass was a fragment of a rivet blasted into his back in the raid over Victoria Harbor more than thirty years earlier. But given that he was not wounded in that raid, in all likelihood what the doctor found was simply a benign lump.

The surgery was successful, and it galvanized Scott into a frenzied round of activities. His behavior became baffling to his family.

To begin with, there was the matter of his father and namesake, then ninety-two and in the early stages of dementia. Every morning the old man picked up the *Macon Telegraph* from the front yard, walked back to his rocking chair on the porch, and slowly read the newspaper. When he finished, he walked down to the curb, urinated on the mailbox post, then walked back into the house, where he spent the remainder of the day.

Sometimes he would walk down to the Dempsey Hotel to read the paper and then urinate on a parking meter outside the hotel. People complained.

Scott came to Macon to talk to his father about confining his urination to his own bathroom. While helping the old man take a bath, Scott saw that he had a hernia and convinced his father to have surgery. Scott's siblings were incensed. "He's ninety-two, for God's sake," Roland said.

To Roland and Elizabeth this was not unlike the time Rob had convinced Roland that he had flat feet. Roland had suffered the pain of wearing unneeded corrective devices. But this was worse: when Robert Senior came out of the anesthesia he was so disoriented and terrified that he suffered a pulmonary embolism and died.

He was buried alongside his wife at Millbrook in Aiken. His grave marker is about the size of a shoebox, dwarfed by that of his wife, and reads simply:

ROBERT LEE SCOTT
SEPT. 4, 1885
JUNE 7, 1978

The second thing Scott did after his surgery was to become obsessive about his next project.

After more than a half century of looking at the long-tattered *National Geographic* photo of the Great Wall of China, after more than a half century of boring dozens of people with his arcane knowledge of its features, after more than a half century of dreaming about following in the footsteps of Marco Polo, he was going to realize his boyhood dream: he was going back to China and he would walk the Great Wall.

Scott returned to Phoenix, where he began working out with weights, doing sit-ups, and running at least five miles every day. If he was not on the road making speeches, he was writing letters to the Chinese embassy. He began studying Mandarin.

Before Scott was ordered overseas in World War II, he had prepared what he called his "war bag" and positioned it near the front door. In the fullness of time the Great Sky Pilot had called upon him, and Scott picked up his bag and walked out the door. Now he prepared a "go bag," a soft duffel bag that he could carry by the handle like a suitcase, or wear over his shoulders like a knapsack.

Into the bag went an extra pair of jogging shoes, clothes, maps, a camera, and a cooking pot. Scott began experimenting with different cookie recipes. He decided that, when the time came, he would live on cookies and water. He found an oatmeal-cookie recipe that called for the addition of either raisins or nuts. He added both.

Scott estimated that, after the cookies, packed two to a plastic bag, were added to the rest of the bag's contents, the go bag would weigh about seventy pounds. He began carrying the loaded pack on his walks around Sun City.

He was ready to go on a moment's notice. Once the word came down, all he had to do was grab his go bag, lock the door, and drive to the airport.

Now it was up to the Big Sky Boss.

Scott says he wrote some two hundred letters to the Chinese government in the next eighteen months; they accomplished nothing. His letters told how he had fought for China in World War II, flew side by side with Chinese pilots, his friendship with the Chiangs. Never mind that the Chiangs had been forced to flee from mainland China to Taiwan when the Communists seized power in 1949.

People in Sun City were curious about Scott, and one day three elderly ladies knocked on his door and asked what he was doing. He had previously traveled a great deal, but now he was home and walking all the time. What was going on?

The curious ladies were about Scott's age, but he thought of them as old. He took a deep breath, but his impatience got the better of him.

"I'm building an airplane," he said.

Eyebrows jerked upward and mouths fell. "An airplane? In your house?"

"In my garage. Anything else?" He shut the door.

A few hours later came a knock and at the door was another neighbor, a man who lived across the street from Scott.

"I hear you are building an airplane in your garage," he said. "Is that right?"

"Yes, that is right."

The man was bewildered. "Well, once you finish it, what are you going to do with it?"

"I'm going to fly it."

"How are you going to do that?"

Scott stepped outside, pointed to his garage, and then swept his arm across the street toward his neighbor's house. "I'm going to open the garage door, rev her up, begin my takeoff roll down my driveway, across the street, and then, if I've figured everything out right, I should clear your roof by about two inches."

He slammed the door and muttered, "These old people are a pain in the ass."

In 1979, *Wings* magazine published a profile of Scott titled "Hollywood's Flying Tiger." In the article Scott was quoted as saying, "All my life it seems like I've been talking when I should have been listening." He acknowledged that he had the reputation of being "arrogantly outspoken."

Self-awareness was slowly coming. Scott had finally acknowledged that he was the Bugler.

Scott returned from a speaking tour to find that his house had been broken into. His pictures of Kitty Rix and Robin had been thrown on the floor and broken, the pages of the manuscript for the book he was working were scattered about, and some personal items had been stolen.

The sheriff of Maricopa County said it was impossible to prevent burglaries in a residence where the owner was gone for weeks at a time.

Scott strung razor wire around his patio, and out front he installed a big sign bearing a picture of a .45-caliber pistol and words warning that he would "Shoot to Kill" anyone who broke into his house again.

Buses filled with prospective buyers of Sun City homes often went past. The prospective buyers were curious. The officials of Sun City were incensed.

Anger over the break-in refueled Scott's determination to get into China. He wrote more letters to Chinese officials.

Some might have said he was an old man with an impossible dream. But Scott believed. And he believed in his heart that a way would open up for him to walk the Great Wall. Scott's job was to be ready when the Big Sky Boss showed him the way.

Now Scott was spending more time on the patio of his house than he was inside. He slept on the patio. Sometimes he pitched a tent in the backyard and slept there.

Now it was 1980 and Scott had still made no headway in gaining entry to China. He had written dozens of letters and the few replies were nothing but bureaucratic verbiage claiming that Scott's requests had been passed on to higher authorities. Thanks to the progress made after President Richard Nixon's rapprochement efforts in the early 1970s, tourism slowly began expanding in China, but there were still no tours to the far west, where the Great Wall began.

Scott realized that he was going about his quest in the wrong way. He would never get permission to enter China and walk the Great Wall. Tourism in China was not set up to deal with solo expeditions.

Taking matters into his own hands, Scott decided to enter China in whatever way he could, and then to simply disappear. He would be on his own.

He found what was called an Explorers Tour, the first time such a tour had been made available to Americans. Scott mailed in his application and was told the tour had been full, but one person had dropped out. Scott was accepted. He mailed his passport to the Chinese embassy, and when it came back, taped on the cover was a piece of paper bearing the number "23," his number in the tour group.

And that is how on August 3, 1980, Scott alighted from a long transpacific flight and stepped onto the warm tarmac at Kai Tak Airport in Hong Kong. He was seventy-two. He had fought off the ravages of time better than most, but now he had the jerky gait, the wide stance, and the high steps that are the mark of the elderly.

Scott at last was back in the country where, in one sense, his life began, where his destiny was realized. He looked up at Victoria Peak. Almost forty years earlier, Scott had led seven P-40s in an attack on the city, fought with enemy fighters arising from this same airport, and strafed the upper floors of the Peninsula Hotel.

As his fellow passengers streamed past him toward the terminal, he continued looking overhead. Later he would write, "There in that vault of sky I had almost died."

The Lone Wolf of the Chindwin had returned to China.

The Great Wall awaited.

# 32

## AT LAST

As Scott stood on the tarmac and watched his fellow passengers stream by, his only thought was *How do I get away from these old people?*

His plan was simple: begin at the westernmost end of the wall at the Gate of Heroes near the city of Jiayuguan, and from there follow the wall more than fourteen hundred miles to the Yellow Sea and the Old Dragon's Head promontory he had flown over so many years ago.

He stayed with the travel group through a train trip to Canton and then flew to Ürümqi, the westward extent of what was called the Explorers Tour, where he planned to break away, put on his blue denim pants and jacket and big sunglasses, buy a train ticket, and pose as a local. But he had two problems. First, Scott was six inches taller than the average Chinese man, and his Occidental features did not exactly blend in with the train's Oriental passengers. Second, he did not have a travel permit. And no one, local or foreigner, could go anywhere in China without one.

We have only Scott's stories as a source for what happened during the next several months. He later wrote a book about the trip but it was never published. One reason might be that Scott was so bedazzled by Chinese place names and geography, and felt so compelled to include numerous mini history lessons, that the manuscript is almost as impenetrable as Marco Polo's *Travels*.

Consider this passage:

"Huang He is the Yellow River. It comes down from the mountains of Qinghai Province near Tibet right through Lanzhou, then turns slightly and flows northward for 400 miles to Inner Mongolia, then east, and finally south, creating a 1000-mile horseshoe-shaped loop known as the Great Bend."

He later condensed his book into a long piece published in *Reader's Digest* for which he said he was paid $20,000.

Scott's story overwhelms us with place names and a time line that may raise eyebrows. At the end, almost as a throwaway story, he provides a moving anecdote about commissioning a memorial to Chennault, along with photos of the monument stone that he says today rests atop a mountain overlooking the old Flying Tiger airfield at Kunming.

The story of Scott's Chinese adventure is confusing and improbable, but there are enough provable details to establish that at least part of his account is true.

And, as always with Scott, the story is a grand one.

Scott flew aboard a commercial airline that crosses the Great Wall. But the weather was cloudy and he could see nothing. Later, aboard a train that was passing through a gap in the wall, he bounced from one side of the train to the other in a futile attempt to see *something*, but to no avail. At one point when the train had stopped, Scott jumped off and climbed a metal tower, camera dangling from his neck, and as the train crew watched in alarm, Scott searched the horizon for a sign of the wall.

Nothing.

During a three-day side trip to Inner Mongolia, Scott found a post office and sent a telegram to U.S. ambassador Leonard Woodcock in Beijing saying he would arrive there on August 21. The telegram asked if the ambassador could obtain permission from the proper Chinese officials for Scott to separate himself from the group and be given a personal travel permit to see the wall from Jiayuguan to the Old Dragon's Head.

On the train ride from Inner Mongolia to Datong, Scott hoped again for at least a sight of the wall. But the trip was at night.

There is a restored part of the Great Wall about forty miles north of Beijing, which Scott dismisses as the "tourist" wall. But he was delighted to see it and jogged along its ramparts for several miles. After that, Scott walked for miles on the unrestored section nearby.

In Beijing, Scott found that not only did the U.S. embassy staff know who he was, many had read the Book and were intrigued by his quest to walk the Great Wall. Scott attended an embassy reception, and he must have been thought to be quite the character. He wore denim trousers, a Mao jacket, and on his feet a pair of two-dollar black silk slippers.

At the gathering, a Chinese official told Scott that a visa and a travel permit would both be forthcoming. George H. W. Bush, then a presidential candidate, was visiting. Bush had been a naval aviator in World War II, and the two men had a long conversation about flying.

Filled with excitement, and knowing that both Bush and a *New York Times* reporter were listening, Scott began bugling. But telling his plan to walk the Great Wall was not enough. Once again he had to make his story bigger.

"My ambition, after I walk the Great Wall, is to return to Kunming where I used to be General Chennault's fighter commander, and put up a small memorial to him."

Until he uttered those words, he had given no thought to such a memorial. It was a throwaway line at a party where he was a big attraction.

The reporter ventured that the Chinese would not permit such a memorial. First, the idea came at a time when China was breaking down the personality cults around such people as Mao Zedong and taking down portraits of Marx, Engels, Lenin, and Stalin. Then there was Chennault's closeness to Chiang—who had fought the Communists harder than he fought the Japanese. And Scott's forceful anticommunist speeches were a matter of record. Scott was proud of being a Cold War warrior, and he still boasted that he had been "fired" from the Air Force because of his speeches against the Red Menace.

The successors of the people whom Chennault and Scott had opposed were now in power. And their approval and cooperation would be needed if Scott was to erect a memorial to Chennault.

As if all this were not enough, the government of the Republic of China had erected a statue to Chennault on Taiwan some twenty years earlier, and it was not likely that the People's Republic of China would emulate the actions of what they considered a breakaway province.

The August 23 article in the *New York Times* was only four paragraphs long. The reporter was clearly skeptical of Scott's proposal. The final paragraph of his story noted that Scott did not have permission from the Chinese government to erect a monument to Chennault. The story nevertheless quoted Scott as saying that he had been in contact by mail with a Chinese person in Kunming who used to serve tea to General Chennault and as a result, "It has been all fixed up unofficially."

Scott did not see the story. By then he had his official documents in hand

and was off to Kashgar, on the far western edge of China. From there he would begin his eastward trek to the Yellow Sea, a route of great significance to Scott in that Kashgar was on the old Silk Road and he would be following Marco Polo's route. And, whether he liked it or not, he would be accompanied throughout by an official guide named Chang Jin.

In his later description of the trip, Scott makes scant mention of Chang Jin. He appears to want his readers to think he traveled alone.

The beginning, as in most great endeavors, was slow, difficult, and demanding. Scott flew back to Ürümqi, where he was told that his trip over the Tien Shan mountains would have to be by bus. What would have been a two-hour flight turned out to be a bus trip of some twenty-four hours. Upon arrival Scott went to a hotel and slept through the night and most of the next day.

When he awakened and walked outside into the desert city that was Kashgar, Scott saw factories everywhere, but it was still a crucial trade city jammed with bicycles, trucks, buses, and all the signs of commerce. Yes, Kashgar was as important as it had been when Marco Polo passed through in 1273, but its fundamental nature had changed. The Industrial Revolution had arrived.

Another dusty and lumbering bus trip across high desert took Scott to Hetian, the end of the line for scheduled travel. Ahead was a nine-hundred-mile segment of the Silk Road along the base of the Kunlun Mountains. Scott talked his way aboard a truck loaded with silk. The truck was part of a ten-vehicle caravan en route to the railroad station at Jiayuguan. The truck drivers were not ones to dawdle, and they drove about twenty hours per day, making the trip in just five days.

Scott was well prepared with maps of every part of China. His maps were the best available, but on this segment of his journey, the maps had some large blank spaces.

On the fifth day, Scott's convoy reached the Caves of the Thousand Buddhas, outside Dunhuang. There was another wall there, but it was not a part of the Great Wall, but rather a much-eroded rammed-earth structure built sometime around 100 BC.

Scott, Chang Jin, and a driver found the western terminus of the old wall at Jiayuguan; all that remained consisted mostly of irregular mounds of mud and the occasional eroded tower. Nearby was a village where camel drivers lived with their herds of camels.

By now Scott's blood was up and he was hard under the spell of the

*National Geographic* picture that showed a boy leading a caravan of camels. Given that he was so close to the wall, he wanted to do as the boy had done in that old *National Geographic*; he wanted to lead a caravan of camels, but they had to be Bactrians just like those in the picture that Scott had filched so long ago.

And so it came to pass that the next morning, Scott found himself in charge of eleven camels, each with its own driver. He was the master of a caravan, surely one of the largest in this part of China in many years.

And at the fortress that marks the beginning of the Ming Wall—as distinguished from Emperor Wu's Great Wall—Scott was introduced to an expressionless middle-aged man dressed in blue denim. The man gave him a blue Chinese army cap and said, "I make you an honorary member of the People's Liberation Army."

And so off they went, Scott aboard the lead camel, leading his caravan along the Great Wall. It was a dramatic touch to the realization of his long dream.

Scott could be a hardheaded man, but he was no match for cantankerous camels. He says his camels did not like the practice of "couching," that is, having the driver tug on the rope leading to a ring in the camel's nose and pulling the camel to its knees so the rider could mount. The command to couch caused his camel to stretch its neck, raise its head to the sky, and utter a shrill and angry cry.

Scott would settle in between the camel's humps as the animal swung its head 180 degrees, looked at Scott, bared its enormous yellow teeth, and—in Scott's mind—tried to find a way either to bite him or spit on him.

Scott rode until he saw something he wanted to examine at close range, and his camel would stop, scream, and kneel, almost pitching Scott forward over the camel's head and onto the ground. A few moments later the process began again.

After several hours of this, when Scott wanted to dismount he simply lifted one leg, drew it over the camel's forward hump, then slid off. And when he wanted to mount he remembered the cowboy movies of a few years earlier and how cowboys sometimes mounted their horses.

Scott had his driver stand at the camel's head with a firm grip on the rope leading to the ring in the camel's nose while he backed off maybe fifteen feet. A running start, a leap, seizing the top of a hump in each hand, a quick twist, and he was settled in between the two humps.

He reports that afterward the camel's disposition was much improved.

No more drooling, head-turning, or attempts to bite. The animal even allowed Scott to stroke its neck.

His caravan continued along the wall for four days. The map showed that except for a few humps of dirt, nothing remained of it until a point north of Lanzhou.

The camel drivers turned around to go home, and Scott's guide arranged a car. They drove along a highway until the map indicated they were near a section of the wall that still stood. They stopped, walked across rough terrain until they reached it, then walked as far along the structure in both directions as they could.

Four days later Chang Jin and Scott saw the Yellow River, and up ahead the wall turned north toward the water.

At a hotel in Lanzhou, Scott made plans to hire another car and continue his trek. But the next morning he came down to breakfast only to find a room filled with tourists. Worse, the Chinese official leading the group had commandeered all the cars in town.

Scott bought a railroad ticket to Beijing with a stop in Datong, the same route he had taken a month earlier with the tour group.

The next morning Scott put on what he called his "tourist shirt," and a baseball cap, and with a camera dangling around his neck, he checked in at the train station. Once aboard, he went to his compartment, changed his outfit to blue denim pants, Mao jacket, and his new Chinese army hat. He strolled down the corridor until he found a railcar designated for those who could pay only the minimum rate. Scott says he sat in the middle of the floor, pulled his hat down around his ears, leaned forward, and waited as the car filled with people dressed just as he was dressed. And there Scott sat, not moving as the occasional uniformed railroad official or security officer passed through the car.

It was almost midnight when Scott felt the train slowing for his destination, Yinchuan. Now came the real test of his disguise. As Scott tells the story, he walked out with the crowd, staying in the middle, and continued to walk with them as they headed east some six miles toward town. Scott claims his disguise was successful.

In town, Scott found a hotel where a sleepy hotel clerk assumed he was a member of a foreign tour group that had just arrived, and assigned him a room.

The next morning Scott joined a Japanese tour group traveling from Yinchuan some 270 miles to Yulin, following the Great Wall. None of the

Japanese spoke English, and Scott spoke no Japanese, yet somehow his enthusiasm for walking the Great Wall was contagious. He pulled out his map of China and with a mixture of English and hand signals, along with much pointing and nodding, the group became as excited about the wall as was Scott.

When he alighted from the bus in Yulin, Scott looked over his shoulder. Suddenly it seemed that from every window two or three arms were waving at him, and the air was filled with what he took to be words of encouragement.

Scott shouldered his pack and began hiking along the wall at a pace he estimated to be about four miles per hour. This is close to jogging, so again, a bit of skepticism is in order.

The wall soon disappeared into dust, forcing Scott to hike on the road through a flat, desolate part of China called the Ordos.

At dusk Scott approached a house where a subsistence farmer was generous enough to give him a melon. Scott retreated a few hundred yards to what he called "my camp," where he built a small fire, boiled water from the nearby river to make tea, and then enjoyed his dinner of melon and tea followed by two chocolate-chip cookies. Scott rolled up in his ground cloth and went to sleep.

The next seven days unfolded more or less in the same manner: two meals a day of melon and tea followed by cookies. Including the distance Scott had traveled with the Japanese tour group, he had now crossed the area framed by the Big Bend of the Yellow River and had approached the river's edge again. That afternoon he reached Shuocheng and, by means he does not explain, rented a car and driver and drove forty miles north to the Great Wall. Scott was back on the main part of the masonry wall again and he could see the equally spaced lookout towers in both directions.

As he had done in every place where he had reached the wall, Scott carved his name in Chinese characters into one of the stones of the wall. On his map he marked an "X" signifying the places on the wall where he had left his mark.

That night Scott was back in Datong. At his hotel he surrendered his passport, visa, and travel permit to the hotel clerk, as was the custom for tourists in China. The next morning he came downstairs to find a security officer going over his documents.

Scott had not disappeared in China as he had thought. He had simply disappeared from the watchful eyes of the hotel clerks and police officers who kept track of all foreigners in China. Now those officials had caught up with him, and they were not amused. Scott's route had taken him near a Chinese missile range, and the security officer was wondering if Scott was a foreign spy.

For days Scott was questioned without end, talking to an interpreter, waiting for the translator to translate his words into Chinese for the benefit of the security officer, waiting as the security officer stared at him, waiting as the security officer spoke in Chinese, and waiting until the question was translated into English. The security officer was particularly interested in Scott's map showing the route of his hike and the occasional "X" along the wall.

One morning Scott was awakened early and herded into a car with the security officer and the translator. The security officer unfolded Scott's map, pointed at the closest "X" on the Great Wall, and ordered the driver to go there. Scott walked him to the tower where he had carved his name, and the security officer studied the carving. The officer then pointed to the next "X" on the map, and the group returned to the car and was off again, backtracking across China, looking for "X"s.

It was after dark when the group returned to Datong, where all of Scott's documents were returned. The security officer seemed satisfied that he was in the presence of a quirky old American who simply wanted to travel the length of the Great Wall. In fact, the security officer seemed to admire Scott's quest, and he pointed out that China offered many other notable sights worth visiting.

The next morning the security officer was waiting when Scott came downstairs for breakfast. With him was a middle-aged man dressed, as was Scott, in blue denim. The security man was introduced to him as "Mr. Li," but Scott had been in the military for too long—in writing of this incident, he said "50 years"—not to recognize another senior officer. If proper military protocol was being followed—and Scott sensed that it was—then, like Scott, the man was a general. Thereafter, Scott thought of the man as General Li.

Outside, General Li and Scott's pack went into the back of a jeep and Scott sat up front with the driver. Scott had no idea of the destination and he feared he was being taken east to Beijing and deported, or worse.

Instead the jeep headed north. As Scott took out his worn and creased map, General Li leaned forward and in excellent English informed Scott, "General, I now become your guide." And then he said, in effect, "You wanted to see the Great Wall. You will see the Great Wall."

The jeep labored along ever-steepening hills until at an altitude of about six thousand feet, the wall crawled along the flanks of the mountains. The jeep stopped. General Li shouldered a backpack similar to that of Scott's and waited. He needed to know if a man of Scott's age could hike, and the first test appeared to be mountain climbing. Off the pair went, hiking along the wall.

At sunset they reached a lookout tower, where General Li unpacked a teapot and a heating tablet and the two men shared tea and a few of Scott's oatmeal cookies. General Li had brought no food, and Scott assumed that was yet another way to measure Scott's ability to survive.

The next morning, General Li and Scott paced the base of the tower, measured it as about forty feet on a side, and General Li delivered a brilliant exegesis of how Ming engineers had laid the foundations and cemented the wall between them.

For the next eleven days the two men hiked the wall, covering—so Scott says—250 miles along the most spectacular sections of the wall and through some of the most spectacular scenery he had ever seen.

Hiking 250 miles in eleven days, walking eight hours each day, works out to 22.72 miles each day. Or 2.38 miles an hour. A stiff pace indeed for two aging men.

Skepticism is in order. Scott does not say so, but he probably rode most of this distance in a military vehicle.

During the day the two rarely spoke. But at night over a fire and a cup of tea, General Li talked of the history and geography of China. And Scott talked of his lifelong fascination with the wall, of that day in 1945 when he had flown a P-51 from the Old Dragon's Head on the Yellow Sea along the wall, Scott following the shadow of his aircraft and praying that one day he might walk where his shadow danced. And now he was on the very part of the wall that he had flown over. Scott told General Li how he had photographed giant Chinese ideographs on a gate tower that later were translated as "First Gate in the World."

General Li nodded in understanding and explained how China once considered itself the only world there was. Beijing was at the center of that world. And the gate on the Yellow Sea was thus the first gate in the world.

By now Scott's cookies were gone, and only a handful of crumbs remained. He and General Li shared the crumbs and several more cups of tea. Scott looked at the last bits of crumbs and said, "That's how the cookie crumbles." Seeing the puzzled expression on the general's face, Scott tried to explain the meaning of the phrase, but he was not sure he succeeded.

Now Scott was about 250 miles from the Yellow Sea, but his travel permit had expired, and he needed to return to Beijing for another in order to continue the final leg of his great dream.

The next morning General Li escorted Scott to the train, followed him to his seat, and talked with him until the train was about to depart. Only then did he give Scott his new ticket. By now Scott and his guide had become friends. Scott asked his new friend if he had waited until the last minute to provide the ticket because he feared that Scott would leave the train and strike out on his own again.

General Li smiled and said, "That's the way the cookie crumbles."


Once Scott had his new travel permit, a Chinese official returned him to the spot where he and General Li had spent their last night together. Scott then walked some seventy miles to a small town called Gubeikou, where he was met by yet another Chinese officer. But this one was a captain and he was in uniform.

The captain did not want Scott to walk the final two hundred miles; he wanted Scott to ride in a truck. Scott says that eventually the captain relented and allowed Scott to walk, but at every place where the road passed through a gap in the wall, one of the captain's trucks was waiting just in case.

Scott said he was hiking almost thirty miles every day (assuming an eight-hour day, this is about 3.75 miles an hour) and that he was coming to the end of a dream that he did not want to end. For the first time in his life, Scott slowed down and sauntered, taking pictures even when there was nothing to photograph.

His goal was to reach Horned Mountain Pass, only fifteen miles from the sea, and a place he had flown over back in 1945. There he would bed down for the final night of his long walk.

It was almost dark when Scott topped a rise and sighted the Yellow Sea. He stopped, took off his pack, and looked at the water and then back over his shoulder at what he called the "rambling old dragon of masonry" he had been following.

Scott says that sleep was a long time coming that night, that his thoughts were filled with memories of Kitty Rix, especially her last words to him.

He said that as she was dying she was trying to talk and he leaned close and placed his ear near her lips as she whispered, "I know you had to do those things your way, and I understand . . . I understand."

In his earlier writings about the death of Kitty Rix, he does mention this exchange. But maybe Kitty Rix's words fit better into Scott's story at the Great Wall than anyplace else.

Scott's last hiking day began early, and by sunup he had reached the First Gate in the World. Then the wall gave out and became a raised mound of hardened earth. Scott was standing on the parapet of Old Dragon's Head just above the beach, and below him the surf pounded on the rocks.

He ran down the dunes and into the waves of the Yellow Sea.

During the past ninety-three days, Scott had walked—by his reckoning—more than fourteen hundred miles. He had realized the last of his boyhood dreams, and he was ready to go home. But upon Scott's return to Beijing he was shown the story in the *New York Times* saying he was in China to honor Chennault.

Scott says he now had no choice. He had to go to Kunming and commission the memorial.

Scott flew to Kunming, and when he got off the airplane he looked to the west, toward the top of a mountain known as Xi-shan, and the place where he and Chennault had gone on numerous occasions to discuss plans for attacks against the Japanese. The top of the mountain was broken off, sheared by an ancient earthquake, and had slid into a lake several thousand feet below.

That's where the memorial to the Old Man should go, thought Scott. Up there atop Xi-shan, and overlooking the lake and what had been the Flying Tiger airfield at Kunming.

Given that an interpreter and guide met Scott at the airport, the Chinese government knew what he was about, and there probably was not the drama attached to all this that Scott tries to impart. What is more likely is that Scott's recent close association with several high-ranking Chinese officers had revealed him for what he really was: an old warrior who still loved the country he had once fought for, and who wanted to honor the general who had been his friend and superior officer. Military people understand such things. The Chinese venerate both the elderly and their heroes. Chennault had fought for China. And of course there was the *Times* story, a story that if borne to completion could only reflect well on China at a time when she was slowly opening her arms to the world.

The young guide, who had not been born when Scott was first in China, nevertheless knew all about Chennault, the Flying Tigers, and Scott.

On his first day in Kunming, Scott found a stonecutter, something he could not have done without the guidance and cooperation of the Chinese government.

On his second day, Scott was again joined by a man he took to be a retired Chinese military officer. It is doubtful the man was "checking me out," as Scott says. At this point Scott has been in China almost three months and there is little left to check out about him. Chances are the retired officer was simply a person of some influence who was there to expedite Scott's endeavor.

But Scott writes of developing a cover story regarding his search for a stonecutter and a piece of marble. He says he told local officials that, as commander of the Twenty-third, he had lost several young fighter pilots during the war and wanted to have a stone cut with their names upon it. He would take a photograph of the memorial in order to record its installation, and he would take the photograph home with him.

Scott climbed up through a tunnel chiseled out of the mountain, up the 371 stone steps to the Dragon Gate, a parapet atop the mountain overlooking the lake and across some ten miles to the old airdrome.

Scott's new friend listened with rapt attention to the stories of Chennault and the Flying Tigers. After one long conversation, Scott asked if he could visit the old airfield where eight Americans were buried. He wanted to revisit the little house where he had lived with Chennault.

His new friend helped find a piece of marble for Chennault's memorial, a piece of native granite, forty-two inches tall, twenty-two inches across, more than six inches thick, and weighing more than a thousand pounds. A monument for the ages.

Scott gave the stonecutter a piece of heavy rice paper on which were written the words he wanted incised on the memorial stone, and he returned to the studio daily to watch the cutter's progress.

One day he received an invitation from a colonel in the Chinese air force. The colonel arrived in a jeep, and took Scott for a drive, through scarred eucalyptus trees and along a road that Scott had remembered driving on many years earlier. Then through a gate, where the sentry saluted. He was back at the old air base, but nothing was the same. The runway was not stone and mud but concrete. He could not find the site where eight of his men had been buried.

The Cultural Revolution had not just changed the city; it had obliterated many signs of the past.

As Scott and the colonel drove around the base, he was distracted by the takeoffs and landing of jet fighters, the Chinese version of the Russian-built twin-engine MiG-19s. No pilot can hear a fighter take off or land and not turn to look, to observe the technique, to see things that only a military pilot sees. A civilian only sees a small jet leaving the ground. A former fighter pilot notices if the aircraft is carrying external fuel tanks, hard points for rockets or bombs. And he can tell by how much runway is used and the attitude on takeoff if the aircraft is lightly loaded. He evaluates the pilot's technique, notices how quickly the landing gear retracts, whether the climb out is straight ahead and slow, or quick and steep.

The colonel took Scott to the flight line, where he introduced him to several fighter pilots. And it was clear from the questions they asked that each had been briefed on who Scott was. These young men knew how many aircraft Scott had shot down, the dates of his victories, and the types of Japanese aircraft Scott had destroyed. These are the things that young fighter pilots around the world know about their older brothers.

Within seconds Scott was in the middle of a group of young pilots, using his hands to communicate, each hand representing an aircraft, showing how he came out of the sun, bounced the enemy and shot him out of the sky.

Scott sat in the cockpit of an MiG-19, examined its controls, and he answered questions about similar American jets. For a brief time there was no American and no Chinese, only the brotherhood of fighter pilots.

The pilots showed Scott a magazine, which he said was a Chinese version of *Life*, containing a story about the Flying Tigers, and they asked Scott to autograph it. He realized that China was recognizing the Flying Tigers as Americans who had fought for China, just under a different regime.


Each day the audience at the stonecutter's grew. The characters in Mandarin were taking shape on the marble.

When the stone was finished, the stonecutter refused to accept payment. This monument honored a foreigner who had fought for China, and he would accept no fee.

The polished stone was lifted to the bed of a truck and driven slowly up to the top of the mountain, unloaded and slid toward the prepared spot, then carefully moved until it fit into a niche in the broken rock. Its calligraphy faced across the lake toward the airfield at Kunming.

Scott stood in front of the memorial and looked at the Chinese characters, which, translated, said:

> General Claire Lee Chennault
> We, your men
> Honor you forever.

Scott stared at the granite memorial and the past came flooding over him. He snapped to attention and rendered a crisp salute as tears rolled down his cheeks.

Now he was ready to go home.

Nephew Roland doubts that his uncle walked fourteen hundred miles along the wall. "He rode more than he walked," Roland said.

But distance was not the important thing. What was far more important, and what we must admire, is Scott's ingenuity, perseverance, and determination; that he was there at all, that he did walk or ride at least several hundred miles along the wall. He was doing something he had wanted to do since he was fourteen. Now, at seventy-two, he had entered China, sneaked off on his own, then walked or ridden at least part of the way from one end of the wall to the other. He had done what so few men are privileged to do: live out a boyhood dream. He had come as close to replicating the route of Marco Polo as any man can in modern China. It may have been a quixotic dream, but it was his dream. For most men, their dreams wither and die. But Scott had been doing what he wanted to do since he was a teenager.

Back home, Scott resettled into the house in Sun City. As he decompressed from the trip to China, he realized that he had accomplished all he ever wanted to do in life, and that he had lived beyond his biblically allotted three score and ten years. He no longer had a purpose in life.

Scott began to slide into a depression; soon he was sleeping for much of every day. Occasionally he would pick up his Bible and invariably he was drawn to one of Mama's favorite verses, a verse from Ecclesiastes: "Whatsoever thy hand findeth to do, do it with all thy might; for there is no work, nor device, nor knowledge nor wisdom in the grave, whither thou goest."

Was the Big Sky Boss sending him a message? Was there something else in store for him, one more job to do? At his age?

# 33

# ONE MORE MISSION

ONE NIGHT IN LATE FEBRUARY 1985, SCOTT RETURNED TO SUN CITY
after making a speech at the National Museum of the United States Air
Force at Wright-Patterson Air Force Base near Dayton, Ohio. He had not
just spoken to a full house; an adjacent room was also filled, with people
who listened in rapt attention as the words of his speech were piped in over
a public-address system. The audience had come from Canada, Maine,
New York, and Massachusetts. One of his former crew chiefs had driven
ten hours to hear the speech, and after the speech he had to drive another
ten hours to return to work on time the next day.

But now Scott was home, back in the little house in Depressionville, and
he was weary. He dumped his stack of accumulated mail on a table in the
living room, and put his suitcase in his bedroom. He sat at the counter in
the kitchen and rustled up his standard dinner of graham crackers, chunky
peanut butter, strawberry preserves, and a glass of buttermilk. Scott looked
across the kitchen through the dining room and into the living room, and
his shoulders slumped. All the reminders of his past life were there in the
living room: the photographs of him with Chennault, the zebra-skin rug,
the wastebasket made from an elephant foot, the teak table from Panama,
a dozen plaques, the mementos of the Book and the movie, all the sign-
posts of a long and active life. But all those things were in the past. And
now the house was empty without Kitty Rix. He saw Robin infrequently.

A doctor had told him he was suffering from "reactive depression," the
diagnosis of a patient who has been active all his life and now has nothing
to occupy his time and no purposes to guide his life.

The words of one of his favorite poets came to him.

*I will not wash my face;*
*I will not brush my hair;*
*I "pig" around the place—*
*There's nobody to care.*
*Nothing but rock and tree;*
*Nothing but wood and stone,*
*Oh, God, it's hell to be*
*Alone, alone, alone!*

Scott pushed his chair aside and got down on his knees. He clasped his hands, looked skyward, and in a voice grown reedy and quivering said, "God, you've left me here for a long time. What did you leave me here for? What do you want me to do?"

Scott had enough experience dealing with the Big Sky Boss to know that his prayer would be answered. And while he would have preferred a pillar of fire by night and a column of smoke by day, he knew that sometimes the answer can be slow coming, subtle in nature, and difficult to recognize. Sometimes the answer is so obvious it is overlooked. But Scotty was confident. "I had radioed in my position report and would continue on until I saw a beacon to guide me," he said.

He stood up and walked into the living room. Now was a good time to sort through the backlog of mail. The letters he thought might be invitations to make speeches, he put into one pile. Bills in another pile. Then a letter with a postmark from Warner Robins, Georgia, drew his attention. He remembered Warner Robins as a little nothing town about fifteen miles south of Macon. Who from Warner Robins could be contacting him and what in the world could they want?

The letter was from a man named Bill Paul and asked if General Scott had a large photograph of himself that he might consider donating to something called the Museum of Aviation in Warner Robins.

Scotty needed to talk to someone back home. He sat down and typed a long personal letter about traveling to make speeches, about China, about living in Arizona, about his depression, and how much the letter from home meant to him.

When Scott had finished typing, he felt energized. He had not been back to Georgia in . . . it was hard to remember the last time. Was it when his dad had died following surgery?

It was not a week later when Scott's phone rang, and the caller identified herself as Peggy Young, director of the museum at Warner Robins. She said a member of her staff had told her about him and that she was surprised because "I didn't know you were still alive."

"Yes, I'm still kicking," Scotty said. He swallowed hard with the realization that some people thought he was dead. But, then, he did not hear the South in Peggy's voice. She was not from around Macon.

Peggy Young said that one of her staff had written Scott about hanging his picture in the museum, that she had seen Scott's response, and that she wanted to work out the details regarding the picture and any other memorabilia the museum might use.

Scott told her he had a large oil portrait that had been painted after he wrote the Book, plus boxes and trunks filled with all sorts of memorabilia from China, his hunting trips, and on and on. He had lots of things. And suddenly the idea of sending souvenirs and trophies and photos to a museum near Macon excited him.

"Can you ship it to us?" Peggy asked.

Scotty was still thinking about the symbols of his life being in a Georgia museum.

"Never mind the shipping," he said. "I'll bring it to you myself."

And thus began the glorious, luminous, and lasting final chapter of Scotty's life.

Peggy Young was from Connecticut. She was a petite bleached blonde with preternaturally bright eyes, bright lipstick, and too much makeup. She was always impeccably turned out. But behind this genteel exterior was the personality of a ferret on steroids.

When her husband, Bob, retired from the Air Force as a major, the couple moved to Warner Robins. Bob had once been stationed at Robins Air Force Base, which abuts the east side of town, and both Bob and Peggy considered the town exceptionally friendly to the military. In fact, a hedge that ran along the road in front of Robins Air Force Base had been trimmed to read "EDIMGIAFAD"—Every Day in Middle Georgia Is Air Force Appreciation Day. And more than sixteen thousand people worked at Robins, making it the largest employer in the state.

Warner Robins was a warm and friendly little town. Sure, it had Southern attitudes that could sometimes make transplanted Yankees uncomfortable, and they would never understand the locals' obsession with the Civil War, bird hunting, and college football. But they had access to all the amenities and facilities at Robins, and Macon was only a half hour up the road. If they wanted to visit a bigger town, Atlanta was about an hour north of Macon.

Even though the Book had been written more than forty years earlier, when driving up I-75 or around Atlanta it was not at all uncommon to see cars with a front license plate reading "God Is My Co-Pilot." The Book's title had long since entered into the vernacular.

Bob was happy with retirement in Warner Robins, but Peggy was not the retiring type. In February 1972, she went to work at Robins AFB as a temporary Civil Service GS-2.

In 1973, Peggy graduated from a local college with a degree in business and specializing in management.

Not only was Peggy aggressive, she was persistent. Now she had the college degree required to climb to the heights she wanted.

Most of the civilians at Robins were local folk and, as the local expression has it, "not et up with ambition." But Peggy was ambitious and she craved the perks associated with being around high-ranking officers. She soon became a management trainee, and in 1975 she began preparing briefings and supervising special projects for generals. Soon she was doing the briefings.

Now that she was hobnobbing with generals, she was embarrassed that Bob had retired as a major, and she asked him not to wear his uniform to social events. Bob agreed.

Peggy operated at one speed: wide open, and damn the consequences and the feelings of others. The mission was all that mattered. Like Hap Arnold, Peggy was the perfect person to start a project and ramrod it through naysayers and over obstacles until the mission was completed. But her manner and her attitude led some to wonder if she thought she had stars on her shoulders. In middle-Georgia parlance, she was "pushy" and "overbearing."

When the Air Force began developing the idea for a Museum of Aviation, Peggy was moved out of her job with the generals and sent to the remote, weed-covered, forty-three-acre southwest corner of Robins to "stand up" the museum.

The museum had twenty dollars in private funds, two displays, and a World War II Butler building handed down from a military base near Atlanta. Often Peggy and her staffers had to dip into their pockets to pay postage and buy office supplies.

Peggy found that the museum's master plan called for raising $10 million for what was seen as a regional museum. But she dreamed bigger dreams. She saw a world-class museum. The problem was that Peggy needed some sort of draw—a big personality who could raise big money.

Then came the day in May 1985 when Scott first arrived at the museum.

He had called in advance to tell Peggy what time he would arrive. Peggy knew that when military people give an arrival time, they will be there. So she and her staff were standing in front of the ramshackle building when they saw a new Cadillac wheel off the road and into the parking lot at considerable speed. Whoever was at the wheel drove like a fighter pilot. The door opened and a tall, gangly, white-haired man leaped out and ran around the car and to the door of the museum.

He was seventy-eight, and he was *running.*

After introductions and pleasantries, Scott opened the capacious trunk of his Cadillac. As he passed out the boxes, he gave a running commentary on the contents. My West Point uniform. A first edition of *God Is My Co-Pilot* inscribed to my parents. Pilot wings from the Chinese air force awarded by Madame Chiang Kai-shek. Lots of Joe E. Brown memorabilia. A fictitious monograph I wrote when I was at West Point. A portrait I had commissioned when the book came out. Photographs from China. Photographs from my safaris. Awards as a certified White Hunter in Africa. A blown-up picture from *Life* magazine in the cockpit of Old Exterminator. And on and on and on.

Bill Paul was ecstatic. "I couldn't believe this was happening to me," he said. Other museum employees acted as if they were in the presence of a rock star, and Peggy, even though she was from Connecticut, quickly figured out that maybe this fellow Robert Scott could become the face of the museum.

And that is how the museum's first major display came to be called the General Robert Lee Scott Jr. exhibit.

Scott returned to Warner Robins to cut the ribbon opening the exhibit. The media reaction was frenzied. CNN came down from Atlanta and shot enough footage to do a long weekend story.

Lengthy front-page stories said that Scott had flown with the Flying Tigers, and that he had shot down twenty-two aircraft, even though he was officially credited with only thirteen. (Scott always disregarded the fact that the Air Force had gone through every pilot's combat records after the war and subtracted victories from many pilots. The U.S. Air Force officially credited him with ten victories.) He said he had thirty-three thousand hours of flying time. The newspaper stories told how Scott carried a seventy-pound backpack for ninety-three days as he walked the two thousand miles of the Great Wall of China.

Hundreds of people showed up. The local newspapers and TV stations and radio stations all attended the event, and the deference they showed Scott was palpable.

People looked at the exhibit and then looked at Scott with tears in their eyes. Part of their reaction was because Scott was from Macon; he was a local boy who had become a war hero and celebrated author. He was history made real. And he was a retired general. In Georgia, a retired general sits on the right hand of the Almighty as a respected and revered figure.

In the beginning, people were afraid to approach Scott. But he laughed and walked closer and reached out and shook every hand he could find. He made everyone comfortable.

People came up and said, "General, you have done so much. How did it all happen?" Scott would shrug and duck his head and say, "I don't know. I was just a guy who wanted to fly."

Grown men wept when they met Scott. With choked voices they told him what they knew of his record in China, and the impact the Book had on their lives, and how they had made a career in aviation because of him.

He was a famous man, and an aura of charisma hung around him. But there was also a vulnerability, a desire to please, a desire to be liked. Late in life Scott had become a gentle man, a nice man, a considerate man.

To the people of middle Georgia, Scott had overcome odds that appeared almost insurmountable. And here he was, a highly decorated combat hero and the man who had written the Book. And he had not gone uppity and tried to change his accent. When he opened his mouth, you knew he was from Macon. His voice was gravelly, syrupy, and diffident, Southern to the core. He did not try to big-time those who came to the opening. He was open and laughing and remembering the old days in Macon.

———

Scott made several trips to Warner Robins and the trips were good for him and good for the museum.

On one of Scott's trips Bill Paul was working as the museum's weekend manager. Scott popped his head in the door and told Bill he wanted to climb the post–World War II flight-line tower that sat outside the museum. He wanted to take pictures.

"Yes, sir," said Bill, thinking Scott wanted to climb into the glass-enclosed cab.

A few minutes later a volunteer rushed into Bill's office and blurted, "Do you know General Scott is up on the tower?"

"Yes, I told him . . ."

"No, Bill, he is on *top* of the tower."

Bill ran to the door and looked up at the tower. Scott had climbed a sixty-foot ladder to the cab, and then climbed up another ladder and was standing atop the cab some seventy-five feet above the ground.

Bill did the only thing he could do. He returned to his office, turned to the volunteer, and said, "I didn't see anything. You didn't see anything." And then they both crossed their fingers.

A half hour later Scott dropped into Bill's office.

"General, did you get your pictures?"

"Yeah, great view from up there."


After about ten days in Warner Robins, Scott had to drive back to Phoenix, where the condo seemed smaller and smaller, and the depression grew greater and greater. He had less and less patience with his neighbors.

One afternoon his phone rang; Peggy was on the line. Others at the museum called him General Scott, but Peggy had picked up on his nickname. She was one of the few people in middle Georgia who presumed to call him Scotty.

She saw Scott's potential as a fund-raiser for her museum and she was not afraid of asking big questions.

"Scotty, why don't you consider moving back home to Georgia?" she asked. "There is a place for you here. We want you to become the museum's national campaign chairman. Raise money for us. Make this a world-class museum. And we would enlarge your exhibit to include General Chennault and the Hump pilots. We want to tell the story of the CBI."

Scotty said he would think about it. He hung up the phone. For a seventy-eight-year-old man to uproot his life and move halfway across the country is no small thing.

Scott called his nephew Roland and said, "They want me to move back to Georgia."

Roland reminded his uncle of how unhappy he had been in Phoenix since Kitty Rix died; he thought a change of scenery might be a good thing.

"I don't know," said Scott. "The bugs and gnats. The heat. I would have to look for a place to live. I'm in the middle of a book." He paused. "They treat me like a king. They are promising me the world; rides in airplanes, a big job."

Roland did not respond. He could almost hear his uncle thinking.

Scott recalled the time when he was about to begin flying the mail, and what a senior officer had told him: "Scott, if you get into a situation where you can't turn back, don't be afraid to go on. Get some altitude and just go on."

Maybe this invitation was the way the Big Sky Boss was answering his prayer.

Scott liked the idea of a museum of aviation. He liked it that a major exhibit would be devoted to him and to the Flying Tigers and Chennault and the Hump pilots. And Peggy was dangling the idea of finding a P-40, rebuilding it, painting it in CBI war paint with a shark mouth, and calling it "Old Exterminator." She said that when new buildings and finances permitted, there could be a major part of the museum devoted to Scott's life.

Scott had lost his wife, and almost never saw his daughter, and his reputation remained tattered. He had lost it all and was a lonely and depressed old man who saw only bleakness in his future. But an exhibit in a museum means a man's deeds will live on. Maybe the museum could be his road to redemption. The basic message of an aviation museum is courage. From the beginning of his life he had manifested courage. In the skies of Burma and China he had manifested courage. When he wrote the Book he had manifested courage. A museum exhibit devoted to his life would be an exhibit devoted to courage. Americans, all Americans, respect courage.

Scott had asked the Big Sky Boss what to do with his life, and the chance to go home and build a museum was his answer.

"I figure we are here on this earth for a purpose," Scott said. "If we run out of purposes, we are just occupying space and shouldn't be here."

And so in 1988, Robert Lee Scott Jr. returned to middle Georgia. He had planned to move to Macon and commute to the museum. But by then he had many friends in Warner Robins, and they all wanted him in their town. The town had adopted him. And Dr. Dan Callahan, a physician closely associated with the museum, had become one of Scott's closest friends. "Dr. Dan," as Scott called him, had found Scott a house at 96 Ridgecrest Place, next door to his own house, in Warner Robins. Scott bought the house. Dr. Dan became his personal physician and their friendship grew.

Robert Lee Scott Jr. was back in middle Georgia; back where he came from.

## 34

# MISSION ACCOMPLISHED

SCOTTY AND PEGGY WERE ALIKE IN THAT BOTH NEEDED A BIG ROOM for their productions. It was natural that Scott agreed with Peggy that the museum they were building should be a national museum.

At first glance the idea seems preposterous. A national aviation museum in podunk Warner Robins, a place a half hour off I-75. The two roads leading to Robins AFB could be models for all the tawdry roads in all the sleazy Southern military towns; roads that seem devoid of zoning laws, roads jammed chockablock with pawnshops, used-car dealers, and outposts of every fast-food emporium in America.

But both Peggy and Scotty saw the goal, not the obstacles. They set to work. Peggy was the work horse, Scotty the show horse. He wrote letters, spoke to any civic group that would extend an invitation, and traveled from one corner of Georgia to the other beating the drum for the proposed museum. He turned over the rights to *God Is My Co-Pilot* to the museum, thus creating a small but steady revenue stream. His name opened a lot of doors that Peggy could never have opened. Political figures, including U.S. senators, came to Warner Robins to play in golf tournaments that would raise money for the museum. Business leaders and defense contractors, all of whom knew of Robert Scott and who wanted to be seen in his presence, wrote checks.

When Scott spoke about the museum, he tapped into the primal patriotic nature of Southerners. This is a national cause, he said. This museum is about America, about American airpower, about heroes and legends.

The unspoken subtext was "We may live down here in middle Georgia, in the middle of the pine trees and gnats, a place that in the summer is hotter than the back corner of hell, and we know that people in other parts of the country make fun of us. But, by God, we are just as good as any sumbitch from New York City, and we can build a first-class museum."

Scott was exhilarated by the speeches, the applause, the adulation. He felt better than he had in months. He ate dinner out often with Dr. Dan and his wife or with Peggy and her husband. If they went to a restaurant in Warner Robins, every head would turn when Scotty walked in. Excited whispers buzzed across the room: "That's General Scott."

People left their tables to shake his hand, to tell him what a hero he had been to them, how important his book was in their life, and would you mind if my wife takes a picture of us together? It was the same in Macon. Peggy and her husband began driving Scott to Atlanta, where he could have a nice quiet meal without being disturbed.

In 1987, the museum hosted a national conference of air museums—it was a first for Robins AFB and it gave the museum credibility and considerable publicity. Peggy, never the shy one, reached out to Tex Hill and Ed Rector and Bruce Holloway and asked them to attend the conference and sit on a discussion panel with Scott.

Until the three men walked into the big meeting room, Scott had not known they were attending. This was their first meeting in years and to have two of the original Flying Tigers, both of whom were squadron commanders under Scott when he commanded the Twenty-third, along with his successor as leader of the Twenty-third, simply overwhelmed everyone in attendance.

Scott, Hill, and Rector forgot about the audience. They were talking to each other, retelling their stories from China, laughing about Bissell's foolishness, speaking reverently of Chennault and Madame Chiang and shaking their heads in bewilderment about Stilwell's thinking the infantry would prevail in the CBI. They wept when they remembered their brother pilots who had died in China.

These were old men who had for a moment become young again; they were fighter pilots waving their hands in the air as they replayed old engagements and relived their glory days.

The crowd was amazed that Hill and Rector attended. These were two of the most famous of all AVG pilots, men of legend. The audience did not know much about Holloway, but he was a retired four-star who had commanded the Strategic Air Command, so he must be a big deal.

But it was Scott who raised the event to a higher level, and not just as a double ace, but as the man who had written the Book that had affected so many lives.

The aviation canon is not large. It is safe to say that almost every pilot knows of the poem "High Flight" and the novel *Night Flight*. And it is safe to say that almost every pilot knows of *God Is My Co-Pilot*.

Scott was aware of what Holloway had written about him, and he couldn't help but wonder how the Flying Tigers felt about him. That Hill and Rector attended gave him the answer. That they spoke so highly of Scott's leadership and courage in battle made this one of Scott's most rewarding days in years.

Holloway's bad mood that day may have been caused by a number of things. He had been retired more than fifteen years and had long since left the public eye. This meeting was a chance for him to appear at a venue where he outranked everyone present.

But at some point during the festivities, perhaps when he saw how the other three men interacted, and how the crowd loved them, he must have sensed that he was different. He had *been someone* but the other three had *done something*. Holloway knew the other three would be celebrated for as long as people talk of World War II, of the CBI, and of the AVG. Their names were in the pantheon of legendary warriors. He would be remembered instead as just another general. And in another generation or two, only his family would know anything more than his name. People would forget or ignore what he had written about Scott, but they would not forget Scott, the Lone Wolf of the Chindwin.

Scott sensed that he was being rehabilitated by his professional brothers, by the new generation of pilots who shrugged at those old stories about masking tape on the gun ports and who cared only that here was a man who had shot down a number of enemy pilots and had written the Book that made them join the Air Force.

And here in the South it did not matter all that much if Scott made little distinction between memory and reality. In the South, the legend is all that is important. Truth can be a pesky appendage. People liked the way General Scott remembered things.

The museum board asked Scott if he would become the honorary chairman of the Heritage of Eagles Campaign, the money-raising arm of the museum. Scott accepted. About half of the support for the museum is from private funds; the other half is in-kind payments from the Air Force.

In 1988 Scott turned eighty, and the museum had a party. Scott had not been enthusiastic about the party, because he thought maybe a few dozen people would show up and he would be embarrassed.

More than four hundred people showed up.

People came to him and said "Tell us the watermelon story" or "Tell us about flying the B-17 when you didn't know how" or "Tell us about talking the Book."

And off Scott would go. Telling stories was what he did. And as he talked the crowd around him became motionless, enraptured, laughing at all the punch lines they knew so well.

And always there were men in the back row, middle-aged men, who listened with tears in their eyes.

A few months after his birthday party, *The Day I Owned the Sky* was published. It is a curious book in that Scott rewrites much of his past; he tells the same stories but makes them better. He again inserts the story about a Romanian princess in the West Point chapter, and about how he and his aircraft were shot up during the raid over Hong Kong. The appendicitis operation in the wilds of Panama now has epic medical overtones.

The opening line to the book is a good one: "Long before any of the Japanese bombers saw us, I saw them."

With the first sentence, he puts the reader in the middle of an aerial gun battle.

The most important thing about the book is what it reveals about Scott's life. William Maxwell wrote, "In talking about the past we lie with every breath we draw." This is not about how speech might become altered, or even how writing may alter events, but rather how the things a person writes begin to blend with and replace the actual experience. How the retelling can overwrite the actual experience and become the remembered truth.

Reality was never good enough for Scott. And now, in his last book, he wrote his life story the way he *wanted* it to be.

And it could not have been better than what Peggy and the museum provided for him.

———

On September 23, 1988, Peggy organized another premiere of the movie in Macon at the Grand Opera House, the same venue where the original premiere was held more than four decades earlier. Dennis Morgan attended, this time without having his clothes snipped by scissors-wielding local ladies. The event raised more than $20,000 for the museum.

By now hundreds of thousands of visitors were coming to the museum every year. When local people came out, they never hesitated to go to the museum's corporate offices and ask if they could see the general.

Scott was very much aware of how he was perceived locally, and he never wanted it said that he was too busy to come out and talk to people. He was very much aware of the place he held in the hearts of so many. He would come out of the back office wearing a shirt patterned from the American flag. A big smile on his face, he would raise his right hand high in the air, say, "How are you?," and begin shaking hands and hugging necks. In five minutes everyone felt they had known Scott for years.

(Scott also went to the archive at the *Macon Telegraph & News*, asked to see all the clippings about him, and then wrote corrective notes and explanations in the margins.)

"General, how many Jap airplanes *did* you shoot down?" was the most common question.

Scott would adopt an aggrieved look, sidle a bit closer to the questioner, and in a conspiratorial whisper say, "Well, you know they gave me credit for thirteen." Pause. "I actually shot down twenty-two." Pause. "But they said the others were probables."

The visitors would nod in agreement, and every one of them believed the general had shot down twenty-two Japanese aircraft.

If Scott had stood on a street corner and announced that the next day the sun would rise in the west, half the people in middle Georgia would have crawled out of bed the next morning with their eyes turned in that direction.

He continued to make speeches, sometimes three or four a week. Scott's speeches were stories woven with patriotism, which always play well in the South, and laced with anecdotes that his audiences already knew by heart. He generated a lot of laughter. He never talked more than fifteen minutes, so that when he stopped, the audience still wanted more.

"Tell us about flying that Army plane from New York to Fort Valley to visit Miss Catharine," someone would shout.

Without missing a beat, Scott would say, "Well, I was just a poor lieutenant who couldn't afford a three-cent stamp, so I flew down and delivered her letter personally."

Many times he said, "The museum and the job they gave me saved my life."


I first met Scott in 1990 and over the next three months spent a great deal of time with him while researching a profile of him for a magazine. I was there when the Air Force put him in the backseat of an F-15, flew off the Georgia coast, and broke the sound barrier. He was thought to have been the oldest man ever to fly supersonic in the F-15.


On June 8, 1995, museum staffer Bill Paul married Barbara Mary Cotton, who worked at the information desk in the museum. Her father had died a decade earlier, and she asked Scott if he would give her away. Scott immediately said yes. Then he stared and paused for a moment and a burst of emotion swept over him. "My own daughter eloped and I never got to give her away," he said. "You will be the daughter I was never able to give away."

And at the wedding, when Scott handed Barbara off to Paul, he whispered, "I'm going to be keeping an eye on you, boy." Afterward he referred to Paul as his son-in-law.

And to this day, when Paul tells people of his wedding and how General Scott gave away the bride, people are amazed. "How did you pull that off?" they ask.


As do many elderly people, Scott was gradually becoming quirky. His obsession with orange juice is one example. He drank freshly squeezed orange juice every day. He discovered that what is sold in most restaurants as fresh orange juice is actually frozen or condensed juice. Once he announced that only two hotels in America served freshly squeezed orange juice: the Beverly Hills Hotel and the Waldorf-Astoria.

Scott bought an electric juicer and began buying oranges by the bag. He carried both in the trunk of his Cadillac, and when he went into a restaurant, the first question he asked was not about the location of his table, but the location of an electrical outlet. He said that every day he drank the juice from ten oranges. When he visited his nephew Roland, he hauled in his juicer and a bag of oranges and said, "I'm a juicing fool."

Along with his orange juice, the breakfast he ate every day was coffee with cream, two strips of bacon, and a sweet roll.

Scott rarely ate lunch, and except for his time in the CBI, his weight had never fluctuated more than two or three pounds away from 168 pounds. He remained trim enough that he could still wear his cadet uniform.

He liked to pick up pinecones in his backyard, because each cone he picked up represented a deep knee bend. Scott still walked two or three miles every day. Occasionally he would walk the seven miles from his house to the museum. And he still inveighed against cigarettes. To him, smoking cigarettes was the sign of a great character flaw.

When Scott went to another town to make a speech, it was customary for a local dignitary to be his driver. With them, Scott liked to demonstrate that his eyes had not lost their acuity. He would read aloud tag numbers from cars up ahead, cars where the driver or other passengers could barely even see the tag. And when the driver sped up to check the tag number, Scott was never wrong.

Scott's nephew Roland identified another attribute that became more pronounced in the years after his uncle had moved to Warner Robins. "Rob was generous to a fault," he said. "And it seemed to me he had an overwhelming desire to please and be loved by everyone he met. He succeeded in most cases."

Scott never lost his sense of impatience, of the need to keep moving. He abhorred stoplights, and when he pulled up to a red light, he would look both ways. If no car was coming, Scott would dart around other cars and continue on his way.

Some people in Warner Robins did not like what they saw as reckless driving and reported to the police that a Cadillac with "23 FG" on the license plate was running red lights.

On November 20, 1995, Chief Deputy Willie Talton of the Houston County Sheriff's Office wrote a "To whom it may concern" letter saying that he had ridden with General Scott to observe the general's driving skills, and that the general was "at all times alert to the traffic and conditions around him and his reflex response is excellent." He said that the general "demonstrated excellent driving skills."

Scott carried the letter for months and delighted in showing it to people. He also continued darting around stopped cars at traffic lights.

In 1996 the summer Olympics came to Atlanta and the torch passed through Warner Robins. Scott carried the torch part of the way through town. He was a tall, gawky, skinny old man with a shock of white hair, faintly bewildered, but smiling and laughing at the wonder of it all, one hand holding the torch aloft, the other occasionally jerking straight up in his trademark wave.

Bags of mail came for him every day in an unending flood, many asking for an autographed copy of the Book. Some writers wanted to call and talk and would leave their phone numbers and ask him to call long-distance for a chat. Some had written books and wanted him to read their manuscript or give them advice on how to get published. Other letters came from World War II pilots who wanted to rehash the white-hot days of their youth. Regardless of the subject, Scott read each letter and typed a personal response.

The Air Force took Scott aloft in a two-seat F-15 fighter on his eightieth birthday, and on his eighty-ninth birthday they took him up in a B-1 bomber. After long weeks of checking out, he also flew in the backseat of an F-16 Fighting Falcon, then one of America's hottest little fighter aircraft. By all accounts, he did most of the flying himself.

For some people flying is a job. When they walk away from an aircraft they have just flown, they never look back. But for some people, flying is a calling, a way of life. And even if they fly every day, when they climb out of the cockpit and walk away, they always look over their shoulder at the aircraft, and from the look in their eyes you know they want to return to the aircraft and fly again.

When Scott walked away from an aircraft, he always looked over his shoulder.

Scott continued to make speeches. When it was time for him to climb the steps up to the stage, the museum staff always flinched. Scott never walked toward the stage and he never walked up the steps: he ran. And as he ran he rammed his right arm upward to wave and looked over his shoulder and smiled at the crowd.

Scott was too old to be running up stairs. But if anyone tried to talk him into slowing down or—even worse—offered a supportive arm, they received a withering glance that only generals have truly mastered.

By now the museum was on firmer financial footing and had grown to include four major buildings, almost one hundred aircraft, and thousands of artifacts. More than 400,000 visitors came in the doors annually, making it one of the most important tourist destinations in Georgia. The General Robert Lee Scott Jr. Golf Tournament drew Georgia political and business leaders while raising around $100,000 annually for the museum. Georgia Highway 247 in front of the museum was renamed the Robert L. Scott Jr. Memorial Highway.

The Museum of Aviation at Warner Robins became the second-largest U.S. Air Force museum in America, second only to the National Museum of the United States Air Force at Wright-Patterson Air Force Base. Museum officials say that Scott personally raised more than $33 million to fund the growth of the museum.

A big part of the second floor of the museum is devoted to Scott's life. And the archival collection of the now-disbanded Hump Pilots Association is based at the museum. Photographs of the dour Chennault grace the exhibit.

Peggy was never bashful about asking Scott for personal items to be placed in the museum. Several times she went to his house, had him haul out boxes and boxes of letters and commendations and photographs. Many of the letters were personal and between Scott and Catharine while he was in China. But Peggy convinced Scott to donate them to the museum and today academic researchers have access to some nineteen boxes of Scott material.

Peggy had done her job well. She was the right person to build the museum. She had everything up and running, and now her bosses wanted her up and running. Pushy and aggressive people are not needed for a mature organization, and now it was time for her to be replaced by a seasoned manager. The museum hired retired Air Force colonel Ken Emery as director.

Scott took a fancy to Emery, who, in addition to running the museum, saw himself as something of an aide to General Scott, to the man who had become the heart and soul of the museum. When Emery took over, Scott went to him and said, "Whatever the museum wants me to do, I will do." He told many people, "This museum provided me with purpose." He said the museum allowed him to escape the boredom of Arizona, where "I was growing older and older without purpose."

After years of trying, the museum finally acquired a P-40, painstakingly rebuilt it, and painted it in Scott's wartime colors—including the shark mouth and the insignia of the Twenty-third Fighter Group. Under the canopy on the left side of the cockpit are painted thirteen Japanese flags.

When Ken Emery was reminded that the Air Force officially credits Scott with only ten aerial victories, Emery said, "He said he got thirteen, so by God, that's how many we put on there."

In middle Georgia, the legend is more important than historical fact.

Scott's younger brother, Roland, died in November 2002, and the funeral was held on December 3 at St. Nicholas Episcopal Church in Encino, California. Scott's nephew, Roland Jr., who prefers the nickname "Scotty," delivered the eulogy and then asked his uncle to say a few words.

Scott stood at the front of the church and looked at his brother's large and close-knit family, at his nephew, his nephew's wife and children, and when he spoke his voice was choked.

"This is what I wanted more than anything else. A family like this. You all are close and you are all here. This is what I never had."

By then Scott had stopped going to his office at the museum. But the people at the museum did not stop going to see Scott.

In late 2003, Bart Ramos, who worked at the museum as a handyman, was assigned more or less full-time duties looking after Scott. He drove Scott around town and occasionally bought him a bottle of Glenlivet or some M&M's. Scott was moderate in drinking his scotch, but he was not so moderate in eating the M&M's. He had developed a passion for them.

Ramos escorted Scott to restaurants and fended off well-wishers. Scott no longer wished to talk to everyone who wanted to talk to him. He was tired of telling the same old stories. By now, he had a fear of falling, and he was embarrassed that he had to hold on to whatever he could find as he walked.

If Ramos grew tired and slumped at the table, Scott snapped, "Sit up straight when you talk to me. I'm almost a hundred years old."

The museum staff worried that Scott was not eating well, and museum employees were assigned to bring meals to Scott's house. But he did not trust the employees, would not let them in, and would order them to leave the meals at the door. They often brought pizza with pepperoni—Scott's favorite meal—and sometimes he would eat it and sometimes he would not.

Ken Emery visited frequently, usually bringing in large amounts of mail addressed to Scott at the museum. He might also bring a pizza. The two would go through the mail and sip on scotch.

Late in 2004, Scott called Emery and asked a favor. He wanted Emery to drive him up to Macon so he could see the old home place at 511 East Napier, and then he wanted to drive down to Fort Valley and see Catharine's house.

When Emery parked in front of Scott's house, Scott leaned over and pointed out features of the house, and what he had done there as a boy. He showed Emery the house he had jumped off to fly a glider.

The two drove to University Avenue in Fort Valley and Scott stared for a long time at Catharine's old house. He talked, almost as if talking to himself, and Emery realized Scott was replaying his early life. Then in a tired voice, Scott said, "I'm ready to go home."

He was deeply appreciative to Emery. The day had meant much to him.

"General, I was honored that you asked me," Emery said.

After that trip, Scott went downhill at a noticeable pace.


Ken Emery tried to keep Scott engaged and would take him out on Saturday nights to see a movie—Scott loved the movies—or to have a steak. Scott believed there was always room for ice cream and often ended his meal with vanilla ice cream topped with chocolate sauce.

Emery supplied Scott with Glenlivet and M&M's. The recipe for the nightly toddy was rigid: a carefully measured jigger of scotch poured over a glass of ice. Scott would nurse the drink for maybe an hour. Then he would put on his silk pajamas, either the pair emblazoned with dozens of American flags or the pair that looked like leopard skin, and he would go to bed.

Scott kept his blinds drawn, stopped reading, stopped watching television, stopped reading newspapers, and spent his days in the gloom as the depression that had haunted him all his life began embracing him.

In the summer of 2005 the museum staff could no longer take care of Scott. Museum officials called Robin and said, "Your father can't live in that house alone. We think he needs to go into a personal care facility."

Bart Ramos, who had been Scott's driver and companion for three years, met Robin for the first time when she flew in to put her father in a personal care facility called Southern Heritage.

Southern Heritage consists of two fifteen-room buildings set on the edge of a pecan grove in Centerville—a small town surrounded by Warner Robins. "Homey" is a word frequently used to describe the facility. The staff addresses people—residents and visitors alike—as "honey" or "baby." After five minutes there, every visitor is a friend.

Administrator Anica Hollar, in whom the qualities of gentleness and toughness abide in harmony, is tall, looks everyone in the eye, and talks straight.

She said that for more than a month, Scott "was the worst resident we have ever had. He was the general, and he was used to giving orders."

Scott considered the facility to be a cage. He thought the place belittled and dehumanized him. He was angry at Robin for placing him there and he ranted and railed to high heaven.

Bart Ramos came out daily to see to Scott's needs, and Scott would lean close and whisper, "Keep your truck running. I've still got the keys to my house. I'll come running out and jump in the truck, and you can take me home."

It took Scott several months to accept that Anica outranked him and he had to take orders. And soon he would deal only with her and do everything she told him to do. She bathed him and got him ready for bed, and when he pulled out his silk leopard-skin pajamas, her eyes widened. "My Lord," she would later say, "I had never seen pajamas like that."

Scott began talking with fellow residents, and sometimes in the evenings he would roll his wheelchair into the lobby, listen to the conversation for a moment, then hold a finger in the air and say, "Now Sam McGee was from

Tennessee . . ." and off he would go, voice rising and falling as he recited the entire poem with all the drama of an actor.

He might be old and frail and confined to a wheelchair, but Scott was still a bugler.

The Robert L. Scott Jr. Heritage Banquet was scheduled for February 10, 2006, in the rotunda of the museum. It is not an annual event, and it is considered the most prestigious banquet held by the museum. Of course the invited guests hoped that General Scott would be there. But except for a few museum staffers, no one had seen Scott for more than a year.

"He's not doing well" was the line often used to explain that he probably would not attend.

Ken Emery urged Scotty to appear. So did Dr. Dan. High-ranking officers at Robins AFB tried. Everyone who knew Scott tried. He said no to them all. Even after Emery went to Scott's house, retrieved the general's mess dress uniform, and hung it in Scott's room, the general demurred.

Scott was a proud man and he did not want people at the banquet to see him in a wheelchair.

Then Anica reminded him of how old he was and how rarely the museum held the banquet named for him, and how "This might be your last chance to attend one of these banquets."

When the general paused, she pushed her advantage. "You dress up for me and I'll dress up for you. Let's go on a date," she said.

The general shook his head. "I am not going."

So, late on the afternoon of the banquet, Anica left the facility and headed home to her family. She told her staff to call if anything changed. She had not reached her home when her phone rang and she heard, "The general put his uniform out on the bed and is waiting for you to dress him. He says he is going to the banquet."

"Oh, my God. I can't believe it," she said. She called Emery and said, "General Scott is coming to the banquet."

After she dressed, she hurried back to the facility and dressed General Scott. He weighed less than a hundred pounds now and his uniform hung in folds from his bony body. His face was wrinkled, his skin was droopy, and his eyes were dim.

"When I tell you I'm tired I want you to take me home," he told her.

At the door to the museum, a red carpet awaited. Emery and museum staffers and half the people in attendance came out to the car to help General Scott into his wheelchair and to escort him into the rotunda. Several people pressed bags of M&M's into his hands.

When Scott entered the museum, it seemed as if a switch turned on. He became fully engaged. His head rose, his eyes brightened, he laughed and waved and pumped his hand high in the air and spoke to everyone he saw. But his main order of business was to show Anica the Robert L. Scott exhibit on the second floor. There he was pushed slowly around the exhibit, explaining in great detail every display. He told her of his childhood in Macon, of jumping off the roof and how his glider collapsed, of West Point, of Catharine, of China, and all the details of his Air Force career, and how he had walked the Great Wall.

"He remembered everything," she said.

At the banquet, when people looked upon General Scott they sensed that this might be the last time they looked upon this legendary man. Every eye remained focused on him.

The evening began with a recording of the national anthem. When the crowd stood, Scott grabbed the handles of his wheelchair with both hands, pushed and struggled and, perhaps aided by the silent prayers of many in the room, finally stood erect, locked his knees, and saluted.

As the meal was served, many dignitaries stood up and offered glowing toasts to the general. He smiled and nodded. He took a few bites of his salad, looked at Anica, and said, "I'm ready to go."

She walked beside him as he was pushed to the door. There he spun his wheelchair around and looked over the hushed crowd. Forks stopped in midair. Faces froze. He smiled that famous smile, gave everyone a thumbs-up, waved good-bye, wheeled around, and was gone.


Six days later, on the morning of the sixteenth, Scott was taken to a hospital to be treated for a stroke. Robin flew in from California and was offered VIP quarters at Robins AFB.

On the twenty-fourth, Scott returned to the personal care facility, where he was placed under hospice care. He could not eat, and he could not speak. His body was shutting down. But Anica looked into his eyes and she knew he could still hear. She said, "Scotty, I'm not going to leave you. I will be here." And the tears in his eyes showed her he understood.

On Sunday night, the twenty-sixth of February, 2006, Anica called Emery and said the end was near. Emery called Robin.

Emery was at Scott's bedside the next morning as dawn was breaking. Scott's breathing was slow and even. Anica turned to Emery and said, "There will be three deep breaths."

She leaned over and lifted Scott's head and shoulders and cradled him and whispered, "Robin loves you. I love you. So many people love you. If you want to go, it is okay. You can go."

Scott took a deep breath and let it out slowly. Another deep breath and a slow exhalation. A third. And then he was still.

Sunrise had always been Scott's favorite time of the day, and at 7:40 a.m., as a new day began over middle Georgia, the Lone Wolf of the Chindwin went west.

In the beautiful phrase of a local columnist, he went to join his co-pilot.

He was a few weeks short of his ninety-eighth birthday.

Emery waited at the facility until Robin drove over from Robins AFB.

On February 28, 2006, the *New York Times* published a lengthy obituary for Scott. It included a picture of him in the cockpit of a P-40 with a white scarf wrapped around his neck.

Scott was later buried at Arlington National Cemetery with full military honors. His cremated remains and those of Catharine were placed side by side under a marker. On the front of the headstone were Scott's name and rank and a listing of the medals he was awarded for his actions in China. On the back of the headstone were Catharine's name and the phrase "His Wife."


How to assess the long full life of a man such as Robert Lee Scott Jr.? Some will want to remember his career as a fighter pilot, some his career as a writer. And there are those in his home state who will forever remember that he built the Museum of Aviation.

Regarding his days as a fighter pilot, this must be remembered:

He was a double ace in the CBI and possibly shot down more aircraft than the record indicates. His bravery in flying solo missions, the abandon with which he engaged superior forces, his extraordinary skill at both aerial gunnery and dropping bombs, all have been documented. Scott was a brave, fearless, and highly decorated warrior.

No matter what else might be said, no one can take that away from him.

But many war heroes eventually fade into the mists of history. It was the Book that brought Scott lasting glory. Were it not for *God Is My Co-Pilot,* Scott would have been just another obscure officer. No other aviation book of World War II had so much influence or was more inspirational than the Book. In 2009, three years after Scott died and sixty-six years after the Book was published, it was described as a "classic" in *Aviation History* magazine. Walter J. Boyne, a famous aviation writer and former director of the Smithsonian's National Air and Space Museum, wrote the review. He said that even today, there is much to be learned from the Book.

No one can take that away from Scott.

At an age when most men are playing golf or playing with grandchildren or telling war stories of their youth, Scott was walking the Great Wall of China.

No one can take that away from him.

In his eighties and nineties, he was responsible, more than any other single person, for building an Air Force museum in a remote corner of America and turning it into a national destination.

No one can take that away from him.

And he was the Bugler. Unfortunately, no one can take that away from him either.

# ACKNOWLEDGMENTS

While researching this project I had the help of various people whose labors became the spine of this book. I owe them much.

I owe the most to retired Air Force historian George Cully. He found documents I did not know existed, provided insight into Air Force people and culture, and explained the significance of various research materials. His comments on the manuscript brought a comfort level regarding a broad slice of Air Force history and the individuals who made that history.

Dr. Daniel Haulman, chief, Organizational Histories Branch at the Air Force Historical Research Agency, helped me understand the controversy around the number of aircraft shot down by General Scott.

Yvonne Kinkaid of the Air Force History Office went out of her way to locate relevant material.

Kristin Wohlleben mined material from the 1940s. She is a focused and smart researcher.

Paul Graham, genealogist par excellence, reinforced my belief that any biographer who does not hire a professional genealogist has not performed due diligence.

Special thanks to a group at the United States Military Academy who were of great assistance in ferreting out details of Scott's time at that magnificent institution: Colonel Isaiah "Ike" Wilson, Colonel Ty Seidule, Major Ed Cox, Suzanne Christoff, and Paul Nergelovic.

Nancy Randle is a writer/researcher who knows her way around Hollywood. She provided important material about Scott's involvement with various movies and his involvement in the Hollywood social scene. The material was made available by Warner Bros. Archives, School of Cinematic Arts, University of Southern California. There is no better source for historical information about the movie business than the Warner Bros. Archives.

Muriel Jackson and Charlotte Bare at the Washington Memorial Library in Macon, Georgia, labored through decades of microfilm to find stories of Robert Scott.

Thanks to the staff at Wesleyan College for guiding me through the Madame Chiang Kai-shek exhibit. Madame Chiang's presence remains strong at Wesleyan.

AnnaLee Pauls of the Rare Books and Special Collections Department at Princeton University Library sent almost five hundred pages of material from the Charles Scribner's Sons archives. The material offered a rare insight into Scott and into the book-publishing process.

Three fine fellows at the Museum of Aviation in Warner Robins, Georgia, were tireless in their assistance: Ken Emery, Mike Rowland, and Bill Paul.

While I utilized the services of many researchers, I alone am responsible for any factual errors.

Finally, I do my work at my studio on Harris Neck, a remote and sparsely populated island on the Georgia coast. Island people are special people and I thank my friends on Harris Neck for their companionship during the writing of this book.

Robert Coram
Moonpie Studio
Harris Neck, Georgia, 2016

# BIBLIOGRAPHY

"Aces Twenty Third Fighter Group." Historical Division, USAF.

*Airmail Creates an Industry: The Army Takes Command.* National Postal Museum, 2004.

Allman, William B. *Successor to the Flying Tigers: The CATF. Aviation History,* March 1977.

"Annual Report of the Superintendent. United States Military Academy. 1932." West Point, NY: United States Military Academy Printing Office.

Baime, A. J. *The Arsenal of Democracy: FDR, Detroit, and an Epic Quest to Arm an America at War.* Boston: Houghton Mifflin Harcourt, 2014.

Barlett, Donald L., and James B. Steele. *Howard Hughes: His Life and Madness.* New York: W. W. Norton & Company, 1979.

"Battle of China: Blood for the Tigers." *Time,* December 29, 1941.

Belden, Jack. *Retreat with Stilwell.* New York: Alfred A. Knopf, 1943.

————. *Still Time to Die.* New York: Harper & Brothers, 1943.

————. "Chennault Fights to Hold the China Front." *Life,* August 10, 1942.

Bell, Raymond E., Jr. "With Hammers & Wicker Baskets: The Construction of U.S. Army Airfields in China During World War II." *Army History,* Fall 2014.

Bergerson, Frederic A. *The Army Gets an Air Force.* Baltimore: Johns Hopkins University Press, 1980.

Bernstein, Richard. *China 1945: Mao's Revolution and America's Fateful Choice.* New York: Alfred A. Knopf, 2014.

"Books: The Year in Books." *Time,* December 20, 1943.

Boothe, Clare. "U.S. General Stilwell Commands Chinese on Burma Front." *Life,* April 27, 1942.

————. "Burma Mission." Parts 1 and 2. *Life,* June 15 and June 22, 1942.

Borden, Norman E., Jr. *Air Mail Emergency: 1934.* Freeport, ME: The Bond Wheelwright Company, 1968.

Borneman, Walter R. *The Admirals: Nimitz, Halsey, Leahy, and King—the Five-Star Admirals Who Won the War at Sea.* New York: Little, Brown, 2012.

Boyne, Walter J. "Tex." *Air Force,* July 2002.

Brannon, Barbara A. "China's Soong Sisters at Wesleyan." *Wesleyan,* Fall 1997.

Buck, Pearl S. *The Good Earth.* New York: Washington Square Press, 1931.

Builder, Carl H. *The Icarus Syndrome: The Role of Air Power Theory in the Evolution and Fate of the U.S. Air Force.* New Brunswick, NJ: Transaction Publishers, 1994.

Byrd, Martha. *Chennault: Giving Wings to the Tiger.* Tuscaloosa and London: University of Alabama Press, 1987.

Caidin, Martin. *The Ragged, Rugged Warriors.* New York: Bantam Books, 1966.

Carrozza, Anthony R. *William D. Pawley: The Extraordinary Life of the Adventurer, Entrepreneur, and Diplomat Who Cofounded the Flying Tigers.* Washington, DC: Potomac Books, 2012.

"Class of 1932: Cadet Service Record." United States Military Academy.

Chennault, Claire Lee. *Way of a Fighter.* New York: G. P. Putnam's Sons, 1949.

Clark, Esther. "From Hero to Zero." *Arizona Days and Ways,* July 5, 1964.

Cockfield, Jamie H. "Robert Scott—God Was His Co-Pilot." *World War II,* January 1996.

Collins, Martin J. *Cold War Laboratory.* Washington, DC: Smithsonian Institution Press, 2002.

Cook, Jud. "Claire Lee Chennault came to China eight years ago to lay the plans for what eventually became the U.S. 14th Air Force. Now he has gone home and for the first time in his 55 years he doesn't know what to do next." *Yank,* September 1, 1945.

Cook, Kevin L. "Flying Blind." *Quarterly Journal of Military History,* Spring 2008.

Copp, DeWitt S. *A Few Great Captains: The Men and Events That Shaped the Development of U.S. Air Power.* McLean, VA: EPM Publications, 1980.

Correll, John T. "The Air Mail Fiasco." *Air Force,* March 2008.

———. "The Flying Tigers." *Air Force,* December 2006.

———. "Over the Hump to China." *Air Force,* October 2009.

Corum, James S. "The Myth of Air Control: Reassessing the History." *Aerospace Power Journal,* Winter 2000.

Donovan, James A. *Militarism, U.S.A.* New York: Charles Scribner's Sons, 1970.

Dunn, Susan. *1940: FDR, Willkie, Lindbergh, Hitler—the Election amid the Storm.* New Haven, CT: Yale University Press, 2013.

Eisel, Braxton. *The Flying Tigers: Chennault's American Volunteer Group in China.* Washington, DC: Air Force History and Museums Program, 2007.

Farley, Robert M. *Grounded: The Case for Abolishing the United States Air Force.* Lexington, KY: University Press of Kentucky, 2014.

Farmer, James H. *Hollywood's Flying Tiger. Wings,* August 1979.

"Flight from Burma." *Life,* August 10, 1942.

"Flying Tigers in Burma." *Life,* March 30, 1942.

Ford, Daniel. *Flying Tigers.* New York: Smithsonian Books, 1991.

Fortun, M., and S. S. Schweber. "Scientists and the Legacy of World War II: The Case of Operations Research." Sage Publications.

French, Paul. *Through the Looking Glass: China's Foreign Journalists from Opium Wars to Mao.* Hong Kong: Hong Kong University Press, 2009.

Frisbee, John L. "Flying Tiger." *Air Force,* April 1993.

———. "They Said It Couldn't Be Done." *Air Force,* September 1963.

———. "Valor: AACMO—Fiasco or Victory?" *Air Force,* March 1995.

Fullilove, Michael. *Rendezvous with Destiny: How Franklin D. Roosevelt and Five Extraordinary Men Took America into the War and into the World.* New York: Penguin Press, 2013.

Fussell, Paul. *Abroad: British Literary Traveling between the Wars.* Oxford: Oxford University Press, 1980.

———. *Wartime: Understanding and Behavior in the Second World War.* New York: Oxford University Press, 1989.

Glines, C. V. "Flying the Hump." *Air Force,* March 1991.

Grant, Rebecca. "Flying Tiger, Hidden Dragon." *Air Force,* March 2002.

Griffith, Thomas. *Harry & Teddy: The Turbulent Friendship of Press Lord Henry R. Luce and His Favorite Reporter, Theodore H. White.* New York: Random House, 1995.

Gurney, Gene. *Five Down and Glory.* New York: G. P. Putnam's Sons, 1958.

Hagedorn, Dan. *Alae Supra Canalem: Wings over the Canal; The Sixth Air Force and the Antilles Air Command.* Paducah, KY: Turner Publishing Company, 1995.

Halberstam, David. *The Powers That Be.* Urbana, IL: University of Illinois Press, 2000.

Hamilton, Virginia Van der Veer. "Barnstorming the U.S. Mail." *American Heritage,* August 1974.

Hammel, Eric. *Aces against Japan: The American Aces Speak.* Pacifica Press, 1992.

Harris, Hunter, Jr. Oral history. United States Air Force Historical Research Center, November 14–15, 1974, and March 1–2, 1979.

Haulman, Daniel L., ed. *Air Force Victory Credits World War I, World War II, Korea, and Vietnam.* Montgomery, AL: United States Air Force Historical Research Center, 1988.

Head, William P., and Diane H. Truluck. *Living a Dream, Building a Vision.* Oral history number 52, Mrs. Peggy B. Young. Office of History, Warner Robins Air Logistics Center, Robins Air Force Base, Georgia, 2001.

"Historical Data Pertaining to the 23rd Fighter Group." Air Historical Office, June 21, 1948.

Hochschild, Adam. *To End All Wars: A Story of Loyalty and Rebellion, 1914–1918.* Boston: Mariner Books, 2012.

Holley, I. B., Jr. "Of Saber Charges, Escort Fighters, and Spacecraft: The Search for Doctrine." *Air University Review.* September–October, 1983.

Holloway, Bruce K. Oral history. Albert F. Simpson Historical Research Center, Air University, Montgomery, AL, August 16–18, 1977.

"Interviews on Japanese Air Tactics and Chinese Capabilities with: Colonel Merian C. Cooper, CATF. January 1943, and Colonel Robert L. Scott, CATF. February, 1943." Intelligence Services. U.S. Army Air Forces. Washington, DC. January 16, 1943.

"Interview with Flight Leader George Paxson, A.V.G." 23rd Fighter Group: January 1941–December 1942. Historical Division, USAF, August 25, 1942.

Johnson, David E. *Learning Large Lessons: The Evolving Roles of Ground Power and Air Power in the Post–Cold War Era.* Santa Monica, CA: RAND Corporation, 2007.

Kaplan, Robert D. *Asia's Cauldron: The South China Sea and the End of a Stable Pacific.* New York: Random House, 2014.

————. *The Revenge of Geography: What the Map Tells Us About Coming Conflicts and the Battle against Fate.* New York: Random House, 2013.

Klein, Maury. *A Call to Arms: Mobilizing America for World War II.* New York: Bloomsbury Press, 2013.

Landfair, David G. "Name That Doctrine!" *Air & Space Power Journal,* July 1, 1997.

Lanphier, Thomas G., Jr. "At All Costs Reach and Destroy." Unpublished manuscript. U.S. Army Military History Institute, Carlisle, PA.

Lavender, Jim. *The Adventures of Robert L. Scott.* Research history thesis, Kennesaw State University, 2000.

Linden, F. Robert van der. *Airlines & Air Mail: The Post Office and the Birth of the Commercial Aviation Industry.* Lexington, KY: University Press of Kentucky, 2002.

Lonteen, J. F. "History of the 23rd Fighter Group. March 1942–September 1943." Historical Office, USAF.

Loomis, Robert D. *Great American Fighter Pilots of World War II.* New York: Random House, 1961.

Lopez, Donald S. *Into the Teeth of the Tiger.* Washington, DC: Smithsonian Books, 1997.

Manstein, Erich von. *Lost Victories: The War Memoirs of Hitler's Most Brilliant General.* Minneapolis: Zenith Press, 2004.

Maurer, M. *Aviation in the U.S. Army 1919–1939.* Washington, DC: United States Air Force Historical Research Center, 1987.

————. "The Irate Citizen and the Air Corps Maneuver of 1931." *Air University Review,* July–August 1985.

McLynn, Frank. *The Burma Campaign: Disaster into Triumph 1942–45.* New Haven, CT: Yale University Press, 2010.

Mitter, Rana. *Forgotten Ally: China's World War II 1937–1945.* Boston: Mariner Books, 2014.

Molesworth, Carl. *P-40 Warhawk Aces of the CBI.* Oxford, UK: Osprey Publishing, 2000.

————. *Sharks over China: The 23rd Fighter Group in World War II.* Washington, DC: Brassey's, 1994.

Moore, Samuel T. "History of the India-China Ferry under the Tenth Air Force." Air Force Historical Research Agency, 1943.

Mueller, Karl P. "Air Power." International Studies Encyclopedia, Vol. I. 2010.

Myers, Gene. "Interservice Rivalry and Air Force Doctrine: Promise, Not Apology." *Airpower Journal,* Summer 1996.

Newell, Clayton R. *Burma, 1942.* U.S. Army Center of Military History.

Nitobe, Inazo. *Bushido: The Soul of Japan.* Lexington, KY: Made in the USA, 2012.

O'Connell, Robert L. *Fierce Patriot: The Tangled Lives of William Tecumseh Sherman.* New York: Random House, 2014.

*Official Register of the Officers and Cadets: United States Military Academy for 1932.* West Point, NY: United States Military Academy Printing Office.

Olson, Lynne. *Those Angry Days: Roosevelt, Lindbergh, and America's Fight Over World War II, 1939–1941.* New York: Random House, 2013.

Olynyk, Frank. *Stars and Bars: A Tribute to the American Fighter Ace 1920–1973.* London, UK: Grub Street, 1995.

Pennington, Reina. "Prophets, Heretics, and Peculiar Evils." *Airpower Journal*, Summer 1996.

"Pilot's Manual for the Curtiss Tomahawk." British Air Ministry.

Polo, Marco. *The Travels of Marco Polo*. New York: Everyman's Library, 1908.

"Recruiting the AVG: Procurement of Personnel for China." Department of the Navy, 1941.

Redding, Stan. "Brig. Gen. Robert L. Scott." *Texas Magazine (Houston Chronicle)*, August 17, 1975.

"Report on Accident to Douglas OA-3 Amphibian at Panama Bay, piloted by R.L. Scott, Jr." January 22, 1936. Air Corps. Form No. 14.

"Report on Accident to Douglas OA-4B Amphibian, Jaque, Republic of Panama, piloted by R.L. Scott, Jr." April 19, 1937. Air Corps. Form No. 14.

Rhodes, Richard. "The Toughest Flying In the World." *American Heritage*, August/September 1986.

Romanus, Charles F., and Riley Sunderland. *United States Army in World War II: China-Burma-India Theater; Stilwell's Mission to China*. Washington, DC: Center of Military History United States Army, 2002.

———. *United States Army in World War II: China-Burma-India Theater; Stilwell's Command Problems*. Washington, DC: Center of Military History United States Army, 1987.

———. *United States Army in World War II: China-Burma-India Theater; Time Runs Out in CBI*. Washington, DC: Center of Military History United States Army, 1999.

Samson, Jack. *The Flying Tiger*. Guilford, CT: Lyons Press, 1987.

Schaller, Michael. *The U.S. Crusade in China, 1938–1945*. New York: Columbia University Press, 1979.

Scott, Robert L. *Boring a Hole in the Sky*. New York: Random House, 1961.

———. "Report of Operations of Twenty Third Fighter Group for Period July 4, 1942 to December 31, 1942." Kunming, China, December 31, 1942.

———. *Damned to Glory*. Garden City, NY: Blue Ribbon Books, 1945.

———. *The Day I Owned the Sky*. New York: Bantam Books, 1998.

———. *God Is My Co-Pilot*. New York: Charles Scribner's Sons, 1943.

———. *God Is Still My Co-Pilot*. Phoenix, AZ: Augury Press, 1967.

———. *Runway to the Sun*. New York: Charles Scribner's Sons, 1945.

———. *Between the Elephant's Eyes*. New York: Dodd, Mead, 1954.

———. *Flying Tiger: Chennault of China*. Garden City, NY: Doubleday, 1959.

———with Ted White and David Hodel. *With Wings as Eagles: The Robert L. Scott Jr. Story*. Unpublished manuscript.

———. "I'm Sorry I Shot You: The Saga of a Safari." *Skyblazer*, March 1953.

———. "The Flying Tigers and Me." *Saga*, February 1959.

———. *Return to the Great Wall*. Unpublished manuscript.

———. Personal Papers. Robert Lee Scott Jr. Collection, Boxes 1–16. Museum of Aviation, Robins Air Force Base, Warner Robins, GA.

———. Interviews by author, Warner Robins, GA, 1990.

Scott, Roland. "The Scott Family." Unpublished monograph.

Scribner, Charles, Jr. *In the Company of Writers: A Life in Publishing.* (Based on the oral history by Joel R. Gardner.) New York: Charles Scribner's Sons, 1990.

Slim, William. *Defeat into Victory: Battling Japan in Burma and India, 1942–1945.* New York: Cooper Square Press, 1956.

Smith, Nicol. *Burma Road.* Garden City, NY: Garden City Publishing, 1942.

Smith, Robert M. *With Chennault in China.* Atglen, PA: Schiffer, 1997.

Snow, Edgar. "China's Flying Freighters." *Saturday Evening Post,* August 1, 1942.

Sorenson, David S. *The Politics of Strategic Aircraft Modernization.* Westport, CT: Praeger, 1995.

Spritzler, Ramon J. "Medical History of the 23rd Fighter Group." Historical Divison, USAF, June 24, 1944.

Svendsen, Leroy W., Jr. Oral history. United States Air Force Historical Research Center, December 9–10, 1985.

Szafranski, Richard. "Interservice Rivalry in Action: The Endless Roles and Missions Refrain?" *Airpower Journal,* Summer 1996.

"Tales of the Tigers: The Flying Tigers Tell Some of Their Stories." www.flyingtigersavg.com.

Tenth Air Force. Interviews on Japanese Air Tactics and Chinese Capabilities. Intelligence Services, U.S. Army Air Forces, January 16, 1943.

"The China Air Task Force." Army Air Force Historical Office, 1942.

"Three Years with the 23rd." Office of the Historical Officer, 23rd Fighter Group, May 31, 1945.

Tuchman, Barbara W. *Practicing History.* New York: Ballantine Books, 1935.

———. *Stilwell and the American Experience in China, 1911–45.* New York: Grove Press, 1970.

———. "The Retreat from Burma." *American Heritage,* February 1971.

———. "Japan Strikes: 1937." *American Heritage,* December 1970.

Tunzelmann, Alex von. *Indian Summer: The Secret History of the End of an Empire.* New York: Picador, 2007.

"USAF Credits for the Destruction of Enemy Aircraft, World War II." Albert F. Simpson Historical Research Center, Air University, Maxwell Air Force Base, 1978.

Vandivert, William. "Joe Stilwell's War." *Life,* April 17, 1942.

Ward, Geoffrey C. "Alsop Ascendant." *American Heritage,* February/March 1992.

Warwick, Adam. "A Thousand Miles along the Great Wall of China." *National Geographic,* February 1923.

White, T. H. "The Greatest Show on Earth." *Life,* November 9, 1942.

———. "China Air Task Force." *Life,* April 12, 1943.

———. *In Search of History: A Personal Adventure.* New York: Warner Books, 1978.

White, Theodore H., and Annalee Jacoby. *Thunder out of China.* New York: Da Capo Press, 1946.

Y'Blood, William T. *Air Commandos against Japan: Allied Special Operations in World War II Burma.* Annapolis: Naval Institute Press, 2008.

Yenne, Bill. *Hap Arnold: The General Who Invented the U.S. Air Force.* New York: Regnery History, 2013.

Zabecki, David T. *God Is Still His Co-Pilot. Aviation History,* 2005.

# INDEX

AACMO. *See* Army Air Corps Mail
    Operation
academics
    slide from, 27–28, 30–32
    at West Point, 26, 29–34
adventures
    camping for, 267
    in China, 262–74
    disguise for, 266
    enthusiasm for, 267
    in India, 174
    strategy for, 266–67
aerial gunnery, 74
aerial snap shot, 76
Aiken, SC, 8–10
Air Transport Command (ATC), 173
airplane building, 257
ambition, 2
    in Army Air Corps, 75
    of Chennault, 70
    for Great Wall of China, 263
    in Panama, 75
    of Young, P., 280
America
    book popularity in, 203
    Britain with, 131
    China with, 130–31
    industrial strength of, 186
    as symbol, 204

*American Mercury*, 205
American Volunteer Group (AVG), 147,
    248. *See also* Flying Tigers
    Chennault training of, 105–8
    dissolution of, 153–56
    flying for, 151–54
    measuring up to, 151–54
    after Pearl Harbor, 114–15
    success of, 155–56
    supply shortage for, 152–53
    during World War II, 114–15
Anchorage, 200
appendicitis boy, 79–81
Arizona v. Scott Productions, Inc., 247
Army
    cavalry in, 34
    China allied with, 105–7
    enlisting in, 21
    Hollywood and, 103–4
    insults to, 237
    Japan and, 115
    life in, 21–22
    pilot in, 3–4
    rebellion in, 5, 30
    salary freeze in, 95
    speaker for, 3–4
Army Air Corps
    ambition in, 75
    beginning at, 39

Army Air Corps (*continued*)
  progress and, 63
  promotion in, 75
  rebellion in, 42, 75–77
  womanizing in, 40–41
Army Air Corps Mail Operation
    (AACMO)
  benefits from, 63
  crash record of, 61
  death toll of, 61–62
  flying for, 58–60
  Hell Stretch of, 59, 63
  organization of, 61–62
  perils of, 57, 61–64
  success of, 61–62
Army Air Forces (AAF), 179–80. *See also*
    Army Air Corps
  confidence of, 186
  insults to, 237–38
  publicity for, 209
  resentment in, 214–15
  resentment of, 239
Army Air Forces School of Applies
    Tactics (AAFSAT), forming of, 200
Arnall, Ellis, 245–46
Arnold, Henry H. "Hap," 62–63, 104, 112
  admonishments from, 194–95, 198, 215
  challenges for, 95
  character of, 94, 187
  complexity of, 187
  dedication to, 205
  derision of, 187, 209
  disagreements with, 210–11
  disappointment for, 205
  doubts from, 198
  military decorations of, 187
  orders from, 185–86, 210, 216
  pleading with, 215
  poor opinion from, 211
  promotion of, 94
  resentment of, 212
  retribution of, 225
Assam, 138
Assam-Burma-China Ferry Command
    (ABC), 137
  disappointment with, 164
  value of, 145–46
authorship, 1
  arrogance as, 191

  demands as, 210
  evolution to, 3–4, 185, 190
  fame as, 205
  income tax from, 208
  one dimension as, 211
  pride as, 193
  of second novel, 196
  work ethic as, 211
  writing as, 192
AVG. *See* American Volunteer Group
AWOL, 43, 194–95

B-17 airplane, 110–11
  experience with, 119–20, 123
  in Task Force Aquila, 123–24
bankruptcy, 247
Battalion Board, 32
Battle of Sandepu, 31–32
Belden, Jack, 136, 139
*Between the Elephant's Eyes* (Scott), 232
  fee for, 236
Big Sky Boss
  doubts in, 95
  faith in, 4, 46, 49, 113, 161, 185, 258
  message from, 275
  plan of, 278, 284
Bishop, Billy, 10
Bissell, Clayton, 47, 88, 134
  arrogance of, 147, 153
  doctrine of, 71
  promotion for, 147, 197
  rebellion toward, 153
  transfer of, 218
blind flying
  benefits from, 58–59
  volunteering for, 51–52
blooded, 104, 161
Boeing, 109–10
Bogart, Humphrey "Bogie," 210
the Book. *See God Is My Co-Pilot* (Scott)
Book of the Month Club, 206
book popularity, 203
Boothe, Clare, 135
Boyne, Walter J., 302
Brett, George, 78, 112, 122–23
  adjutant to, 81
  approval from, 81
  premonition of, 77

Britain
America with, 131
Burma rule of, 130–31
Japan and, 115
Brown, Don, 103
death of, 175
dedication to, 175–76
as golden boy, 89
Brown, Joe E.
antics with, 239
appreciation from, 175–76
as father, 98
of Hollywood, 98–99, 103, 175–76
Buck, Pearl, 95–96
the Bugler, 258, 302
bugling, 31–32, 35–36, 120,
189–90
Burckhalter (grandfather), 19, 121
Burckhalter, Jarrett D. (great-
grandfather), 10, 20
burglary
anger from, 258
security for, 258
burial, 301
Burma
British rule of, 130–31
Japanese invasion of, 130, 133
story of, 142–43
Bush, George H. W., 263

C-47 airplane "the Goon," 137–38
Cadillac, 244
Caidin, Martin, 146
Callahan, Dan "Dr. Dan," 285
camels
mounting of, 265
story of, 265–66
trouble with, 265–66
career, 241
cavalry
in Army, 34
mockery of, 34–35
at West Point, 34
cave surgery, 207
Chamberlain, John, 205
character
of airplane, 83
of Arnold, 94, 187

arrogance of, 66, 104, 117–18, 146,
219, 223, 226–27, 228, 232
audacity of, 237–37
of Bissell, 147, 153
charm of, 25–26
of Chennault, 88
of Chiang Kai-shek, 131
complexity of, 230
conceited in, 231, 235–36, 240, 263
confidence in, 278
distinction of, 231
dramatics of, 1–2, 98, 230
evil of, 231–32
flair of, 164–65, 188, 294
humility of, 206, 223, 282
as husband, 82–84
impatience of, 75, 228, 293
independence of, 52–53, 274
insecurities of, 4–5, 289
integrity of, 231–32, 236, 239
of Lewis, 196
of Madame Chiang, 90
of Mama, 199–200
mixture of, 81
optimism of, 138
paranoia of, 98, 101–2, 122, 143,
151–52, 180, 207
perseverance of, 143, 208
in poetry recitation, 30–31
scarf as, 188
of Scott, O., 199–200
self-awareness of, 257–58
self-centered in, 70, 75
of Stilwell, 132
stubborn in, 265
transformation of, 217
vanity of, 244, 246, 284, 291, 299
work ethic and, 21–23, 41, 51–54, 59, 77
of Young, P., 295
Chennault, Claire Lee, 132, 185
ambition of, 70
AVG trained by, 105–8
biography of, 239, 244–45
career of, 87–88
character of, 88
in China, 238
of China, 245
of Chinese air force, 87–88, 90, 97,
104–8, 218

Chennault, Claire Lee (*continued*)
  commonalities with, 147
  death of, 245
  dependency of, 177
  disfavor for, 87
  doctrine of, 71
  fame of, 163, 197
  first meeting with, 146
  Flying Tigers of, 114–17, 134, 146–48,
    158
  forced retirement of, 88
  friendship with, 70–71, 146–47, 168,
    174–75, 177–78
  as gardener, 158
  genius of, 167–68
  hobbies of, 87–88
  homecoming of, 221–22
  honoring of, 222–23, 271, 274
  idolizing of, 215
  introduction of, 205
  leadership of, 167
  memorial to, 263, 271, 273–74
  as mentor, 172–73, 244–45
  physique of, 197
  promotion for, 147, 197
  respect for, 108, 116–17, 168
  retirement of, 221
  salary of, 89
  strategies of, 212
  training by, 105–7
  trouble for, 219
  worship of, 147
Chiang Kai-shek, 146, 175. *See also*
  Madame Chiang
  character of, 131
  as Chinese leader, 87–89
  demands of, 218
  despair of, 89
  extortion of, 89
  nepotism of, 89
  religion of, 90
  ultimatum from, 212
childhood, 1, 8–20. *See also* Lanier High
  School
  scars of, 2
  storyteller of, 26–28
China. *See also* Great Wall of China
  adventures in, 262–74
  air force of, 87–88, 105–7

alliance with, 88–89
America with, 130–31
Army with, 105–7
camels in, 265
Chennault in, 238
Chennault working for, 87–88, 90, 98,
  104–8, 218
Communists in, 89
disappointment in, 272–73
Explorers Tour in, 259
fame in, 273
fears of, 130–31
Flying Tigers of, 107–8, 114–17
Japan and, 115, 129–30
Japanese invasion of, 91, 130
memorial in, 272–74
memories in, 272–73
return to, 259
storytelling of, 179–80, 188, 262
China trip, 262–74, 264
China-Burma-India (CBI)
  challenges in, 130
  changes in, 218
  combat in, 130
  defense of, 131–33
  fall of, 219
  fighting in, 129–30
Chinese air force
  Commission on Aeronautical Affairs
    on, 87–88
  Madame Chiang of, 89–91, 105
Chinese government
  acceptance from, 271–72
  caught by, 268
  correspondence to, 257
  documents from, 263–64
  evading of, 266–68
  fear of, 268
  manipulation of, 259
  permission from, 258–59
  questioned by, 268
  reaction of, 268
  relationship with, 272
  suspicion from, 268
  treatment by, 267–74
Chucunaque Indians, 79–80
church, 182–83, 189–90
Churchill, Winston, 115, 197
  leadership of, 132–33

Civil War, 2, 9, 16
  terrors of, 99
Cold War, 237
combat flying. *See* fighter pilot
Communism, 89
  in China, 89
  opinions on, 237
  speeches on, 241
community
  relationship with, 257, 283
  security in, 258
  treatment of, 257
Cooch Behar, 173
cooking, 69, 112
Cooper, Merian
  intervention from, 119–20
  of *King Kong*, 104
  of Task Force Aquila, 121, 123
Coram, Robert, 292
correspondence
  attention to, 294
  with Chinese government, 257
crashes, 59–60
  in AACMO, 61
  in Panama, 74, 81–82
  storytelling of, 82
Cully, George, 122
Curtiss-Wright Corporation, 188

*Damned to Glory* (Scott), 209
*The Day I Owned the Sky* (Scott), 290
dead reckoning "DR," 58, 125–26
death, 301
  of Brown, D, 175
  of Chennault, 245
  of Kitty Rix, 251, 270–71
  of Mama, 248–49
  of Roosevelt, 217
  of Scott, Robert Lee, 255–56
  of Scott, Roland, 296
decorations. *See* military decorations
demerits
  as observation pilot, 50–51
  at West Point, 30–31
depression, 2, 248, 274, 284
  beginning of, 118
  of Kitty Rix, 82–83, 136–37, 216,
    243–44, 246

progress of, 283
  as reactive depression, 277
  religion in, 275
  running for, 253
Depressionville, 253, 277
destiny, 4
  as fighter pilot, 70, 100–101, 160
determination
  as fighter pilot, 70, 113
  of Kitty Rix, 68–69
  of Stilwell, 14–141
  for West Point, 21–23
Dictaphone, 191–92
diet, 277
  for breakfast, 293
  for Great Wall of China, 256, 267
disgrace, 18–20
Doolittle, James "Jimmy"
  as bomber, 123
  competition with, 137, 156, 205
doubts, 23
DR. *See* dead reckoning

Eagle Scout, 11, 15, 26
  Scott, Roland, as, 20–21
East African Hunters Association, 232
Eisenhower, Dwight "Ike"
  as fisherman, 232
  inquiries from, 233
  recommendation from, 233
  relationship with, 233
Ely, Eugene, 7–8
emergency airstrips, 78
Emery, Ken, 295–96, 299, 301
  friendship with, 297
engineer, 75
Explorers Tour
  challenges on, 261
  in China, 259
  escaping from, 261–62

failure, 17–23
fame, 179, 188, 217, 238
  as author, 205
  challenges of, 214–16, 226
  of Chennault, 163, 197
  in China, 273

fame (*continued*)
  as fighter pilot, 144, 152, 164–65,
    168–69, 173, 194
  of Flying Tigers, 207–8, 273
  good use of, 189–90
  of Haynes, 163
  for health, 288
  impact from, 219, 288, 300
  in *Life*, 195–96
  in Macon, GA, 171, 180–83, 212–13
  as speaker, 243–44
  in Warner Robins, GA, 282
family, 8–10, 36
  influence from, 1–2
  love for, 240
  vacation as, 229
fans, 4
fears
  of China, 130–31
  of Chinese government, 268
  of missing World War II, 99
  of Training Command, 98, 120, 122,
    124, 180
fighter pilot, 1, 159
  challenges of, 162
  destiny as, 70, 100–101, 160
  determination as, 70–113
  longevity as, 230–31
  mortality and, 126
  reactions as, 273
  skill as, 160–61, 167, 171–73, 175
flight instructor, 93
  at Cal-Aero, 98–102
  dismay as, 85
  unhappy as, 98
flight school, 39–40, 43–45
  acceptance into, 33
  challenges with, 41–42
  graduation from, 46–47
*Flying Tiger: Chennault of China* (Scott), 245
Flying Tigers (Fei Hu), 152
  of Chennault, 107–8, 134, 146–48,
    158
  of China, 107–8, 114–17
  fame of, 207–8, 273
  Imperial Army of Japan against, 134
  in *Life*, 120
  morale from, 115–16
  pilot for, 148–49

storytelling of, 188
  stunt men from, 211
forced retirement
  aftermath of, 243–44
  choices of, 241
  storytelling of, 240
fortune's child, 141
Foulois, Benjamin D., 57, 61
The Fourteenth Air Force, 218
Fraser, Bruce, 244
Fraser, Robin. *See* Scott, Robin Lee
friendships
  with Callahan, 285
  with Chennault, 70–71, 146–47, 168,
    174–75, 177–78
  with Emery, 297
  with Hollar, 298–301
  with Li, 269–70
  with Paul, 283, 292
  with Ramos, 296–98
  with Young, P., 283

Generalissimo. *See* Chiang Kai-shek
genius, 167–68
Gentry, Tom, 178
Georgia National Guard, 15–16
Germany, 101
  assignment in, 230–33
  hobbies in, 232
Glorious Cause, 2
God. *See* Big Sky Boss
*God Is My Co-Pilot* (Scott), 4
  affirmations from, 204
  alienation from, 254
  as best-seller, 206
  for Book of the Month Club, 206
  conception of, 191
  confidence in, 191
  cost of, 205
  cultural impact of, 207, 246
  editing of, 200–201
  exaggerations in, 204
  fees for, 201, 227
  flaws of, 206–7
  glory from, 302
  King in, 213
  military impact from, 207
  Morgan in, 210, 213

as movie, 197–98
movie contract for, 194
movie flaws of, 211
movie release of, 211
for Museum of Aviation in Warner
    Robins, 287
paranoia in, 207
popularity of, 203–4
premiere of, 212–13
problematic title of, 191, 200–201,
    205–6
promotion of, 206
publisher for, 194
publishing of, 201
reviews of, 203, 206, 214
sales from, 214
solidarity with, 204
success of, 205, 219
title of, 191, 200–201, 205–7, 214,
    250, 280
tone of, 204
visions of, 207
writing of, 192
*God Is Still My Co-Pilot* (Scott), 247
golf, 93
Great Wall of China, 5, 13
    ambition for, 263
    anticlimax from, 274
    camping to, 267
    diet of, 256, 267, 269
    documents for, 263–64
    domination of, 274
    first sighting of, 220
    hiking, 267, 269
    markings on, 267
    obsession with, 14–15, 21, 26, 29, 33,
        256, 258–59
    preparation for, 256–57, 264
    route to, 266
    scenery at, 269
    story of, 262
    test for, 269
Great Wall of China markings, 267–68
Green, Catharine Rix (Kitty Rix),
    36–37, 39. *See also* marriage
    absolution from, 270–71
    break for, 200
    challenges of, 93–94, 111, 122,
        136–37, 163–64

courting of, 42, 44–45, 46–47, 53–55,
    64–66
death of, 251, 270–71
depression of, 82–83, 136–37, 216,
    243–44, 246
determination of, 68–69
disappointment of, 210, 216
disillusionment of, 225–26, 229–30
doubts of, 60
dream of, 200
engagement to, 66
failures to, 251
first flight for, 231
first proposal for, 53
gifts for, 163–64
grief of, 222
growing resentment of, 76–77
health of, 250–51
honeymoon with, 67–68
loneliness of, 251
Mama with, 169–70, 181, 183, 229–30
meeting of, 26–27
memories of, 270–71
miscarriage for, 222
missing of, 173–74, 277
as mother, 251
pleading of, 250–51
regrets of, 246
regrets to, 251
story of, 270–71
treatment of, 25, 231–32, 241, 243,
    248, 251
vices of, 69, 82, 111, 119–20, 216,
    229–330, 240
wedding to, 67
wifely duties of, 68–69
Green, Glenmore, 26–27
Green, Sadie, 26–27
guilt, 183

Harris, Hunter, 31
Hartley, Sadie. *See* Green, Sadie
Haynes, Caleb V., 138–41, 146
    fame of, 163
    of Task Force Aquila, 121, 124
health
    exercising for, 256
    fame for, 288

health (*continued*)
  of Kitty Rix, 250–51
  of Lee, Robert, 255
  in old age, 299–301
  religion for, 255
  surgery for, 255
Hemingway, Ernest
  meeting of, 206
  respect from, 206
Heritage of Eagles Campaign, 290
hero, 1
  challenges as, 215–16
  in Panama, 80
  at war, 2–3, 5, 144
high-velocity aircraft rockets (HVARs),
  220
Hill, Tex, 288
Hiroshima, 222
Hitler, Adolf
  rise of, 96–97
  suicide of, 217
hobby
  cooking as, 69, 112
  in Germany, 232
  golf as, 93
  hunting as, 93, 112, 174–76, 223, 232
  photography as, 50
Holden, William, 228
Hollar, Anica, 298–301
Holloway, Bruce, 176, 178, 288
  accusations of, 254
  despair of, 289
  disapproval from, 254
  jealousy of, 255
  retirement of, 254
  slap from, 248
  vanity of, 289
Hollywood, 98, 101–2, 112
  Army and, 103–4
  Brown, J., of, 98–99, 103, 175–76
  in Macon, GA, 213
  movie contract in, 194–95
  obsession with, 227
  womanizing and, 109, 111
*Hollywood Reporter*, 214
homecoming, 225, 274
  guilt from, 183
  hope for, 222
  to Macon, GA, 180–83

humiliation, 238
hunting, 93, 112, 168, 174–76, 223, 232

Imperial Army of Japan
  advancement of, 139
  Army and, 115
  attack of, 91
  attack on, 143
  Britain and, 115
  brutality of, 91, 115–16
  Burma invasion of, 130, 133
  China invaded by, 91, 130
  China surrendered to, 115, 129–30
  fading of, 168
  against Flying Tigers, 134
  occupying by, 145–46
  revolution of, 29–30
  on the run, 221
  surrendering of, 222
  threats from, 157–58
income tax
  loans for, 208
  problems with, 208, 216, 227
independence, 52–53, 274
India, 174
insurance salesman, 245–46
Internal Revenue Service (IRS).
    *See* income tax
international travel, 17, 33, 37–38
intertropical convergence zone (ITCZ),
  124–25k

Japan. *See also* Imperial Army of Japan
  China and, 129–30
  tyranny of, 94–95
Japanese, 116. *See also* Imperial Army of
    Japan
javelina, 83–84

Karachi, 127
*Keep 'Em Flying*, 111–12
King, Andrea, 213
Kipling, Rudyard, 28
Kirk, Phyllis, 227
  affair with, 240
Kitty Rix. *See* Green, Catharine Rix

La Venta Inn, 76
Langewiesche, Wolfgang, 205–6
Lanier High School
  flunking out of, 4
  ROTC at, 12–13
Lanphier, Thomas G., Jr., 112–13
Lee, Robert E., 2, 67
legacy, 5–6, 302
LeMay, Curtis, 237
Lewis, John, L.
  character of, 196
  as labor leader, 196
Li (general)
  friendship with, 269–70
  as guide, 268–70
  meeting of, 268
  stories from, 269
  storytelling of, 269
*Life,* 120, 135
Lindbergh, Charles, 57, 61, 97
  as Nazi sympathizer, 101
Lone Wolf of the Chindwin, 189, 259,
  289, 301
loneliness, 277, 284
  of Kitty Rix, 251
Long Rampar, 13–14
Luce, Henry
  as publisher, 135
  as war correspondent, 135–36
Luke Air Force Base
  assignment to, 238
  community at, 246
  rebellion at, 240–41

machine gunner, 76
Macon, GA
  fame in, 171, 180–83, 212–13
  Hollywood in, 213
  homecoming to, 180–83
  last visit to, 297
  life in, 2–3
  Madame Chiang and, 89–90
Madame Chiang, 101
  approval of, 156–57
  character of, 90
  of Chinese air force, 89–91, 105
  demands of, 218
  education of, 89–90

jade gift from, 148–49, 156–57
leadership of, 132
Macon, GA and, 89–90
power of, 89–90
religion of, 89
at Wesleyan College, 89
Wilkie and, 170–71
Mama. *See* Scott, Ola Burckhalter
Manstein, Erich von, 131
manufacturing
  in America, 186
  Bell Aircraft Corporation for, 188
  Curtiss-Wright Corporation for, 188
  Packard for, 188
  of warplanes, 186, 188
marriage
  challenges of, 82–83, 111, 122, 136–37,
    163–64, 215–16, 226
  commitment to, 122, 154, 186, 240,
    241, 250
  failures in, 246
  to Kitty Rix, 67–70
  Mama and, 69–70
  unraveling of, 164, 168–70, 183, 186,
    210, 216, 226, 240–41
Marshall, George C., 95–96, 105, 112
*The Maverick General* (Scott), 250
Maxwell, William, 290
media blunder, 196
melon bombs, 228–29, 244, 290
memorial
  to Chennault, 263, 271, 273–74
  in China, 272–74
memories, 277, 288
  in China, 272–73
  of Kitty Rix, 270–71
  visiting of, 297
mentor, 70–71, 146–47, 168
  Chennault as, 173–73, 244–45
Meyer, Wallace, 236
military decorations, 179, 181, 217, 227
  of Arnold, 187
Mitchell, Billy, 10, 26
M&M's, 296, 300
Moffitt, Jack, 195, 210
monument, 301
morale, 185–87
Morgan, Dennis, 210, 213
Morrow, Elizabeth, 97

motorcycle pilgrimage, 37–38
Mountbatten, Louis "Dickie," 133,
    218–19
movie contract
    fee for, 195
    in Hollywood, 194–95
Museum of Aviation in Warner
    Robins
    arriving at, 281
    donation to, 287, 295
    fund raising for, 287
    *God Is My Co-Pilot* for, 287
    growth of, 295
    memorabilia for, 279, 295
    P-40 for, 296
    plans for, 287
    salvation from, 278, 292
Mussolini, 96

naive
    as Arizona v. Scott Productions, Inc.,
        247
    in business, 247
    in "From Hero to Zero," 247
*National Geographic*, 264–65
National War College (NWC)
    assignment to, 233
    class president in, 235
    dismay in, 233
    leverage at, 235
    popularity at, 235–36
    prestige of, 235
    stakes at, 235–36
    storytelling at, 235
navigation
    challenges from, 125–26
    skill for, 125–26
Navy, 237
*New York Times*, 301
*New Yorker*
    endorsement from, 205
    reviews in, 214
NWC. *See* National War College

observation pilot
    demerits as, 50–51
    life as, 49

obsession
    with Great Wall of China, 14–15, 21
        26, 29, 33, 256, 258–59
    with Hollywood, 227
    with M&M's, 296
    with orange juice, 292–93
    with piloting, 254
    with Polo, 28–29, 31, 33, 35
old age. *See also* health
    drinking in, 297
    embarrassment of, 296–97
    memory in, 300
    mood in, 297–300
    pilot in, 294
    Scott, Robert Lee in, 255
    storyteller, 298–99
*One World* (Wilkie), 203
orange farmer, 212
orange juice, 292–93
O'Sullivan, J. Reilly, 176

Panama
    ambition in, 75
    challenges in, 78–79
    Chucunaque Indians of, 79–80
    community-relations in, 80
    crash in, 74, 81–82
    culture of, 73–74
    emergency airstrips in, 78
    exotic cuisine in, 81
    government of, 73
    hero in, 80
    life in, 73–85
    living quarters in, 73
    social life in, 74
    storyteller about, 79–81, 84
    work ethic in, 74–75, 77
paranoia
    of being grounded, 143, 207
    of big lie, 122–24, 127
    of character, 98, 101–2, 122, 143,
        151–52, 180, 207
    in *God Is My Co-Pilot*, 207
    from pranks, 228–29
Pardue, Austin "Dean," 188–89
Paul, Bill
    friendship with, 283, 292
    wedding of, 292

Pearl Harbor
  attack on, 97, 113–14
  AVG after, 114–15
  revenge for, 133
People's Republic of China, 263. *See also*
  China
photography, 50
physique, 244, 294, 299
  challenges from, 261
  of Chennault, 197
  consistency of, 293
  impact of, 16, 26, 44, 70, 124, 136,
    182
pilot. *See also* fighter pilot
  in Army, 3–4
  checklist for, 110
  evolution to, 8, 10–12, 19, 21–23
  for Flying Tigers, 148–49
  instructing of, 25–26
  obsession with, 254
  in old age, 294
  pay for, 47
  rebellion as, 231
  record hours as, 233, 241
  work ethic as, 63–64, 143, 151–52,
    172, 230–31, 233
poetry, 28, 30–31. *See also* Service,
  Robert
Polo, Marco
  admiration of, 274
  obsession with, 28–29, 31, 33, 35
  route of, 264
  writings of, 261
pride, 193
Princess. *See* Madame Chiang
promotion, 217
  in Army Air Corps, 75
  Bissell, 147, 197
  to brigadier general, 236–37
  for Chennault, 147, 197
  to colonel, 117
  to Director of Training, 117
  of *God Is My Co-Pilot*, 206
  rejection from, 229
  from Talbott, 236–37
publicity magnet, 253
  blunder as, 196
  love as, 209
  regularity as, 238–39

Quarles, Donald
  anger of, 237–38
  assignment from, 238


Ramos, Burt, 296–98
Rawlings, Marjorie Kinnan, 206
*Reader's Digest*
  fee from, 262
  writing for, 262
rebellion, 4, 142–43, 161, 283
  in Army, 5, 30
  in Army Air Corps, 42, 75–77
  toward Bissell, 153
  at Luke, 240–41
  as pilot, 231
  at Training Command,
    239
reckless driving, 293–94
Rector, Ed, 288
regrets
  for family, 296
  of Kitty Rix, 246
  regarding Kitty Rix, 251
rejection, 229
religion, 4, 83, 181–83
  of Chiang, 90
  in depression, 275
  for health, 255
  of Madame Chiang, 89
  in prayer, 278
  war and, 189
reviews
  of *God Is My Co-Pilot*, 203, 206,
    214
  in *Hollywood Reporter*, 214
  in *New Yorker*, 214
  in *Time*, 214
Richardson, Robert C., 35
Richthofen, Manfred von, 10
Rickenbacker, Eddie, 10
The Robert L. Scott Heritage Banquet,
  299–300
Robins Air Force Base, 279–80
*The Role of Defensive Pursuit* (Chennault),
  71
Rome, GA, 43
Roosevelt, Franklin D., 57, 61, 77, 97
  death of, 217

*Runway to the Sun* (Scott), 211
  circulation of, 223
  criticism of, 223
  exaggerations in, 223–24

San Antonio, TX, 40
  trip to, 43
Sawyer, Edward, 30
School of Applied Tactics, 196
Scott, Catharine. *See* Green, Catharine
  Rix
Scott, Elizabeth (sister), 1, 9
  birth of, 8
  tutoring from, 20
  at Wesleyan College, 36
Scott, Ola Burckhalter "Mama"
  (mother), 18, 21–22, 36
  adoration of, 248–49
  character of, 199–200
  death of, 248–49
  education of, 9
  grave of, 249
  to impress, 222, 230
  Kitty Rix with, 169–70, 181, 183,
    229–30
  on marriage, 69–70
  philosophies of, 8–9
  pressure from, 1–6, 8–9, 11, 15, 20
  as teacher, 9
Scott, Robert Lee (father), 15, 18–19,
  21–22, 36
  career of, 8–9
  death of, 255–56
  health of, 255
  in old age, 255
  pressure form, 26, 30
  relationship with, 255
Scott, Robert Lee, Jr. (Rob) (Scotty).
  *See specific topics*
Scott, Robin Lee (daughter), 241,
  300
  birth of, 101
  at college, 244
  estrangement from, 210
  relationship with, 277, 298
Scott, Roland (brother), 1, 9, 19, 28
  birth of, 8
  death of, 296

decorative eye of, 199
as Eagle Scout, 20–21, 36
in England, 198–99
high school graduation of, 36
hospitalization of, 199
mission of, 198–99
reaction of, 250
training of, 198
wounding of, 199–200
Scott, Roland, Jr. (nephew), 240, 248, 250
  doubts of, 274
  relationship with, 284
Scott, Roland, Jr. "Scotty" (nephew), 296
Scott, Roland B., Jr. (nephew), 30
Scott, William Thomas (great-
  grandfather), 9
Scribner, Charles
  breaking up with, 226
  dissatisfaction with, 226
  doubts of, 200–201
  as editor, 190
  gift to, 208
  meeting with, 190–92
  patience of, 223
  reactions of, 191–94
Scribner's. *See also* Scribner, Charles
  harassment of, 236
self-pity, 251
Service, Robert, poetry of, 28, 37–38,
  40, 99, 278
Sherman, William Tecumseh, 2–3, 99
smoking, feelings about, 69, 111, 122,
  136, 229, 293
Snow, Edgar, 136, 144
solo fight, 159–61
Soong, May-ling. *See* Madame Chiang
Southern Heritage, life in, 298–99
souvenirs, 277
speaking tour, 293
  fee for, 243
  for morale, 185–87
  travels of, 186–87
  work ethic on, 244
Stilwell, Joseph "Vinegar Joe," 96, 197
  character of, 132
  determination of, 140–41
  failure of, 179, 212
  opinions of, 212
  story of, 140